S0-BHR-077

Developing
Musical
Intuitions

GIFT

GIFT

Developing Musical Intuitions

A Project-Based Introduction
to Making and Understanding Music

Jeanne Bamberger
Massachusetts Institute of Technology

Incorporating **Impromptu**
An interactive software application
by Jeanne Bamberger and Armando Hernandez

New York   Oxford
Oxford University Press
2000

Oxford University Press

Oxford   New York
Athens   Auckland   Bangkok   Bogotá   Buenos Aires   Calcutta
Cape Town   Chennai   Dar es Salaam   Delhi   Florence   Hong Kong   Istanbul
Karachi   Kuala Lumpur   Madrid   Melbourne   Mexico City   Mumbai
Nairobi   Paris   São Paulo   Singapore   Taipei   Tokyo   Toronto   Warsaw

and associated companies in
Berlin   Ibadan

Copyright © 2000 by Jeanne Bamberger and Armando Hernandez

Published by Oxford University Press, Inc.
198 Madison Avenue, New York, New York 10016
http://www.oup-usa.org

Oxford is a registered trademark of Oxford University Press

All rights reserved. No part of this publication may be reproduced,
stored in a retrieval system, or transmitted, in any form or by any means,
electronic, mechanical, photocopying, recording, or otherwise,
without the prior permission of Oxford University Press.

Library of Congress Cataloging-in-Publication Data

Bamberger, Jeanne Shapiro.
    Developing musical intuitions : a project-based introduction to
making and understanding music / Jeanne Bamberger.
        p.   cm.
    Includes index.
    ISBN 0-19-510571-0
    1. Impromptu (Computer file)   2. Music—Theory, Elementary—
Software.   3. Music appreciation—Software.   I. Title.
ML74.4.I47B36   1999
781—DC21   99-11123
                                                       CIP

9 8 7 6 5 4 3 2 1

Printed in the United States of America
on acid-free paper

To the memory of my dear friend
Don Schön
who could find an elegant idea in a bramble of details

Contents

Foreword

As forms of communication go, music has its problems. In many ways the most human of activities, it "speaks" in amplitude and duration, in sounds and rhythms which, taken literally, signify nothing other than themselves. Music is clearly the product of the mind, yet nothing moves the body so immediately or so well; it exists in the material world, but its existence is purely ephemeral, transmitting through the air and then disappearing. What ever gave us the idea that we could understand it, speak through it, use it to say something?

Not that this has stopped anyone from trying. Generations of theorists, musicologists, program note annotators, visionaries, prophets, and opera buffs all have rushed to the fore to tell us how to listen to it, how to make sense of it, how to hear it telling us what we're told it ought to be telling us. The need to explain music is apparently almost as universal as the need to make music, and, to be fair, the explanations are often not only illuminating but self-fulfilling. Pythagoras and the ancient Greeks had it all figured out; so, as it turns out, did classical China and India, and they all got their facts straight: the acoustical principles of sound have been clear for thousands of years. But one man's consonance is another's dissonance, and a mode that denotes nobility in one culture may well denote the opposite in another. Music is what we make of it, both in the sending and the receiving. Endlessly malleable, it can be used toward any number of ends, and it usually ends up fitting the bill. Whether it be uplifting the spirit in a concert hall or shaking the body in a dance hall, accompanying a wedding or relieving the boredom of doing the dishes, music can fit the bill. And somehow, not only can we generate theories to make it all make sense, but composers can then write music powerful enough to prove any theory right.

Music is a cultural product, to be sure: the ears of the average American are not those of the average Viennese of the late Eighteenth Century, let alone of the average Balinese villager. As with everything, we make sense of music largely through what we already know—that is, through music we already know. In other words, musical meanings build upon one another, generating themselves through previously established meanings. Each of us comes to the musical table with different musical experiences and memories, as well as different aptitudes and areas of focus. Unlike language, music doesn't necessarily refer to anything outside of itself, so it's inevitable that even within a single culture, a piece of music will engender different responses and different meanings. Perceptually, each of us creates our own musical culture, in our mind and imagination.

How, then, does one teach people how to listen to music? Too often, the approach is diagnostic and prescriptive. Budding music students are bombarded with arrays of terms and concepts, all telling them what they should be hearing, and leaving those who get confused to self-select out of the course, out of the program, and perhaps into another area of study. To be sure, lack of education doesn't stop one from having a full musical life, but it seems clear that the discrepancy between people who love music and people who feel equipped to study it is far too wide.

It is worth considering what the implied message of most music theory is: music is presented as something objective, a rune to be gleaned for esoteric knowledge. Standard musical analysis (we won't mention any names here) takes music as a natural phenomenon like a rock formation— something to be divided into the sum of its unquestioned parts: it is what it is, and it's up to us to divine its parts. Music appreciation, on the other hand, takes music as a quasi-divine work of perfection to be interpreted— marvelled at. It's a perfect message from a genius and, again, it's up to us to rise to its level. In either case, there's something to get, and you either get it or you don't.

Jeanne Bamberger's life's work starts from a very different premise. She assumes that we all know quite a lot about music, having lived with it our whole life, and that the way to deepen our musical understanding is to examine what we already know, to reflect on what we already hear. Influenced by the work of Jean Piaget, and having emerged from the rigors of the MIT Artificial Intelligence Lab, Bamberger has spent much of the last 30 years grappling with first principles: what do you hear, and when do you hear it? All of her extremely substantial work stems from these basic questions. She has used this approach with inner-city preschoolers and with MIT graduates, with nonmusicians at conferences and budding concert artists at the New England Conservatory. The basis of her work is so simple, intuitive, and necessary that one wonders why it is so rare and why no once ever thought to do it before—that is, to get people to pay attention to what they already know and how they come to know it.

This book presents a pragmatic, working introduction into Jeanne Bamberger's methods. The games and exercises provided by the Impromptu software are nothing more or less than exercises in self-knowledge: through manipulating basic musical objects, one discovers what one already knows, and one builds on that. The program is built on musical "simples," Bamberger's term for the children's songs, common rhythms, etc., which are our musical common denominators and the building blocks of musical thought. The program is methodically organized around explorations of the ways in which music is organized: melodic structure, rhythm and meter. Each set of tasks is designed to be of interest to any musical thinker, from the concertmaster to the grade-schooler. The reason for this is the essential lesson of Bamberger's work: that the depth of our musical thought is not related to the scope of our musical knowledge. We are all musical thinkers, although we use a variety of mental tools to do the work.

You can verify this statement simply by attending to your own thought processes as you work through the book. As you do, questions will continually emerge: Why does this version of this song sound better than that one? Why does this one feel more regular? These questions lead to more questions, and suddenly you realize that tunes you have known your whole life—tunes that never seemed even remotely interesting—are endlessly fascinating and explorable. Walk away from Tuneblocks and put on a Brandenburg Concerto, and you realize that a lifetime of musical exploration awaits you, merely by developing your own innate musical intuitions.

Evan Ziporyn
Massachusetts Institute of Technology

Introduction: Framing the Questions

Almost everybody can make sense of the folk and pop music they have grown up with. But what is it in the music that makes the sense we so easily hear? And why is it that sometimes a piece of music doesn't seem to make sense, or that one person hears a piece as making perfect sense, while another does not? What, indeed, is the relationship between sense making and liking or disliking?

To help in answering these questions, consider the following proposal: In listening to music, the sense we seem simply to find, we are in fact making. Sense making is not in the music alone, it is an active process—a kind of ongoing "conversation" with listener, performer(s), and the piece as participants.

Given that this proposal is plausible, it then suggests another: If the sense we find is indeed a constructive interaction between listener and piece, then differences in the "hearings" we make could be traced to differences in the means we have available for musical sense making. For instance, individuals may differ as to the aspects of music they choose or are able to attend to. What if, for example, you are used to focusing your attention primarily on melody, giving less attention to harmony, or maybe finding it difficult even to hear harmonic change? What happens, then, when you are confronted with a composition whose melody is relatively static and uninteresting, while there is a lot going on in the harmonic dimension? With your attention on the melody where there is little action going on, you would most likely find the piece simply boring.

It's a little like watching a baseball game and focusing attention only on the batter. If you are not yet able to see the many other dimensions of the game, and thus unable to shift attention when the action is somewhere other than with the batter, you will most likely conclude that baseball is a boring sport. But as you gradually learn how to see what's happening where, and learn appropriately to shift attention to where the action is, the game will obviously become more exciting. Similarly, in learning how to move freely among the multiple dimensions of music, and also how to shift your attention to wherever the action might be in a piece—melody, rhythm, harmony, instrumentation—your hearing of the same piece and your feeling about it will probably change, too; what was initially a boring piece that you didn't like could become a piece that you liked a lot and even found quite exciting.

But how can you learn to do that? One way is to listen more actively and to be guided by analyses that help differentiate among the various dimensions, highlighting those that are important at different moments in a given piece. Another way is to design and build musical structures yourself—melodies, rhythms, and eventually larger pieces. For in actually making musical structures, as in learning to play baseball yourself, or in learning to build a sand castle or a model bridge that will stand up, you need to solve problems and confront practical questions. As you do so, features and relations are liberated that otherwise may remain hidden within the undifferentiated total meld of a piece as it unfolds continuously in time.

Think of the process of learning as a conversation with the materials of music. By "conversation" I mean the usually silent conversations we have with materials as we are building, fixing, or inventing. As we handle these materials, arranging and rearranging them, watching them take shape even as we shape them, we learn. The materials "talk back" to us, remaking our ideas of what is possible. The back-talk leads to new actions on our material objects in a spiral of inner and outer activity; our inner intentions are reflected back by the results of our actions, leading to new outer actions and often to changing of our intentions. It is a kind of "re-search"—one that is as familiar to the scientist designing a theory as to the painter or composer designing an artifact.

Arnold Schoenberg, juxtaposing the technique of musical composition with carpentry, puts it this way:

> For if the carpenter knows how to join pieces of wood securely, this knowledge is based no less on fruitful observation and experience than is the knowledge of the [composer] who understands how to join chords effectively. And if the carpenter knows which types of wood are required by a particular job and selects accordingly, he is thus taking natural relationships and materials in account, just as does the [composer] when, appraising the possibilities of themes, he recognizes how long a piece may be.*

Thus, I have designed the projects that you will be working on as a workplace in which to explore, experiment, and question the materials and relations that help to give musical structure its coherence. The projects begin with the most common tunes, but these tunes also include the

---

*Arnold Schoenberg (1874–1951) was one of the composers who had the greatest influence on the music of the twentieth century. He is best known for formulating the principle of composition with twelve notes related only one to the other. Schoenberg also wrote several books on music including a text, *Harmony*, and a collection of essays, *Style and Idea*, from which this quotation is taken.

basic structures from which the greatest musical complexity grows. As you work, you will be making explicit what you know how to do already—that is, making sense of the shared structures embodied by our most familiar music, while at the same time expanding your "hearings" to include the multiple intersecting dimensions of more complex compositions. The process begins with relatively easy, composition-like projects, and each subsequent project builds on the previous ones. Putting all of that to work, you will make longer and more complex compositions within design constraints that derive from listening to a variety of music from different historical periods and different cultures.

Each project includes some or all of the following kinds of guidance:

1. The Tasks: A description of the goals of the task and specific directions for how to do it.
2. Info Boxes: Directions for how to get started with a project or exploration.
3. Notice Boxes: Suggestions for avoiding common difficulties and how to remedy them if encountered. They are indicated by the following icon:

4. Explorations: Questions, probes, and puzzles that suggest broader musical implications of the tasks.

To get the most out of working on the projects, it is important that you actively question your own spontaneous, intuitive responses as you go along. For instance, the most significant learning often happens when you confront surprising or puzzling results. Surprises reveal expectations, and expectations are clues to the powerful musical intuitions you are already using in making sense of familiar music. Becoming aware of these healthy intuitions is an important step in developing them further. For example, in building a melody or even just a rhythm, you may be surprised as you listen again to the sound of the results of your descriptions—that is, the instructions you give to the computer. Sometimes the surprising result is more interesting than what you intended, and these are just the moments to stop and ask, "I wonder why *that* happened?"

These are the moments of most important learning, but they are also moments that quickly disappear from view and from memory; once you have an insight, and have learned to use a new idea, it is very difficult to remember what it was like before—life without that idea is as if wiped out. Try to imagine what it was like, for instance, before you knew how to read, or before you knew how to count.

So, in order to track your progress, to be able to look back at what you have learned, and to reflect on it, you will be asked to keep a running log as you work through the Impromptu projects. These logs will then become the basis for the papers you will be writing. There will be more about log keeping in the context of each Project.

Interspersed with the projects, you will find sections titled "Listening Examples," examples recorded on the audio CD included with this book. Instructions to listen to a specific example are indicated by the following icon:

In the text, discussion of each example guides you to the specific features of the music that require your particular attention at that point.

The sequence of projects and Listening Examples may look irregular, but in fact they are carefully arranged in accordance with the pedagogical objectives of the text. In some cases, the Listening Examples illustrate a concept you will need in order to carry out an upcoming project; other times they are designed to show how the concepts you learned in the foregoing project are applied in the "real world" of making and hearing music.

At the ends of Parts 1, 2, 3, and 5, you will find sections titled "Some Basics." These discussions are designed to lead you from the concepts you have learned to the "nuts and bolts" of how these concepts are expressed in musical performance and in the written language of music.

Getting Started with Impromptu

Impromptu software is designed to be closely linked with the musical activities of the projects; thus, only the bare basics for getting started with the software are introduced here. Further instructions for using the software will be introduced as they become relevant to specific projects. Included here is just what you need to know to begin work on Project 1.1. For more information, select Help in the Edit menu.

Software

The Impromptu folder on your computer includes the following:

1. The Impromptu application
2. Tunes folder: A folder of prepared material, one folder for each of the following Impromptu environments: Tuneblocks, Drummer, Rounds, Harmonize, 4-Voices
3. Synthesizers folder: A folder that includes setups for several kinds of synths, including General MIDI

4. PatchBay 2.0: An application that helps connect your computer to a synthesizer if you use one

5. Help folder: A folder that contains the files used by Impromptu's Help feature

Starting Impromptu

To start Impromptu, follow the instructions in the Info Box.

Impromptu gives you two different options for generating sound: Internal Sound, which uses Quicktime Instruments, and MIDI Sound, which links to any MIDI synthesizer. The default is Internal Sound—that is, when you load Impromptu you are automatically using the internal QuickTime Instruments. Using the Internal Sound option, your Macintosh computer with its built-in speaker running Impromptu can stand alone for working on most projects. To improve the Internal Sound, you can connect any amplifier/speaker system to the audio output on your computer. If you select the MIDI Sound option, you will need to connect a MIDI synthesizer to your computer and couple it with an amplifier/speaker. Using MIDI will result in better sound, especially for projects that include more than one instrument playing at once. Impromptu includes menus of instruments for both Internal Sounds and MIDI Sound. You will find information on selecting instruments as you get into the projects.

INFO BOX

Starting Impromptu

Using Internal Sounds
1. Turn on the computer
2. Double-click the Impromptu folder
3. Double-click Impromptu
4. Connect and turn on your amplifier and speakers (optional)
5. Plug in your headphones (optional)

Using MIDI
6. Connect and turn on your synthesizer
7. In the Options menu
8. Select MIDI sound

Part 1

Using tuneblocks to reconstruct a melody is like using jigsaw puzzle blocks to reconstruct a picture. This puzzle, *A Palette of Pieces* by Steve Malavolta, includes approximately 350 hand-cut and hand-finished pieces. (Photo courtesy Steve Malavolta)

Melodic Structure

Introduction: Constructive Analysis

IN LISTENING TO MELODIES, AS IN LISTENING TO CONVERSATION, WE MOST OFTEN follow the sound unfolding in time by grouping it into meaningful "chunks." For instance, we don't generally pay attention to syllables but rather group them into meaningful words, the words taking on particular meaning as they group into phrases and sentences. Similarly, in listening to melodies, we don't hear individual notes but rather the groupings of these notes into *motives,* or small "figures." Thus, it is more intuitive to start your work in building melodies by using these intuitively meaningful motives as the basic building blocks.

The basic building blocks with which you will be working are actually preprogrammed, short melody segments called *tuneblocks.* Each tuneblock is a meaningful structural element of a given tune. Using tuneblocks to reconstruct melodies is much like doing a jigsaw puzzle: By putting together the given "pieces," you can reassemble the whole tune. Sometimes you may find that in programming the blocks, we have broken the melody into segments that are different from the ones you hear on first listening to the whole tune. That raises some interesting questions: What features make boundaries that delimit the structural elements we hear? What are our intuitive strategies for noticing these boundaries? How might these differ from one person to another? We will return to these questions as you go along.

Project 1.1 involves reconstructing given tunes, while in Project 1.2 you will construct your own original tunes using unfamiliar sets of tuneblocks. Reconstructing tunes can be a rather mechanical, mindless task, especially if you just play with the technology. But if you listen carefully to the results of your experiments and think about the decisions you make, some important general aspects of musical structure will emerge that are shared by all these common tunes. As you work, try to listen for these shared aspects of musical structure. You will return to these structures in the Explorations sections.

Project 1.1

*Reconstructing Melodies with Tuneblocks**

THE TASKS

INFO BOX Starting Project 1.1 In the Playrooms menu, select Tuneblocks

1. Using a given set of tuneblocks, put them in order so as to reconstruct the given tune.
2. Learn to play your completed tunes on the keyboard.

A Practice Session

To get a feel for how to play tuneblocks, work through the following practice session. The tune to be reconstructed in this practice session is "Did You Ever See a Lassie," which we will call "Lassie" for short. To begin work on "Lassie," scroll down the Tunes Catalog and double-click LASSIE.†

---

*Instructions in the Info Box assume that you are using the internal instruments included in the Impromptu software (actually, QuickTime Instruments). If you wish to use a MIDI synthesizer, you must connect the synthesizer to your computer, pull down the Options menu and select MIDI Sound. For more details, please select Help from the Edit menu.
†Notice that the *status bar* in the upper right corner of the Tools area tells you where you currently have the cursor positioned. For example, while you are in the Tunes Catalog, the status bar says "Select Tunes."

The three patterned icons you see in the Tuneblocks area on the right of the screen are the three blocks you will use to build "Lassie." The LASS icon plays the whole tune "Lassie." The FP and SP icons play, respectively, the first part and the second part of "Lassie."

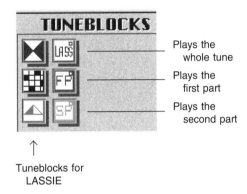

Tuneblocks for
LASSIE

So that you can refer to the blocks in writing your log and in the analyses of the tunes, make a chart for yourself numbering the blocks from the top down as they appear in the Tuneblocks area—that is, call the top block "1," the next one down "2," and so forth.

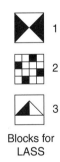

Blocks for
LASS

As you work on this project and on all the future projects, keep a running log of your thoughts and of your progress. Just get into the practice of jotting down your comments in an informal way. You may use a notebook or you can type your comments into Impromptu's text screen. To use Impromptu's text screen, simply click the Log button at the bottom left corner of the screen.

The Log icon

    This will open a small text screen, which you can later print and also save. The informal comments in your personal log are important in helping you reflect on your work. Your comments will also serve as the basis for tracking the progress of your developing musical intuitions. Later, you may use your log as the basis for writing up your work in a more structured way.

Procedure for Playing Tuneblocks

    The *hand cursor* is used for listening to blocks and also for dragging blocks into the Playroom area. As you move the mouse, the hand cursor will follow you.

The hand cursor—for listening to blocks and dragging them

1. *Listen to the whole tune:* Using the hand cursor, click the block marked LASS, which plays the entire tune "Lassie."

Listen to "Lassie" as many times as you like. As you listen, think about how the whole tune is organized. Make note of the following in your log:

- How are you segmenting the tune? What are the basic blocks that you hear?
- Which blocks are repeated? When are blocks repeated?
- When are new blocks introduced?
- How do blocks group together to form bigger blocks?

2. *Listen to each tuneblock:* Using the hand cursor, click each of the blocks in turn.

As you listen to each block, make note of the following:

- Do the given blocks segment the tune as you expected? If not, how do the blocks differ from yours?
- What is the possible function of each block—for instance, does it sound like an ending, a beginning, or a middle?
- What is the "contour" of each block—going up, going down, going up and down? Make a sketch of the contour as you hear it.

3. *Find the block with which the tune begins:* Listen to just the first part of "Lassie" by clicking the FP icon. Then listen once more to each block and find the one that matches the beginning of the tune.

4. *Drag the beginning block into the Playroom area:* Position the hand cursor on the beginning block, click and hold the mouse button down, and drag this block into the Playroom. You can release the mouse button anywhere in the Playroom; the block will find its way. *Note:* Block 3 is the beginning block.

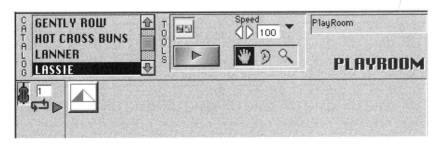

Block 3 in the PlayRoom area

5. *Listen to your tune so far:* Click Play in the Tools area at the top of the screen.

The Play button

As you listen, follow the pitch contour graphics for Block 3 in the graphics window at the bottom of the screen. Does the contour match the one you drew?

Pitch contour for Block 3

6. *Build up the rest of the first part of "Lassie":* Listen to just the first part of the tune (click the FP icon). Then, listening to each of the blocks, find the sequence of blocks that matches FP. As you find each block in the sequence, drag it into the Playroom. Remember to click Play to listen to your tune so far, and follow the pitch contour graphics as you do so.

Graphics for Blocks
3 1 3 2

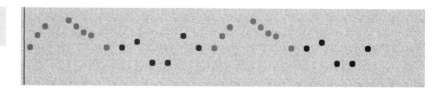

  If you make a move that doesn't work, you can drag a block into the Trash (in the lower left corner of the Impromptu screen).

Trash

  You can rearrange blocks in the Playroom area and insert blocks between blocks that are already present.

7. *Build the second part:* Listen to SP, then drag blocks into the Playroom area to build it. As you go along, click Play to listen to your results.

8. *Check your results:* Click the magnifying glass cursor at the top of the window.

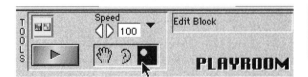

The magnifying glass cursor—for checking the "contents" of a tune

Now place the magnifying glass cursor over the LASS icon. Click LASS and hold the mouse button down. A small window will pop up showing the contents of "Lassie"—that is, the sequence of blocks that plays "Lassie."

Sequence of blocks for LASSIE

Check to see whether your sequence of blocks matches this sequence. Using the numbering convention, you would describe the sequence of blocks as: 3 1 3 2 1 1 3 2.

You can choose different instruments to play melodies. To do so, use the Instruments menu just to the left of the Playroom. Click the violin icon, hold down the mouse button, and select an instrument. Click Play to hear how your selected instrument sounds.

You may also select alternate graphics. The default graphics are called Pitch Contour. To see another kind of graphics, select Piano Roll in the Graphics menu.

Instrument menu $\rightarrow$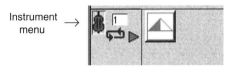

Going on

Now go on to reconstruct the following five melodies for Project 1.1:

Tune*	Number of blocks
"Hot Cross Buns"	2
"Austrian"	4
"Susanna"	5
"Early"	6
"Ode"	7

Begin with "Hot Cross Buns," following the same procedure as in the practice session.

1. Scroll down the Tunes Catalog and double-click HOT CROSS BUNS. The two patterned blocks in the Tuneblocks area are now the blocks you will need, and the HOT icon plays the whole tune of "Hot Cross Buns." Listen to HOT, listen to the two blocks, and as you find each block in the tune, drag it into the PlayRoom area until you have reconstructed the whole tune.
2. Check your result using the magnifying glass cursor and write down in your log the numbers for the blocks in your completed tune.
3. After you have built the tune, try to pick out "Hot Cross Buns" on a piano or on an electronic keyboard. Use the pitch contour graphics as a guide.

Now go on to build "Austrian." When you have completed "Austrian" and checked your result, teach yourself to play the completed tune on the piano or electronic keyboard.

Playing Tunes on the Keyboard

To learn to play "Austrian" on the keyboard, use the tuneblocks as the units of work. Follow these steps:

• With the whole tune built up in the Playroom, double-click the first block. Watch the pitch contour graphics as you listen. The graphics for the block you selected will be darkened.

---

*Some of these tunes will sound quite familiar, others probably will not. "Austrian" is an Austrian folk song; "Susanna" is "Oh! Susanna"; "Early" is "Early One Morning"; "Ode" is the melody Beethoven used to set Schiller's poem "To Joy" to music, familiarly called "Ode to Joy."

- Using the memory of the block in your mind's ear and the pitch contour graphics as a guide, pick out the pitches for the first block on your keyboard. Notice that the relative *horizontal distance* between dots in the pitch contour graphics corresponds to the relative *time* (duration) of the pitches. If you choose piano roll graphics, the length of each pitch line corresponds to the time (duration) of the pitches.
- Pick out the next block on the keyboard following the same procedure.
- Now play this first pair of blocks on the keyboard, one after the other.
- Since this first pair of blocks is repeated to form FP, you can now play the whole first part of the tune.
- Go on to play the next pair of blocks. This pair makes the middle part of the tune—that is, the beginning of SP.
- Since the first block comes back again at the end, you are now ready to play the whole tune. Play it on your keyboard just as you built it up in the Playroom.
- In writing up your log, be sure to include the steps in your progress as you learned to play "Austrian" on the keyboard.

Remember to keep a log of your work, following the preceding suggestions for log keeping.

Before going on to "Susanna," "Early," and "Ode," read Explorations 1 and try the experiments that are suggested.

Boundaries and Other Structural Functions

While you may have segmented the tunes differently from the way I did in making the tuneblocks, it is likely that your "chunking" and mine shared important aspects. For instance, you may have heard larger segments than those played by the tuneblocks, but yours were probably made up of groupings (most often pairs) of the given, smaller blocks. And that raises an important question, which we will return to in later projects: What elements do we hear as generating *structural boundaries*, and what makes the difference when people's hearings differ in this regard?

While there are individual differences among our hearings, there are also deeply shared intuitions that form a common basis for making meanings and for constructing coherence—even in much larger works where composers expand and elaborate on these relations.

So learning to hear these structural relations by constructing them yourself—by making them happen—will also help you hear how composers create the complexity that characterizes more extended compositions.

Repetition, Function, and Context

Folk tunes usually include a good deal of repetition. For instance, in reconstructing each tune, you had to use the same block in more than one place. Repetition presents an interesting paradox: It helps us define what we hear as an entity—but, strangely, repetition is not always obvious. Why? One reason is that the same block can appear in different contexts, and when it does, it can assume different *structural functions.* For instance, in building "Lassie," tune builders will often finish building FP, listen to SP, and then say, "But I need another block; the next one isn't here." Why do they not recognize that they already have the block that begins SP? As one student put it, "The last block in the first part, Block 1, sounded like a sort of half-ending; how come the same block sounds like a beginning when it's in the second part?" What, then, do we mean by "the same" when "the same" block may change function? In other words, why, at one moment and in one context, may a block function as a beginning, while at another moment, in a different context, it may function as an ending?

Even in the simple tune "Hot Cross Buns," the same block—the same set of pitches and durations—changes function. The sequence of blocks, **2 2 1 2,** plays the whole tune, but Block 2 clearly changes function: It functions as a "beginner" at the outset, while in its final appearance after Block 1, everyone hears Block 2 clearly as an "ender." Why? Think about it and we will return to that question later.

Interestingly, we are all able to hear these situational-functional changes without anyone explicitly teaching us to do so. Indeed, it is often easier to recognize structural functions, such as beginning or ending, than to recognize that the same block with all the same properties (same pitch and time) is occurring again. Just in listening to the music all around us, our musical intuitions have come to include this powerful ability to hear the structural function of figures in response to their surroundings—the musical context in which they occur.

Sequence

In addition to literal repetition, blocks are related to one another in more subtle ways as well. For instance, select "Austrian" again in the Tunes Catalog and drag Blocks 3 and 4 into the Playroom. Listen to them again and pay special attention to the pitch contour graphics. What makes these two blocks similar?

Looking at the pitch contour graphics, you can see and hear that Blocks 3 and 4 are both similar and different: They have the same melodic shape or contour, but Block 4 is a "moved-down" version of Block 3. This kind of similarity relationship between two figures or blocks is called a *sequence.* A sequence can be defined as a series of repetitions in which the pitch contour and rhythm of a figure stays the same but the whole figure is repeatedly moved down or repeatedly moved up so as to form a kind of "chain" of linked figures. Sequences are found in compositions that date from as early as the sixteenth century up to the present. The Listening Examples on your CD include excerpts that illustrate some of the many different ways in which composers have used sequences in the midst of changing musical styles.

Now go on to reconstruct "Susanna," "Early," and "Ode." Use the same procedure as in "Austrian," including learning to play each tune on the keyboard. As you rebuild these tunes, listen for how these familiar aspects of melodic structure are used:

- Repetition
- Function and context
- Sequence

When you have finished "Susanna," "Early," and "Ode," go on to Explorations 2.

Comparing Tunes

EXPLORATIONS 2

While the tunes you have reconstructed may have seemed almost too simple to be interesting, this very simplicity carries within it the "generative primitives" from which much larger and more complex compositions grow and develop. Composers depend on these generative primitives for essential coherence and also for creating complexity. In anticipation of your work with more extended pieces, it is worthwhile to continue making some of these common structures more explicit.

Structural Hierarchies

An aspect shared by all of these tunes is their hierarchical structure: Each tune includes several levels of structural elements, with each level nesting within the next. The blocks that you were given in each set are the smallest, lowest structural elements of a tune, conventionally called *motives*. These motives group together to become parts of bigger blocks or mid-level structural elements usually called *phrases*. These phrases, in turn, can be grouped together to form still-higher-level structural elements, usually called *sections*. The difference you may have found between the "size" of entities you heard in "chunking" a tune and the "size" of the given tuneblocks is an instance of focusing on different levels of the structural hierarchy.

In the following diagram, you see the given, lowest-level blocks (motives) for "Austrian" grouped together to form larger, mid-level structural elements (phrases). These phrases are conventionally labeled *a* and *b*, respectively—where *a* is the name for one kind of phrase and *b* is the name for a different, contrasting phrase. Using these names for the mid-level structural elements, the whole structure of "Austrian" can be described as *a a b a*. This structure and varied versions of it occur frequently in folk and pop tunes and, in more expanded form, in larger compositions as well. Listen to "Austrian" again while you follow the diagram.

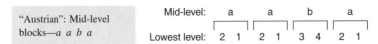

"Austrian": Mid-level blocks—*a a b a*

Mid-level:	a	a	b	a
Lowest level:	2 1	2 1	3 4	2 1

The phrases of "Austrian" can be further grouped together to form the highest-level blocks (sections). Sections are conventionally named with capital letters— A and B. At this highest level of structure, "Austrian" would be described as having simply two sections, A and B, as shown in the following diagram:

"Austrian": Top-level blocks—A B

A	B
a a	b a

Impromptu will let you make these bigger blocks and listen to them. As you do so, you are moving up a level in the description of the structural hierarchy, as compared with the level of small melodic figures played by the given tuneblocks.

To make the mid-level block that we called *a*, follow these steps:

1. Put Blocks 2 and 1 in the Playroom—that is, the tuneblocks that form the contents of phrase *a*:

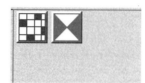

Blocks 2 and 1, the contents of phrase *a*

2. Select Blocks 2 and 1 by clicking each of them *once.* The selected blocks will be darkened.

3. Click the Block-It button—this will make a single, new block that contains Blocks 2 and 1.

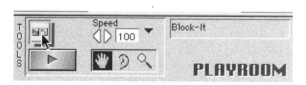

The Block-It button

4. Blocks 2 and 1 disappear from the Playroom and a new block that contains them both takes their place.

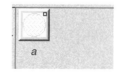

Mid-level block *a*

5. Click Play to hear the phrase called *a*.

6. Notice that this new block has also been added to the blocks in the Tuneblocks area. Drag another copy of the *a* block into the Playroom to make the repetition *a a*.

Mid-level blocks *a a*

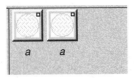

Before continuing, click any empty spot in the Playroom to deselect the darkened blocks. All darkened blocks will be "gobbled up" by Block-It.

7. Build the middle section, *b*, in the same way:

• Add Blocks 3 and 4 to the Playroom. Notice that you now have a mixed-level description of "Austrian"—*a* and *a* blocked together are at the middle (phrase) level of the structural hierarchy, while Blocks 3 and 4 are at the lowest (figure or motive) level of the hierarchy.

A mixed-level description

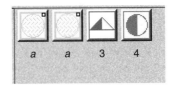

• Select Blocks 3 and 4 by clicking each of them *once*.

• Click the Block-It button to make Blocks 3 and 4 into the single mid-level block we called *b*.

Adding mid-level block *b*

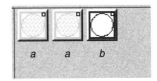

8. Recall that "Austrian" ends with a return to the opening phrase, *a*. So you can finish "Austrian" by just adding a copy of *a* at the end.

Mid-level structure:
a a b a

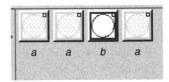

The whole tune is described at the middle (phrase) level of the structural hierarchy—*a a b a*. Does this new description that you created change your hearing of "Austrian"?

You can continue upward in the structural hierarchy by grouping these mid-level blocks to make just two top-level (section) blocks. (Click any empty spot in the Playroom to deselect the darkened blocks.) The procedure is exactly the same: Select the appropriate groupings of mid-level phrase blocks and click Block-It to make the top-level section blocks we called A and B.

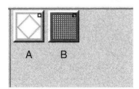

Top-level structure: A B

The whole structural hierarchy for "Austrian"—top-level blocks (sections); mid-level blocks (phrases); and tuneblocks (figures or motives), represented by the Impromptu blocks—is shown graphically in the following diagram:

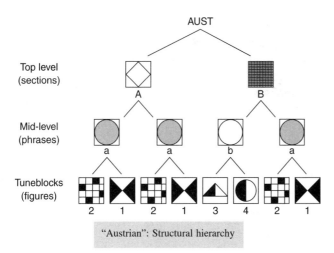

"Austrian": Structural hierarchy

The hierarchy can also be represented as an inverted tree structure—inverted because the branches increase downward instead of upward like those of a real tree.

A growing tree with branches expanding upward. (Image ©
Shai Ginott)

The whole tune "Austrian" is at the apex. Top-level blocks, A B,
the sections of the tune, are shown as two branches coming off the
whole tune. In turn, mid-level blocks, *a a b a*, the phrases, are
shown as branches coming off the sections—A and B, respectively.
The given tuneblocks (figures or motives) form branches coming off

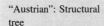

"Austrian": Structural
tree

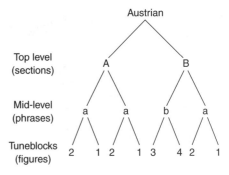

the phrases. The tree diagram is a more general representation of hierarchical structures. Can you think of other structures in other media that can be represented as trees? Examples might include poems (sections, stanzas, sentences) or the hierarchy of animals (vertebrates, mammals, primates, etc.).

Listen once more to "Austrian," following the hierarchical diagrams. Which representation seems best to capture the tune as you hear it? Which level seems best to match the focus of your intuitive hearing of the tune? For instance, which level matches the blocks that you heard in initially listening to "Austrian"? Can you shift your attention from one level to another—that is, from detail to larger design and back? This ability to shift your focus among levels as well as among the different dimensions of music will become increasingly important as you listen to longer, more complex pieces.

What about higher-level blocks for "Susanna"? Select "Susanna" from the Tunes Catalog and use Block-It to group the given tuneblocks into mid-level blocks and then top-level blocks.

The tree diagram for "Susanna" is shown in the following diagram. Why does the diagram for "Susanna" include a block labeled *a'*? What is the relationship between *a* and *a'*?

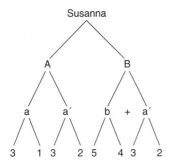

"Susanna": Structural tree

Comparing Four Tunes: Structural Functions

If you compare the structural trees for "Austrian," "Susanna," "Early," and "Ode," subtle differences in their organization emerge, despite the general similarities among them. These structural differences also help to account for the differences in character among the four tunes.

As you look at the structural trees and sing the tunes to yourself,

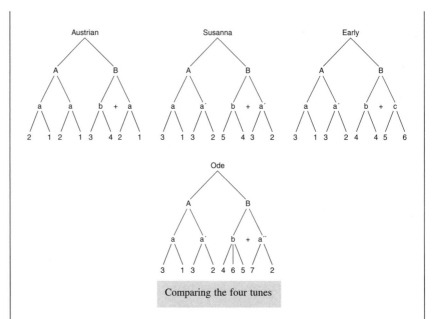

Comparing the four tunes

it's obvious that the larger structural relations are much the same—each includes two large sections (A and B). However, the mid-level elements (phrases) within them differ somewhat. For instance, focusing your attention at this mid-level of structure and moving your eye across the four tunes from left to right, you can see (and hear) a small progression toward increased complexity: Within the A section, "Austrian" is limited only to literal repetition (*a a*), while "Susanna," "Early," and "Ode" include varied repetition within their A sections. This varied repetition is represented as *a a'*. Within their B sections, "Austrian" and "Susanna" include a literal return to material already found in A. The B section of "Austrian" returns to *a* (*b a*); the B section of "Susanna" returns to *a'* (*b a'*). But the B section of "Early" does not include a return at all; instead it introduces new material (*b c*) that continues to elaborate material from the first A section. The B section of "Ode" is more complex—it includes three small blocks (figures) in the *b* phrase, and returns to a still different version of *a* (*a"*).

Equally important are differences in the functional relations among these mid-level elements. For example, within the A sections of "Susanna," "Early," and "Ode," the varied repetition (*a* and *a'*) creates a complementary relationship: *a* and *a'* begin exactly the same but they end differently—3 1 and 3 2. The differing endings create different functions and different feelings for the two phrases:

The first phrase, *a*, sounds incomplete, "left hanging," while the second phrase, *a'*, feels more complete. Thus *a* leads into *a'* with *a'* resolving the tension created at the end of *a*. This relationship of both similarity and complementarity between two phrases is called an *antecedent-consequent* phrase relationship. In its most constrained form, an antecedent-consequent relationship is defined as that between two phrases that begin the same (similarity) but end differently (complementarity); the first phrase ending sounds incomplete, while the second phrase ending sounds complete (tension to resolution). Antecedent-consequent relations can be heard and seen quite clearly by listening and looking at the pitch contour graphics for the A section of each tune.

In all four tunes, the *b* phrase functions as a contrast by introducing new material derived from material in the previous A section. And in all four, *b* runs right on into the final phrase. The final phrase functions as a resolution to all that has gone before. To indicate this close joining of the *b* and *a* sections, we use a plus sign (+) to connect them.

It is now quite clear that in "Austrian," "Susanna," and "Ode" the B section includes a return (*b + a* or *b + a'*), but in "Early," there is no return. Instead, the B section of "Early" includes a new phrase, which still achieves resolution, but by extending the previous material rather than returning to it. We will come back to these structural functions and to the pitch and time relations that generate them in subsequent projects and also in the Listening Examples that follow Project 1.2.

Last Words

It's fun to make new tunes out of old blocks. Take a set and try rearranging the blocks to make a whole new tune. What happens to the structural functions of blocks as you do so? For instance, try building "Early" so it has a return, like "Austrian" and "Susanna." Or try making a new tune with the blocks for "Twinkle, Twinkle, Little Star" (scroll down in the Tunes Catalog and double-click STAR) so that it includes a sequence.

Project 1.2

Composing Melodies with Tuneblocks

INFO BOX
Starting Project 1.2
· In the Playrooms
  menu, select
  Tuneblocks
· In the Tunes Catalog,
  select FRENCH

FOR PROJECT 1.2 YOU WILL BE COMPOSING YOUR OWN TUNES, BUT AS IN Project 1.1, you will still be working within the constraints of precomposed tuneblocks.

THE TASKS

1. Using a given set of unfamiliar tuneblocks, make a tune of your own that makes sense and that you like. Try to use all the blocks in the set in making your tune. There is no given tune to match; there is no right answer.

2. Play your completed tune on the piano or electronic keyboard.

3. Analyze the structure of your completed tune using the models of structural analysis (such as structural trees) from Project 1.1.

4. Keep a running log of your progress. These notes and your analysis of your tunes will be the bases for your paper on this project.

There are five sets of blocks to work with for Project 1.2.

Group 1:	French,	English,	Vienna
Group 2:	Portals,	Ambrosian	

Begin with the French set and choose at least one other set from Group 1. Do at least one of the sets in Group 2. The blocks in Group 2 are more challenging.

Note: If you find that a block in Group 2 just doesn't work for you, you can experiment with making a few changes in some of its pitches and/or durations to make it work better (see the section titled "Viewing and Editing the Contents of Blocks" later in this project). But if you do so, you need to account for why the block(s) didn't work and how your changes helped.

Procedure for Composing Tunes with Tuneblocks

To compose your tune, follow these steps for each block set:

1. Scroll down in the Tunes Catalog and double-click the name of the set you wish to work with (FRENCH, ENGLISH, and so on).
2. Listen to each block in the Tuneblocks area.
3. As you listen to each block, jot down your impression in your log. Note distinctive features that you hear and possible structural functions (beginning, ending, and so on), and make a sketch of the block's pitch contour. This will also help you remember each block.
4. Experiment with possible sequences of blocks: Drag blocks into the PlayRoom and arrange them in differing ways. Listen carefully to each of your experiments, remembering that you want to end up with a tune that you like and that makes sense.
5. In your log, keep track of your progress:
   - List the blocks you tried.
   - Record what worked, what didn't, and why.
   - Note any surprises or shifts in possible functions of blocks.
   - Try to account for the decisions you make along the way.

You can repeat blocks, insert blocks between other blocks, and rearrange blocks within the Playroom area; also, you can always drag blocks into the Trash.

6. When you have completed your tune, play your whole tune on your piano or electronic keyboard using the procedure described in Project 1.1.

7. Describe the structure of your tune. Your description can take the form of a diagram. It should also include the functional relations among the blocks as you use them in your tune—antecedent-consequent relations, repetition, return, middle, ending, and so forth. Also describe how you hear tuneblocks (motives) grouping together—that is, move up the structural hierarchy to form bigger blocks (phrases and sections).

8. When analyzing your tune and playing it on the keyboard, pay attention to recurring structural patterns that could help to account for your decisions in composing your tune.

Things to Think About in Composing Your Own Tunes

The Compositional Process

Composing your own melody with tuneblocks is a rather different process from simply reconstructing a given tune. You will need to experiment, listening carefully as you try various arrangements of the given blocks. As you experiment, you may be surprised to discover that you are usually able to hear quite intuitively what you like and what you don't, what sounds good and what doesn't. This is good evidence that in listening to the familiar music around you, you have developed a kind of intuitive model of a sensible tune. To search for and make explicit the characteristics of this intuitive model—that is, what you know how to do already—is a primary goal of the projects in this book. Paying attention to the decisions you make while building your tunes will help you move forward. For example, when writing notes in your log, consider the following questions as you listen to and experiment with the blocks:

- What specific features and relations differentiate one block from another?
- What musical features seem to generate the possible structural function of each block (beginning, ending, middle, and so on)?
- Which blocks seem to go well together and why? Why do you dislike a particular sequence of blocks? What did you do to fix it, and why is the new sequence better?

As you go along, pay attention to surprises. For example, notice that putting the same block in a new context may change the way it sounds to you. The blocks obviously remain exactly the same, but as you arrange and rearrange them, the same block may take on differing functional meanings. These are moments to take out your log, to stop and ask:

- I wonder why *that* happened?
- Why didn't this series of blocks sound like I expected it to?
- How would I describe what I just heard?
- What are the differences between what I expected and what I heard?
- How can I make use of what just happened?

Common Organizing Principles

In analyzing the tunes you composed using Group 1 blocks, you may find that you have quite spontaneously used some of the organizing principles found in the tunes for Project 1.1. This is partly because of the structure of the materials you are working with—the given tuneblocks. But your use of these shared organizing principles also supports the notion that you were strongly influenced by the intuitive knowledge you have developed through familiarity with the structures of these and other common folk songs. For instance, in looking back at your completed tune, make note of whether you had built in some of these common organizing principles:

- *Repetition:* Did you intuitively repeat blocks and perhaps even repeat whole phrases?
- *Sequential relations:* Did you juxtapose blocks that share the same pitch contour to form a sequence?
- *Antecedent-consequent phrase relationships:* Did you create phrases that begin the same but move from tension to resolution in their respective endings?

Strange Blocks

The two sets of blocks in Group 2, Ambrosian and Portals, may have sounded "strange" or unusual. The question is, why do they sound that way? Thinking about what makes some melodies sound "strange" can help you to think about what sorts of features and relations you are taking for granted as generating coherence in the tunes you find "ordinary." Consider the following questions and note your answers in your log:

- In what ways are the features (rhythm, pitch relations) of these "strange" blocks different from those of the others?
- What can these differences tell you about the kinds of relations that you are used to and that you have come to take for granted as generating coherence?

• In composing with these blocks, did you discover some new ways of generating coherence?

• Do these ways of generating coherence relate in any way to the organizing structures you used to make tunes with the blocks in Group 1?

Viewing and Editing the Contents of Blocks

To view the contents of blocks

1. Click the magnifying glass cursor at the top of the screen.

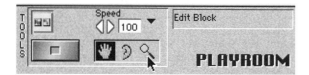

2. With the magnifying glass as your new cursor, click the block that you want to look into.

3. The Edit window will open.

The Edit window

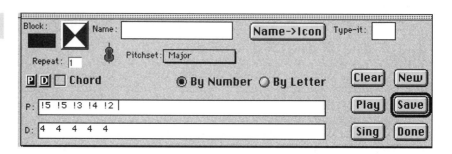

There is a lot of information in this window; we will come back to it shortly. Right now, notice particularly the two lists of numbers: one labeled P, for pitches; the other labeled D, for durations. A good way to explore the meaning of these numbers is to see what happens if you change them. To experiment, you can change some of the pitches and/or durations of a block to make it work better if you find that a block just doesn't work for you (see the list titled "To edit blocks" that follows). But if you do make changes, keep track of the changes in your log. In your paper, you will need to say what you didn't like about the original block and how your changes improved it.

To edit blocks

1. To change the given pitches, drag the cursor over the number (s) you want to change. The pitch number(s) will be highlighted.

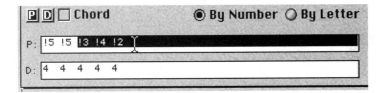

2. Type the new pitch number(s) that you want to try.
3. Click the Play button in the Edit window to hear the result. If you are not satisfied, try some other changes.
4. Experiment with durations in the same way.
5. When you are happy with the results of your experiments, make a new block that incorporates them.
6. To do so, click New.

Do not just click Save; that will incorporate your changes into the original block.

Notice that a new block has been added in the Tuneblocks area, but it has the same icon as the block you just edited. To make your own icon for your new block, follow the instructions below.

Naming Your New Block
In the Name box, type the name you choose, then click Name → Icon. The name you type will appear on the block icon.

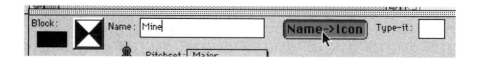

Making Your Own Icon

To make your own icon, you have several choices. To begin, click the icon
in the upper left corner of the Edit window.

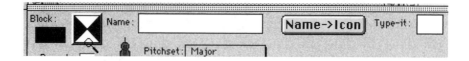

The EditIcon window will open.

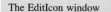
The EditIcon window

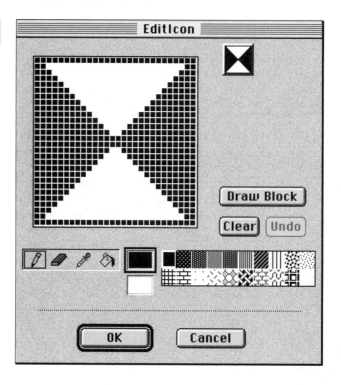

Now you have several options:

• You can select a new pattern from the assortment shown at the bottom of the EditIcon window. Just click your chosen pattern and the

new pattern will replace the old one. Click OK to return to the Edit window.

- You can see a pitch contour picture of the block. Click Draw Block, then OK.

- You can design your own icon. The icon is a *bit map;* you can draw the icon just as you would in any drawing program, such as MacPaint. If you click and drag shaded pixels, they will become white; if you click and drag white pixels, they will become shaded.

- You can choose a color for your block. In the Edit window, click and hold down the mouse button on the colored rectangle just left of the small icon. Select a color from the menu that appears.*

After making a new icon for your block in any of these ways, click Done. You will be prompted to select Save or Don't Save to return to the Tuneblocks window. Clicking Don't Save will leave the new block just as it was before. If you select Save, you will see that the new block that has been added in the Tuneblocks area now has an icon with your chosen color, and your chosen pattern or name. You can use your new block just as you do the given blocks.

> **To change the icon on a bigger block (one that you have assembled with Block-It), use the magnifying glass cursor as before. But now, as you click your bigger block, also hold down the Command (Apple) key. The Block Info window will open. Follow the preceding instructions to give your block a new name or to select a different pattern for the icon.**

Repeating the Blocks in the PlayRoom

You may repeat (up to ten times) all the blocks that are currently in the Playroom area. Experimenting with the repetition of a group of blocks often creates surprising results. To repeat the blocks in the PlayRoom:

- Click the small box to the right of the violin icon. Up and down arrows will appear.

---

*For more editing features, go to Help in the Edit menu.

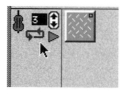

• Click the up arrow till you have the number of desired repetitions. Click the down arrow if you selected more repetitions than you wanted.
• Click Play.
• Notice that the graphics also include the repetitions you have indicated.

There are more new things to do using the Edit window, which we will return to later.

Saving Your Work

Be sure to save your finished compositions so that you can play them in class. To save your work on the hard disk of the computer you are using, follow these steps:

1. Pull down the File menu, select Save.
2. Click the box labeled "Save tune as."
3. Delete "#0" and type your name.
4. Click Save.

To save your work on a floppy disk, follow these steps:

1. Insert your own floppy disk.
2. Pull down the File menu, select Save.
3. Select Desktop and double-click the icon for your floppy disk.
4. Follow steps 2–4 from the preceding list.
5. Remove your floppy disk by dragging its icon to the Trash on the desk-top.

Your paper for Project 1.2 should include at least the following:

• A summary of the log you kept that tracks your composing process— your block requests, your initial comments on each block, the sequences of blocks you tried
• Your process of decision making: expectations, surprises, new hearings, how you account for what "worked" and what didn't

- Examples of how you fixed a problem and why you like the new sequences better.
- A list of the sequence of blocks in your completed tune and an analysis of the structure of your tune, following the models in Project 1.1
- A beginning speculation on what features seem to generate differing structural functions
- A discussion of issues that came up in learning to play your tune on the keyboard

---

LISTENING EXAMPLES: ELABORATING SIMPLE STRUCTURES

Example 1.1: Beethoven, Symphony #9, Fourth Movement, ("Ode to Joy") (1824)

Example 1.2: Beethoven, Symphony #9, Fourth Movement, Variations (1824)

Example 1.3: Haydn, Symphony #99, Minuet, A section (1793)

Example 1.4: Haydn, Symphony #99, Minuet (1793)

Example 1.5: Vivaldi, The Four Seasons, "Winter" (c. 1730)

Example 1.6: Bach, Partita #2 for Solo Violin, Gigue (c. 1720)

Example 1.7: Liszt, Faust Symphony, First Movement (1854)

Introduction

As you listen to the musical examples on your CD, you will recognize many of the same structures you have used in composing your tunes. However, composers also toy with these structural simples; using them as scaffolding, they deviate, elaborate, and expand on these norms to make much larger and more complex compositions. These deviations contribute to moments that we hear as special, as particularly exciting, in the continuous unfolding of a piece. It is interesting that composers who may have been most popular during their lifetime, but whose compositions have not survived in the repertory (for instance, the infamous Salieri), tended to write music that stayed closer to our shared norms. And that is exactly what we mean when, in listening to these forgotten pieces now, we describe them as "banal."

So far you have focused primarily on melodic structure. The recorded examples will give you an opportunity to become familiar with some of the many other means and possibilities composers use in making larger and more complex pieces. For instance, you will be introduced to other dimensions of music such as texture, instrumentation, range, and register. You will find brief definitions of these terms in the section titled "Some Basics: Texture and Instrumentation" at the end of Part 1.

Experiments and explorations can be part of the listening process, too. Listening to a composition is also a performance of sorts; the meaning that you seem just to find in the music, you are actually helping to make. And it is exactly because listening is a process of constructing meaning that you are also able to come to hear in new ways.

It will be most useful to move back and forth between listening to an example, reading the comments and questions, and listening again. Just listening to the examples by themselves or reading the commentary without listening will not do much good or even make much sense. As you work through these examples, keep a log, much as you did in working through the projects. Consider such things as moments of confusion, how your hearings change, your own personal discoveries, and your reactions to the comments and questions in the text.

Note: You may listen to the recorded examples on a regular CD player or, preferably, on the CD-ROM player on your computer. If you use your CD-ROM player, you can control the selections from within Impromptu. To do so, follow these instructions:

1. Insert the CD in the CD-ROM player.
2. In the CD menu, select Play CD Examples. The CD window will open.
3. Notice that you can choose to view the examples by example number, by composer, or by part.

4. Click the example you wish to hear. For instance, to begin listening to the examples for Part 1, click Example 1.1.

5. The CD-ROM player will automatically move to the selected example.

6. To play the example, use the usual CD player button shown on your screen.

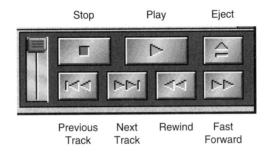

7. To listen to an example again, use the Rewind button or click the selection you wish to hear again. You can select a different example at any time.

Playing with Structural Simples

Building on your experience thus far, we will take as the first example a melody with which you are already familiar. The tune called "Ode" that you reconstructed in Project 1.1 was actually a synthesized version of a melody familiarly known as "Ode to Joy," which was composed by Beethoven on the text "To Joy" by the poet Schiller. Beethoven used it as the theme for a set of variations in the fourth movement of his Ninth Symphony. Listen to it now performed as Beethoven wrote it. The recorded excerpt begins a bit before the familiar melody appears. What is it that gives this same melody such a remarkably different character from the version you worked with?

> **Example 1.1: Beethoven, Symphony #9, Fourth Movement ("Ode to Joy") (1824)**

The hushed quality of the low instruments certainly helps to create the very special mood of the melody—solemn, distant, almost unreal. Cellos and basses, the lowest string instruments in the orchestra, play the melody by themselves; one can almost feel the breathing presence of the live performers. Comparing this performance with the synthesized, mechanical, computer-generated "performance" that you worked with before, it is hard to say that it is even the same melody.

The situation—the context—in which the melody appears is also critically important. Just as context is important in giving particular meaning and function to a phrase, even to a single note within a phrase, so the larger context in which a whole melody appears also influences its effect. Beethoven prepares and sets off the melody to create dramatic contrast. Before the melody begins, we hear fragmentary, unsettling bits of melody which anticipate melodic figures of "Ode." These are interrupted by aggressive and expectant chords, the last ones resolving to frame the quiet entrance of the melody.

What, then, is the same? Having reconstructed the tune, you heard, in the midst of these differences, the same familiar structure:

"Ode" Structural tree

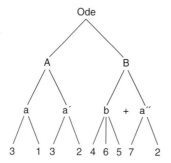

There are two large sections (A and B), with the A section relatively stable and complete through its paired antecedent-consequent phrases. B begins with a feeling of moving onward. The three brief, melodic fragments that make up the *b* phrase help create a feeling of unrest and moving on. The *b* phrase resolves into the return, which includes only the consequent phrase. This phrase is also slightly but significantly varied right at the beginning and is thus labeled *a"*. In the recorded performance, the B section is repeated, as Beethoven indicated in the score.

"Ode to Joy": B is repeated

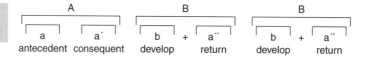

Listen to Example 1.1 again while following the diagram showing structural functions. Pay particular attention to the moment of return—the "joint" between *b* and the return to *a"*.

Beethoven is often most creative in playing with our expectations at boundaries such as the joint between *b* and *a"*. Beethoven prepares and marks the return to *a"* by introducing a large downward leap. The leap stands out in what has been mostly stepwise (conjunct) pitch motion in all of the preceding sections. At the same time, this leap moves the melody beyond its previously limited range. The leap and the move outside the prevailing range can be seen clearly in the pitch contour graphics.

"Ode to Joy": The boundary is marked by a large leap

Notice, too, that the return seems to arrive precipitously, before we expect it and a bit off balance. As evidence that this return is unusual, unexpected, consider that you may have heard arrangements of the "Ode" melody (in supermarkets, for instance) that simply rewrite the joint between *b* and *a″*. The rewriting smooths out the arrival of *a″* in just the right way so as not to disturb our normative expectations. We will return to this passage in Part 2, focusing there on the rhythmic means Beethoven uses to generate this precipitous arrival while also creating complexity— complexity that is evidently too disturbing for shoppers in supermarkets. Listen to Example 1.1 once more before going on to Example 1.2.

Variations on "Ode": Same and Different

Beethoven uses the "Ode" melody in the fourth movement of his Ninth Symphony as the basis for building a larger structure called a *theme and variations*. Each variation in a set of variations is a distinctive and self-contained little piece, with the progression from one variation to the next carefully crafted to create a meaningful whole. As the name suggests, each variation carries over some aspects of the theme while others change. Example 1.2 includes the theme and three variations. Listen to the excerpt several times. Pay particular attention to, and jot down in your log, which aspects of the theme Beethoven keeps the same in each variation, what he changes, and also how the changes progressively transform the character of the original theme.

Example 1.2: Beethoven, Symphony #9, Fourth Movement, Variations (1824)

With respect to what stays the same, the entire "Ode" melody is clearly heard in each of the three variations, and thus the overall structure of each variation also remains the same. Yet each variation presents a striking contrast as Beethoven "dresses" his theme in ever new ways.

For instance, the melody is played by different instruments in each variation. Starting with the lowest strings in the theme, Beethoven moves the melody progressively up through the string section: Cellos and basses play the theme, violas (the mid-range string instruments) play the melody in variation 1, and variation 2 introduces the violins, the highest string instrument. Finally, after a surge in loudness, the whole brass section plays the melody in variation 3. The progression from the theme through the three variations creates a feeling of the gradual emergence of joy: up and out from the low, solemn theme to the brilliance of the brass in variation 3.

But you probably noticed other changes as well. Indeed, in composing the variations, Beethoven has exploited, just in these brief moments, many of the possible means available to composers for creating contrast in sound and character—instrumentation, texture, dynamics, register, and range.* Notice, for example, that moving from the theme to variation 1, the number of instruments participating increases (the texture becomes thicker, more dense). Also, in variation 1, the texture becomes more active: The bassoon plays a countermelody at the top of its normal range, thus competing for attention as it weaves in and around the melody of the theme played by the violas and cellos. In the repetition of the B section in variation 2, the small *crescendo* (increase in loudness) that has consistently marked and reinforced the precipitous joint between *b* and *a"* becomes much more forceful as it leads into the entrance of the brass in the majestic variation 3. And yet, through all of this, the basic structure, just as you reconstructed it and as it was represented by the tree diagram and the structural function diagram, remains the same. It is as if we learn about the hidden potential of the theme and its structure through the many ways Beethoven finds to elaborate on and change it, while still keeping it the same. Listen to Example 1.2 once more. Do you notice other changes, perhaps some that you hear as more important than those included in these comments? Remember to keep notes in your log.

Listen to Example 1.3 now and compare the means Haydn uses to create complexity with those Beethoven used in his theme and variations.

Example 1.3: Haydn, Symphony #99, Minuet, A section (1793)

---

*For more information on instruments of the orchestra and on terms such as *texture, range, register,* and *dynamics,* see the section titled "Some Basics: Texture and Instrumentation" at the end of Part 1.

In Example 1.3, Haydn also plays with structural simples to create complexity, but he does so rather differently from Beethoven in his theme and variations. As you listen, ask yourself questions just as you did in first listening to the tunes in Project 1.1: How are you segmenting the excerpt? What are the basic blocks that you hear? Where do you hear contrast and what means does Haydn use to create it? Do you hear repetitions? If so, when do they occur? Try to make a pencil sketch of what you hear as the basic structure of the excerpt.

Motivic Development: Transformations

The excerpt from the Minuet movement of Haydn's Symphony #99 begins much as Beethoven's theme did—with coupled phrases that function as an antecedent-consequent pair. But instead of going on to complete a full-fledged, self-contained theme, Haydn takes off. He immediately goes on to develop his opening phrases by building on and transforming this initial melodic material. Just as we learned about Beethoven's theme from what happens to it in each variation, so we learn about Haydn's opening phrases through their continuing transformations. Indeed, the whole Minuet movement grows out of this opening material. The complexity that results, in turn, requires you to listen even more attentively as Haydn extends and plays with common structural simples.

This excerpt could be "blocked" in several ways, depending on the level of detail you are focusing on and the kinds of contrasts you are paying attention to. On the largest level, at the top of the structural ladder, you probably heard that the whole excerpt, the first part of the Minuet, is repeated exactly. Moving down the structural ladder, the antecedent-consequent phrases can be heard as forming an initial group—an opening stable statement. Following this, there is a more active, less stable "working out" of motives derived from the opening phrases. This moving-on section is bounded by the arrival of a more stable passage, resolving the previous, less stable, moving-forward section. On this hearing the excerpt might be roughly sketched as shown in the following diagram. Does this sketch match *your* hearing? If not, how does it differ?

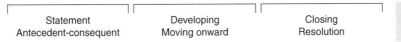

| Statement | Developing | Closing |
| Antecedent-consequent | Moving onward | Resolution |

Minuet structural functions: An initial sketch

Moving down into the details, listen now to just the antecedent-consequent pair. As you listen, pay particular attention to the structural details of these opening phrases.

Zooming In: A Novel Departure

Zooming in on the details, did you notice that Haydn begins the Minuet with an interesting twist on the conventional antecedent-consequent relationship—that is, as compared with those you heard in "Lassie," "Susanna," and "Ode"? The functional relationship between Haydn's two opening phrases is quite clearly the same: The first phrase ends with a feeling of incompleteness, needing to move on; the second phrase ends more completely, thus resolving the previous tension. What, then, is the twist? Recall that in all the traditional antecedent-consequent phrases you have heard, both phrases began exactly the same. In the Minuet, Haydn mimics but plays with this sameness: He gives the beginning of each phrase the same general pitch shape and rhythm, but uses somewhat different pitches. Thus, we hear the same basic structural relations, but with a novel departure from the norm, which can be seen quite clearly in the pitch contour graphics:

Minuet: Opening phrases

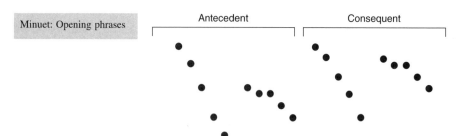

The pitch contour graphics help us move still farther down the structural ladder, zooming in on finer details. You can see and hear, for instance, that each phrase has two quite distinct inner figures—like the two tuneblocks you needed to make each antecedent and each consequent phrase in reconstructing "Ode." But unlike "Ode," Haydn makes a noticeable contrast between these two inner figures: The first figure in each phrase moves down through a large pitch space, and it does so by leaps (*disjunct motion*); the second figure moves through a smaller pitch space in the same amount of time and with the same rhythm, thus it necessarily must move by steps instead of leaps (*conjunct motion*).

The contrast between the two inner figures is made even clearer by a coinciding contrast in texture and instrumentation: The leaping figures are played by only part of the orchestra—strings and winds (clarinets) playing in *unison.* Unison texture is created when the composer writes the same pitches and same rhythm for all the players, but the instruments play in different *registers*—some high and some low, much like men and women singing the same song together. The stepwise figures, in contrast, are played by the whole orchestra with everyone playing the same rhythm but with a rich combination of different pitches (*rhythmic unison*). Thus, to reinforce the contrast within each phrase (not visible in the pitch contour graphics), each phrase moves from a relatively thin, unison texture to a texture that includes more instruments, which are also playing different rather than the same pitches. Can you make a sketch of these contrasting textures?

Listen to Example 1.3 still again. This time continue on, focusing on the means Haydn uses to transform the figures in his opening phrases and how these transformations help to create a sense of moving onward in this developing section.

Motivic Development: Fragmenting

Looking now at pitch contour graphics for the beginning of the onward-moving elaboration, you can see and hear that Haydn has truncated the normative phrase length established by the two opening phrases. There are two shorter figures, each half as long as the previous phrases. These two brief figures form another familiar structural simple, a sequence—two figures that have the same pitch shape and rhythm, with the second moved down a few steps from the first.

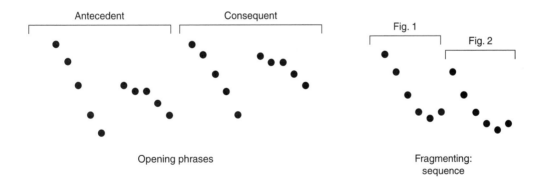

Opening phrases

Fragmenting:
sequence

Haydn compresses the time span in the sequence by using only fragments from the leaping block and from the stepping block. These fragments are joined to form each of the new figures. As a result of this development strategy, Haydn still keeps the contrast between leaps and steps within each of these two brief figures.

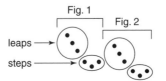

Minuet: Fragments combined

The contrast in pitch motion (leaps and steps) is again reinforced by contrasts in texture: thin, then thick; unison, then rhythmic unison.* And as a result of the compression and fragmentation, contrasts happen more quickly—the pace seems to speed up. All these compositional ploys play a big role in creating the feeling of moving onward, of developing.

Finally, listen to all of Example 1.3 once more. Using what you have learned thus far in listening to the Minuet and especially the ways Haydn develops and transforms musical material, listen for other new ways Haydn finds to intensify the feelings of moving forward as this developing section continues. Going on to the closing section, ask yourself what Haydn does to make this section sound so much more stable than the developing section. Why does it function so effectively to resolve the developing section and, indeed, to provide a fitting close to the whole excerpt? Pay attention to texture—especially melody in relation to accompaniment, and to the relationship between the two large phrases that make up this closing section.

In your log, jot down any discoveries you have made in listening to the Minuet. Also, expand your initial sketch to include more aspects that you think are important to representing your hearing of the Minuet.

Now that you have gone so deeply into the workings of this beginning excerpt of Haydn's Minuet, you will appreciate hearing the whole movement.

Example 1.4: Haydn, Symphony #99 (1793)

The entire movement is a large A B + A' structure—a much expanded and elaborated version of the small *a b + a'* structures you are familiar with from the common tunes in Project 1.1.

Minuet: Structural functions diagram

You will recognize the A section as the portion of the Minuet you have already heard (but now played without the repeat). B is an extended development of the motivic material you heard in A. Notice that Haydn begins this development process with a feeling of taking off. How does he do that? Haydn takes the descending, disjunct pitch shape with which

---

*This is a little like taking the brief fragments of phrases you overhear in a distant conversation and turning them into a new, shorter phrase to make new meaning.

the Minuet begins, and turns it upside down. Now an ascending, disjunct figure, the upward motion sets off the onward, restless feeling that pervades the entire development, which subsides only as the movement approaches A', the return.

A' emerges out of B with hints of return, as if through a process of becoming; almost after the fact we realize that we are already there in the return. But once again Haydn plays with our expectations. No sooner do we recognize the familiar opening motivic material than Haydn takes us through a new elaboration of it—a sequence built from a two-note rising fragment. But rather than arriving at a stable goal, Haydn seems to simply stop, suspending us as if in midair. The suspense gives way to a quiet *coda* (an Italian word meaning "tail"), which resolves and completes the movement. As you listen to the whole movement again, focus on all the ingenious means Haydn uses to transform his opening melodic material.

Can you hear that the entire movement really does grow out of its initial germinal motives? Arnold Schoenberg, a composer of the twentieth century, describes how this process of germinal growth occurs even in simple songs:

> Even the writing of simple phrases involves the invention and use of motives, though perhaps unconsciously. . . . The motive generally appears in a characteristic and impressive manner at the beginning of a piece. . . . Inasmuch as almost every figure within a piece reveals some relationship to it, the basic motive is often considered the "germ" of the idea. . . . However, everything depends upon its use . . . everything depends on its treatment and development.*

Continuous Structures: The Sequence

The next Listening Examples give particular significance to Schoenberg's final sentence. Many of the tunes that you reconstructed in Project 1.1 and composed in Project 1.2 included sequences. There was, for instance, a sequence in the middle of "Austrian," and students usually notice and make use of the sequential relations among blocks in the French and Vienna block sets. Sequential relations are easy to see in the pitch contour graphics, as the pitch shape of a figure always remains the same while it is moved up or down. The following diagram shows representations of sequences from "Austrian" and the Vienna set.

---

*Schoenberg, *Fundamentals of Music Composition,* St. Martin's Press, p. 9.

Austrian   Vienna

A sequence is a particular use of a germinal figure; it differs, for instance, from fragmenting or embedding in new textures such as you heard in the Beethoven and Haydn examples. The sequential repetition of a melodic figure is similar to the repetition of visual shapes in the designs of tapestries, in the patterns of nature, and particularly in *fractals*—complex geometric shapes that exhibit the property of self-similarity.

Sequential repetition is mirrored in this example of a computer-generated fractal shape. (Courtesy Serguei S. Sidach)

In the Classical period (c. 1750 to c. 1820), composers such as Beethoven, Haydn, and Mozart tended to use sequential figures to craft more continuous passages. In most of the melodies you have worked with, as in the Haydn and Beethoven examples, sequential passages occur in the middle, more onward-moving, developing sections. And, as in the Haydn Minuet, these passages were usually surrounded and contained by more stable, statementlike passages with balanced, clearly articulated phrases. The larger organization of these Classical-period works can be described as *sectional*, since each section of a piece is relatively bounded, and each has a distinct structural function within the whole. The initial diagram of the Haydn Minuet reflected this sectional structure on a small scale: Clearly defined antecedent-consequent phrases formed an initial statement section; the developing section with its sequences based on fragments of the previous phrases formed a second more *continuous* section; this was followed by the stable closing section, in which complete phrases were again clearly defined and balanced. At this more detailed level of the structural ladder, there may be contrast between relatively sectional and relatively continuous passages, but at the top of the structural ladder, each of these passages is a section that contributes to the clearly bounded, sectional organization of the whole.

Composers have used sequential progressions in different ways and for different purposes throughout the history of music. In the Baroque period (c. 1600 to c. 1750), composers including Vivaldi, Bach, and Handel used sequential passages as a primary and pervasive means for carrying their compositions forward. As a result, compositions of the Baroque period tend to be more continuous than sectional. Indeed, to make an analysis such as that reflected in the diagrams of the Haydn Minuet would be inappropriate as a representation of the structure of these continuous Baroque pieces. What, then, would constitute an appropriate analysis of such continuous compositions?

Listen to Example 1.5 with this question in mind. Try to make a sketch of how the excerpt proceeds, paying particular attention to the sequences and how they help to organize it.

Example 1.5: Vivaldi, The Four Seasons, "Winter" (c. 1730)

In contrast to the clearly bounded phrases of Beethoven's "Ode" melody, this violin melody accompanied by the string orchestra is made up almost entirely of sequentially repeated figural patterns—small shapes evolving in a kaleidoscopic way. But the process is still hierarchical, although in a different way than in the folk songs or in the Haydn and Beethoven works. In those sectional pieces, you could follow phrases to their goals and group phrases together to hear sections, with each section serving a larger structural function. In contrast, Vivaldi asks you to follow a single figure as it repeatedly winds its way up or down until it gives way to another figure, a new beginning with its own sequential repetitions. Rather than the clear boundaries of phrases and sections, each new figure and its sequential repetition moves almost seamlessly into the next.

Try to follow these subtle changes: The excerpt begins with the whole string orchestra playing together in rhythmic unison. This orchestral passage is followed by the first sequential section, with the solo violinist moving into the foreground. Listening in detail to the pattern that is repeated sequentially, you will hear that it includes within it three smaller figures, each of which is repeated twice—first a disjunct figure, then a conjunct, faster figure followed by a relatively static but again disjunct figure that turns around on itself.

"Winter": Three contrasting figures

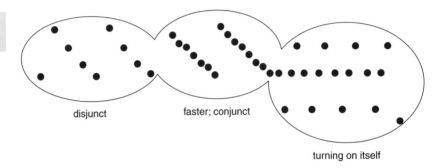

These three short figures are followed immediately by a series of repeated chords played by the whole orchestra. This whole pattern is then moved up and repeated, and once again moved up and repeated.

"Winter": The three figures moved up and repeated

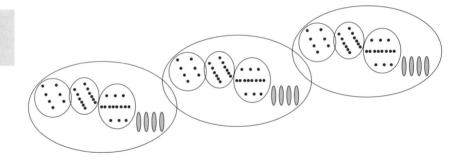

The whole sequential passage culminates in a short passage played by the orchestra, marking the close of the larger section. Vivaldi's organization is perhaps best described as a *nested structure*: Small, inner figures are grouped together to form a single larger pattern, which is in turn nested in repetitions of itself.

Another sequential passage follows: A shorter and more dramatic figure forms the "template" of this sequence, played by the violinist together with the full orchestra. There are four repetitions of this figure, with each repetition shifting downward this time. Still another sequence follows, played by the violin soloist now with minimal accompaniment from the orchestra.

The entire first half of the movement is made up of these ever-growing, nesting structures: single melodic figures nested within their sequential repetitions; a series of sequences, each nested within a clearly bounded section and each "personalized" by a particular repeated pattern; and the entire set of sequences, in turn, nested within the large section bounded by the return of the thematic material played by the full orchestra with which the movement begins. As you listen, you will hear that motion is continuous within sections through the subtle eliding of one repeating figure to the next, but the larger structure is sectional, each subsection bounding the continuous motion within it, and each subsection separated from but directly juxtaposed to the next.

Example 1.6: Bach, Partita #2 for Solo Violin, Gigue (c. 1720)

The process of continuously unfolding is heard in its most intense and complex form in the partitas Bach wrote for solo violin. A partita is a suite of dancelike pieces, and this excerpt is from one movement, called the Gigue, of Partita #2. Bach's use of sequences differs from Vivaldi's in an important way: While Vivaldi clearly marks off one continuous section from another, making a kind of striated structure, Bach's sequential passages lead continuously onward—the violinist is hardly given a chance to "breathe."

While the Gigue starts off with two relatively bounded gestures, followed by another briefly settled moment, the rest of the excerpt moves forward with hardly a pause. Moreover, after the opening two gestures, nearly the whole excerpt proceeds without any rhythmic change—that is, all the notes are of equal duration. Surely you will feel lost, the music seeming just to go on and on, if you are listening for the regular arrivals of phrase endings as in the melodies you have been working with or the compositions by Beethoven and Haydn. What, then, can you focus your attention on? What gives shape and coherence to the Gigue? Listening again, closely, you may begin to hear momentary arrivals and departures, even changes in the rate of motion. What can generate these apparent changes in motion, and what can articulate this seeming continuousness?

As in the Vivaldi example, Bach is also playing with sequences, but now relentlessly—each unwinding and evolving into the next. The movement begins with two well-articulated gestures resembling antecedent-consequent phrases—as if Bach is helping listeners get their bearings. This pair is followed by a first sequential passage, with each repetition marked especially by its highest note—which, along with each sequential repetition, moves down one step each time, coming to rest momentarily in a short closing figure.

Gigue, the first sequence: Each repetition moves down one step

As shown in the graphics, the contour of this sequential figure makes the series itself continuous—the ending of each sequential figure melodically merging with the beginning of the next one.

Gigue: Each figure merging with the next

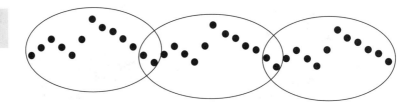

Going on, notice that in the midst of freer passages and an ever-cumulating energy, the sequential passages serve as moments of relative stability, of regularity that you can hold on to. Notice, too, that the excitement of the movement is also created by the enormous variety among the sequential figures—in the length of the "template" and in the shape of the figures, together with never knowing how long a sequential passage will last, when it will give way to a freer passage, or when the freer passage will evolve once again into a sequence. Listen for these sequences, but then try to hear them as moments through which Bach makes the music become one seamless web of organized motion.

Go back and listen to Haydn's phrase-oriented Minuet and compare the role that sequences play in that piece with the role that sequences play in the continuous Bach Gigue.

Example 1.7: Liszt, Faust Symphony, First Movement (1854)

We now jump ahead 134 years to a work composed in the middle of the nineteenth century. The Faust Symphony by Franz Liszt begins with a sequential passage, but one that is surely a far different kind of thing from previous examples of sequences—both in feeling and in form. What accounts for the differences and how are feeling and form interconnected?

The excerpt is continuous but, again, in ways that differ from either Vivaldi or Bach. Beginning with a three-note, rising sequential figure, each of its four repetitions creeps down. The violins take over the sequential figure from the cellos, stretching out the initial figure into one continuous line that quickly expands the range upward. The melody goes directly onward to its high point, rather than turning in on itself as before. At this top point, the oboes sneak in, taking over the pitch from the violins to introduce a new, disjunct, more jagged figure. The ending fragment of this new figure is repeated sequentially. As the figure passes from oboes to bassoons, the bassoons now stretch it downward, extending the melody to its lowest pitch—and almost to theirs.

The diabolical feeling of the Faust Symphony is thus created by a number of factors: the large range, the movement of the melody through this often empty-sounding expanse, the use of solo instruments—especially the oboes and bassoons—and the restless character of the sequential figures, which seem never to settle down or to imply a pitch that would bring the melody to rest.

Some Basics: Texture and Instrumentation

Composers use instrumentation and texture as a painter uses the colors of the palette: Sometimes these "colors" support inherent structural relations; sometimes they become the means for actually creating structure. The difference is illustrated by a comparison between, for example, Haydn's use of instruments mostly to support other structural means, and Liszt's use of instruments in the beginning of his Faust Symphony, where the "colors" of the instruments he selects play an important role in shaping the character and mood. Beethoven, in the variations from his Ninth Symphony, does both.

Recall that Beethoven creates a feeling of increasing intensity through the variations. He does so by modifying the texture in two primary ways:

- By adding more instruments, thus increasing the *density or thickness* of the texture.
- By increasing the inner *activity* of the texture by making instruments move more independently of one another.

This progression can be heard, but it can also be seen quite clearly by looking at the score.

Think of the score for the moment as an abstract painting that captures the textures of material—single or multiple layers, relatively still or actively moving internally. Then compare the score of Beethoven's theme with the score of variations 2 and 3.

The thin, inactive texture of the theme is clearly reflected in the score-as-picture—just the cellos and basses playing in unison. The second variation not only sounds but also looks much more active—individual instruments can be seen freely moving around and in competition with one another. The texture of the third variation looks and sounds much "thicker"—more instruments take up more space on the page as Beethoven adds woodwinds, brass, and timpani to complete his entire orchestra.

Looking more closely at the score of the third variation, you will see at the left of the page the names of the full complement of instruments— each instrument on one of the twelve lines (called *staves*) of the score. Brackets (called *braces*) group the staves into the four traditional groupings of instruments:

1. *Woodwinds*—here, flute, clarinet, oboe, bassoon, and contrabassoon (saxophone and English horn are also woodwinds)
2. *Brass*—here, French horn and trumpets (trombone and tuba are also brass)
3. *Percussion*—here, timpani (there are also many others, such as snare, tom, cymbals, gong, and so on)
4. *Strings*—violin, viola, cello, bass

The composer specifies the number of players on wind and brass instruments (two on each, in most cases); the total number of players will depend mostly on the number of string players involved. The total number in a symphony orchestra can vary between 40 and 80 performers.

While the particular technology of each group of instruments and their characteristic means of producing sound can be described, to become familiar with the sounds of each instrument, you need to listen. The synthesized sounds you have been working with give you a flavor of these instruments, but they are only electronic approximations of the real thing. At best, you should listen to live performances by going to concerts by an orchestra, band, or other group. Or you can listen to one of the many CD-ROMs that show you pictures of the instruments and give examples of the instruments actually playing typical passages.

Dynamics and Expression

Dynamics

The term *dynamics* refers to the relative loudness or softness (intensity) of musical tones. Markings derived from Italian are generally used to indicate dynamics. The basic signs are as follows:

p	*piano,*	soft
f	*forte,*	loud

Beethoven, Symphony
#9, Fourth Movement:
(a) Beginning of the
theme "Ode to Joy"
(measures 92–99); (b)
Beginning of variation 2
(measures 140–147); (c)
Beginning of variation 3
(measures 164–171).
(See the section titled
"Bar Lines and Beams"
in Project 2.2 for an ex-
planation of measure
numbers.)

THEME

VARIATION 1

VARIATION 2a

VARIATION 2b

VARIATION 3

Modifications of these serve as very rough dynamic indications for the performer:

pp	*pianissimo,* very soft
ppp	even softer
pppp	still softer
ff	*fortissimo,* very loud
fff	even louder
ffff	still louder
mp	*mezzo piano,* "half soft" (less soft than *piano*)
mf	*mezzo forte,* not as loud as *forte*
$<$	*crescendo,* gradual increase in loudness
$>$	*decrescendo* or *diminuendo,* gradual decrease in loudness

Expression

Composers also use Italian terms to indicate their intentions concerning expressive feelings and character to be projected by the performer in a given piece or passage. Just how performers are to do this is pretty much left up to them. However, it is taken as a given that pitches as notated will remain unchanged and that durations will have a certain "give and take," but still remain within the bounds of their notated values. This is much like the actor who must find ways of speaking the author's words (pace, accent, dynamics, and so on) so as to project the emotions of the passage as he or she interprets them.

Some of the Italian words more frequently encountered as expressive terms are the following:

animato	animated
appassionato	passionate
cantabile	in a singing style
con brio	with spirit; brilliantly
con moto	with movement (moving along)
dolce	sweet; tender
espressivo	with expression; expressive
grazioso	graceful
legato	smoothly connected; bound together (as in a sung melody)
sforzando (sf)	a single note strongly accented
staccato	detached (opposite of *legato;* notes are separated)
tenuto	held (the full value of the note or a bit more)

Obviously these indications of dynamics and expression are vague and subjective, thus demanding interpretation by performers. For example, the term *appassionato* (to be played in a passionate manner) may have reflected a particular hearing of a piece or particular passage when the composer wrote it into the score. But the term is going to be interpreted and projected in many different ways by performers. The score, even with the composer's dynamics and expressive markings included, is still only an approximation. The challenge to the performer is to develop a "hearing" of the work (for instance, figural groupings, larger structural boundaries, and the contrasts they create) while still remaining true to the information—the notations—given in the score. At the same time, through experiment, practice, and listening back to themselves, performers must find ways of projecting their hearings by using subtle means particular to their instrument.

Part 2

Rhythmic complexity: Each instrument plays its own rhythmically independent line. (Image: Charlie Chaplin in *Modern Times*)

Rhythmic Structure

Introduction: Making and Breaking Rhythmic Structure

The word *rhythm*, as used in everyday language and also in science, usually refers to some kind of periodicity—a series of events that recur at regular time intervals. We speak, for instance, of the rhythm of the seasons or of day and night; the rhythm of breathing, of the heartbeat, of walking; the rhythm (period) of a pendulum or of the vibrations of a string.

Rhythm as a musical term has a much broader meaning; it is used to refer to the many different ways in which *time* is organized in music. Indeed, since all music moves continuously through time, its structure is uniquely dependent on the means composers develop to regulate, articulate, group, constrain, and confound the passing of musical time. In turn, the temporal structuring of music is probably the aspect to which we respond most viscerally and most directly.

Musicians use the term *rhythm* to refer to periodic structures like those mentioned here, but rhythm also applies to aspects of temporal organization that are not easily heard as a simple recurrence of events at regular time intervals. For example, the relative time spans of motives (as in tuneblocks) and the relative time spans of larger entities such as phrases generate *structural rhythms*, and these may or may not be periodic in their relationships. Or we speak of *harmonic rhythm*, referring to the rates at which chords change in an accompaniment. And on a more detailed level, there is the rhythm of a tune—the particular and usually varied durations of notes in a melody. For instance, try clapping just the rhythm of "Hot Cross Buns" or "Oh Susanna."

But of all the ways in which musical time is structured, the most fundamental, and the one that is shared by the musics of most cultures, is the presence of an underlying beat or pulse. The term *beat* refers to that aspect of music that marks off time into regularly recurring units. To mark a pulse or keep a beat seems to be an ability we are all born with—for instance, the newborn baby's rhythmic sucking or rocking. This innate ability may be the earliest sign of our capacity to segment continuous phenomena (especially the flow of time), and as such it is thought to be the beginnings of our abilities to construct units and to measure.

Indeed, it is in relation to this regularly recurring beat that all the other dimensions of rhythm are felt and heard. The beat serves most specifically as the temporal unit in relation to which we measure varied durations of a melody or rhythm. But there is a paradox here: Unlike other units of measure (an inch, an hour, a pound) which remain fixed, external, and uninfluenced by the matter that is being measured, a beat is continuously being regenerated as a piece is performed. Relations among events internal to each piece of music generate the beat, and the beat, in turn, serves as the unit for measuring these events that create it.

This paradox raises a number of intriguing questions, which you will be exploring in Part 2. For example, while almost everyone can feel the beat generated by a piece, it is not so obvious just what kinds of relations among performed events function to generate this beat. Moreover, we will want to ask, what are the interactions between the piece and the performer of that piece with respect to the underlying beat? Does the performer *follow* a beat or *create* one as he or she goes along? And what are the relationships between these underlying, invariant temporal units and the boundaries of melodic motives (figures), phrases, and sections that you listened to and worked with in Part 1?

Metric Hierarchies

In your work on Projects 1.1 and 1.2, you found that tunes generate multiple structural levels called *structural hierarchies.* We represented these hierarchies as tree structures, with smaller structural elements (figures/tuneblocks) grouped together to form larger structural elements (phrases); these elements grouped together to form still larger structural elements (sections). Similarly, most of the melodies that we hear every day generate *metric hierarchies.*

Both structural hierarchies and metric hierarchies are actually generated by the relations among performed events. However, there are significant differences between them. The elements of *structural* hierarchies—figures, phrases, sections—are the particular musical gestures of a melody, those that we follow from one goal of motion to the next. The elements of *metric* hierarchies are the regularly recurring time units we call beats; the proportional relations among rates of beats at each level determine the metric hierarchy of a piece.

We might compare figures and phrases to the elegant and varied figures and shapes that form both details and the large design in Leonardo da Vinci's anatomical drawings. The time units (beats) that form a metric hierarchy might be compared to the spatial units that Leonardo sometimes used as a grid to measure and guide the relations among the shapes he drew.

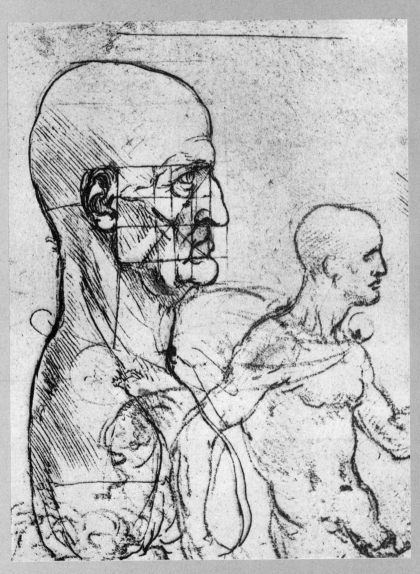

Compare the use of a spatial grid in this drawing by Leonardo da Vinci with the way metric hierarchies work in music.

Just as Leonardo's grid marked off proportional relations in space, so metric hierarchies mark off proportional relations in time. But there is also an important difference between Leonardo's spatial grid and the temporal metric of music. While the spatial grid is given beforehand, the temporal grid is not; rather, as suggested earlier, a temporal grid is generated by the relations among pitch and time events as a piece unfolds. Moreover, in looking at Leonardo's drawings, we can ignore the spatial grid; it may be part of the anatomy of Leonardo's drawing process, but it is certainly not generated by Leonardo's unique spatial gestures through which he forms figures and shapes. In contrast, temporal grids in music are generated by the unique sound gestures of a composition, and they are continuously regenerated by the musical relations the composer has created.

This process of regenerating time units creates the underlying temporal framework of a piece against which particular temporal relations are heard to conform or conflict. Thus, unlike Leonardo's grid, which remains static, always the same, and unaffected by what is drawn in relation to it, the metric hierarchy is a regenerating, living constituent of the piece as it moves through time.

Another interesting paradox emerges here: While time is continuous in its essence, our experience of organized time depends on the boundaries that segment this continuousness. On one hand, the flow of time is marked off into discrete, invariant units—the metric dimension of temporal structure; on the other hand, the continuous flow of musical time is marked off by the arrivals and departures of figures and phrases.

The Projects

In your work with melodic figures (especially when editing the given tuneblocks in Project 1.2 to make them conform to your intuitive preferences), you learned that both pitch and duration contribute to "shaping" figures and to the coherence of melodies of which they are a part. Working on the projects in Part 2, you will focus primarily on varied durations played by nonpitch percussion instruments. In Project 2.1 you will play and work with the structure and function of metric hierarchies. In Project 2.2, you will use Impromptu and the synthesizer's percussion instruments to reconstruct the metric hierarchies that you hear in familiar tunes. Once built, these temporal frameworks will become the basis for composing more interesting and varied percussion accompaniments. In Projects 2.3 and 2.4 you will compose your own original percussion pieces.

The large goal of these projects is to help you appreciate the many ways in which composers play with temporal frameworks to create exciting complexity and surprise.

The specific, smaller goal of each task is to give you more intimate experience with the musical means that create this rhythmic interest and surprise.

Project 2.1 focuses on helping you notice and make explicit your very basic sense of "keeping time"—of moving along with the beat of a piece. In turn, this project will help you hear and play metric hierarchies—the several layers of beats that are going on simultaneously.

The metric hierarchy is certainly not something you ordinarily listen to by itself, separate from compositions that are generating these structures. But the hierarchy, often running in the background, serves as a critical organizing frame not only for a melody, but also for events in all other parts of the texture. Indeed, once established by the events in a composition, this frame creates expectations for continuation, while deviations from the metric frame are noticed as surprising.

But you can't be surprised unless you have expectations, and establishing expectations is what metric frameworks are all about. A composition in which the framework is established but never "attacked" is like a mystery story that is boring because you can predict every move. Once the metric framework is established in a composition, then there is a potential for surprise as conflict is introduced in relation to that norm. This is like a more exciting mystery story in which the author builds a firm structure of expectations and then introduces that brilliant twist that carries you off in a direction that you could never have anticipated.

It would be a mistake to think that all music generates a beat or groupings of beats. Indeed, composers can use the presence or absence of a beat as a means for creating contrasting feelings and also different structural functions. Further, in the musics of other cultures, the organization of time is often quite different from what we take for granted as "making sense." It is useful to listen to some examples of music that is organized differently from ours with respect to temporal structure. By moving away from what we know best and then looking back, we can often discover what it is we know so well.

So before beginning your work on actually building meter, listen to some examples of music in which time is organized in differing ways.

LISTENING EXAMPLES: BEAT, METER, RHYTHM

Example 2.1: "Bhimpalasi" (sitar played by Ravi Shankar)

Example 2.2: Hindemith, Kleine Kammermusik, Fourth Movement (1922)

Example 2.3: Porter, "Night and Day" (Billie Holiday, vocal) (1937)

Example 2.4: Lanner, "Styrian Dances" (1840)

Example 2.5: Sousa, "Stars and Stripes Forever" (1888)

Each of these examples comes from a different place and a different musical culture. It is not surprising, then, that in each piece, time is also organized quite differently. Listen particularly for the beat and the different role it plays in organizing the music. For instance, do you immediately feel the presence of a beat, does it appear gradually, or is a beat entirely absent?

Example 2.1: "Bhimpalasi" (Ravi Shankar, sitar)

"Bhimpalasi," a traditional piece from India, begins with a free improvisatory feeling. Ravi Shankar, playing the sitar, is accompanied by the tamboura, a stringed instrument that is plucked continuously so as to make a drone. As the piece goes on, the two performers are joined by a third playing an Indian drum called a tabla. Listen for the change in sound when the tabla comes in. Can you hear the increasingly strong presence of a beat? How would you describe the difference in feeling between the opening part and the later continuation of the excerpt?

Example 2.2: Hindemith, Kleine Kammermusik, Fourth Movement (1922)

Kleine Kammermusik (German, "A Little Chamber Music") was composed by Hindemith for five wind instruments: flute, oboe, clarinet, horn, and bassoon. As you listen, notice the alternation between passages where all the instruments are playing together in rhythmic unison (same rhythm, different pitches), and solo sections where each player, in turn, is given a chance to show off his or her instrument. What creates the difference in feeling between the unison sections and the solo sections? How do these contrasts relate to the presence or absence of a beat?

Example 2.3: Porter, "Night and Day" (Billie Holiday, vocal) (1937)

There is no question about the presence of a strong beat in "Night and Day." But notice how Billie Holiday plays with, almost teases this underlying pulse. While she moves elegantly around and against the bass player's ever-present beat, she always comes out just right at the end of phrases and sections. This is an example of a beat providing a strong framework within which an artist performer can be free to wander but is never lost.

In fact, performers of all kinds of music rarely play a mechanically exact beat, such as we hear in computer-generated music. Rather, performers "bend" the beat, subtly stretching or contracting it so as to animate the motion toward musical goals and to emphasize the arrival at boundaries of structural events. Indeed, this flexibility makes the difference between what we feel is a *musical* performance in contrast to a *mechanical* performance.

Example 2.4: Lanner, "Styrian Dances" (1840)

Lanner's dance represents popular music of another time and place—the Vienna coffeehouses of the mid-nineteenth-century. Again there is a clear and present beat, but if you listen closely, you will hear that these performers are also "bending" the beat. They are doing so in a quite different way from Billie Holiday, but one that is typical of the performance of Viennese waltzes. As you listen, make a little experiment: Move with the beat that you feel (clap or tap along). Then listen again and make a steady but *slower* beat, and then an equally steady but *faster* beat. What are the relations among these three rates of beats? How could you find out?

Example 2.5: Sousa, "Stars and Stripes Forever" (1888)

The Sousa march brings you to music that is probably most familiar. Listening to it after your experience with music of other cultures and different times, how would you describe what is so comfortable about the organization of time in this march? There is no question about the presence of a beat. But what else is going on? Move along with the beat, just as you did with the Lanner dance. Then listen again and clap a *slower* beat; then, as you listen once more, clap an equally steady but *faster* beat. Are the relations among the beats the same as in the Lanner dance?

The internal relations among these beats, which you can feel and follow, make up the metric hierarchies of the two pieces. The structure of metric hierarchies is the topic of Projects 2.1 and 2.2. We will return to the differences between the metric hierarchies of the waltz and the march after you have completed Project 2.1.

Project 2.1

Building Meter

1. Listen to and build metric hierarchies.
2. Differentiate between and build duple and triple metric hierarchies.
3. Determine various ways to make music move faster or slower.

Project 2.1 focuses on helping you make explicit your very basic sense of "keeping time"—of moving along with the beat of a piece. In turn, this project will help you hear and play the several layers of beats that are going on simultaneously. The project begins with a series of guided experiments that will help you hear and feel some of the basic elements of rhythmic structure as well as some of the ways these elements can be represented.*

In the Drummer Playroom, with the sound file named METER in your workspace, click METER in the Blocks area. To get a feel for the basic temporal relations of "Anya," you will need to feel the beat with your body. So, as you listen to "Anya," move to the beat—tap or clap a steady beat along with the music, much as you did in clapping along with the Sousa march and the Lanner dance. If you listen again, you will also be

INFO BOX
Starting Project 2.1
· In the Playrooms menu, select Drummer
· In the Tunes Catalog, select METER
· In the Graphics menu, select Rhythm Bars

---

*The Drummer activities are more effective if you can use MIDI Sound instead of the default Internal Sound.

able to hear and to clap a slower beat. On one more listening, try to clap a faster beat that also goes with the tune.

Now click Play and listen to "Anya" accompanied by three percussion instruments. Each percussion instrument is playing a beat that is going at a different rate, but each beat also fits with the tune. In fact, these are probably the same three rates of beats that you clapped just now when you were keeping time to "Anya." All together, these three rates of beats make up the three levels of "Anya"'s metric hierarchy. Listen again, and this time clap along with the beat that feels most comfortable to you.

The Drummer Environment

Now that you have a feeling for the metric hierarchy, take a moment to familiarize yourself with the setup of Impromptu's Drummer environment before going on to actually play with the hierarchy. The Drummer environment differs in several ways from the Tuneblocks environment. Looking at the Drummer screen, notice that the Blocks area includes two kinds of blocks—the familiar tuneblocks and also drumblocks. Tuneblocks, as always, play tunes such as "Anya" and "Lanner." Drumblocks have numbers on them and they play percussion instruments. The meaning of the numbers will become clear in a moment.

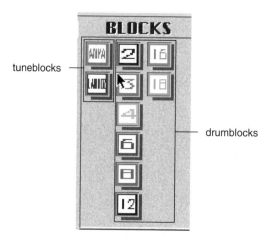

Now look closely at the following annotated picture of the Playroom and compare it with the Playroom on your screen.

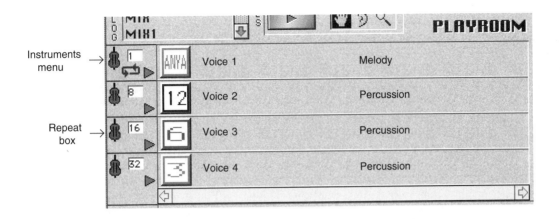

While you could work with only one instrument and one "voice" in the Tuneblocks Playroom, you can work with four instruments, each in a separate voice, in the Drummer Playroom. The four separate "strips" in the Drummer Playroom correspond to the four separate *voices* that you will be working with in the Drummer projects. Voice 1, as you have heard, is a melody voice for tuneblocks, which play pitch-playing instruments—clarinet, vibes, piano, and so on. Voices 2, 3, and 4 are for drumblocks, which play non-pitch percussion instruments such as conga, bongo, or snare.

The Repeat box at the left of each voice tells Impromptu how many times to repeat the drumblock(s) in that voice. For instance, the 8 in the Repeat box for Voice 2 tells Impromptu to repeat the 12-block in that voice eight times. Thus in the graphics you see eight vertical lines in Voice 2, each line representing a repetition of the sound for the 12-block.

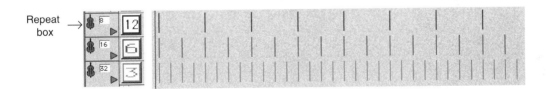

Repetitions of the same block mark off the continuous flow of time into regularly recurring units. Marking off time into equal units creates a beat. Thus, repetitions of a single block in each of the voices creates a beat and each of these beats is going at a different rate. What are the proportional relations among these rates?

From Action to Description: Graphic Representations of Time Relations

Hearing and feeling the temporal relations among the three levels of beats is a primary goal of Project 2.1. However, time is always going by and events happening in the present disappear into the past. Unlike sound events, graphic representations hold still—past and future are both visible in the present. Click Play again, and this time follow carefully the graphics at the bottom of the screen.

Impromptu's Rhythm Bars notation represents time relations through analogous space relations. For instance, the unequally spaced vertical lines in the top row of the graphics window represent the varied durations of the rhythm of "Anya." Focus your attention just on "Anya" and, while watching the graphics, clap the varied durations that make up the rhythm of the tune. Notice that melodic events that take up more time (go slower) also take up more space. Similarly, melodic events that take up less time (go faster) also take up less space.

In contrast to the unequally spaced lines representing the rhythm of "Anya," the other three rows of vertical lines are all equally spaced. The equal spaces between these lines represent the equal durations played by the percussion instruments in each voice. They also show that each percussion instrument is playing a steady beat. These are the steady beats that you clapped when you first listened to "Anya." However, the spaces between lines differ at each level to show the differences in the rate of beats played by each instrument.

Spaces between lines show the rate of beats

Turn off the melody voice of "Anya" (Voice 1) so you can listen more closely just to the percussion instruments.

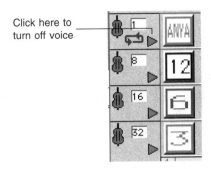

Click here to
turn off voice

Click Play and focus your attention on the slowest beat. The slowest beat is represented by the lines at the top level of the percussion (Voice 2). Remember that more space between lines represents sound events moving more slowly. Can you distinguish this slowest beat from the others? Listen again and clap along with the slowest beat.

Now listen for the fastest beat, shown by the lines at the bottom level (Voice 4). Clap along with the fastest beat. Notice that these lines are closer together than those at the top level. Notice, too, that your hands also move less distance from one another in clapping a faster beat.

Finally, focus your attention on the mid-level beats. This is the beat that usually feels most natural—the beat that you probably clapped when you were first keeping time to "Anya." Of course, you may have found that a different beat was more comfortable to keep time to—for instance, the faster or the slower beats at the outer levels. That is a matter of individual preference. For now, try to focus your attention on this mid-level beat. The mid-level beat is called the *tactus* (Latin for "touch"). The tactus is the beat that usually serves as the temporal reference in relation to which beats at the other levels of the hierarchy are measured.

Playing the Numbers: How Much, How Many?

In seeing and hearing the differences among the rates of beats at the three levels of "Anya"'s metric hierarchy, you were probably also getting a feel for how drumblocks work. In general, numbers on drumblocks determine the rate at which events follow one another. The numbers and Impromptu's notation for time relations are based on two general principles:

1. Larger numbers represent longer durations; smaller numbers represent shorter durations. The smaller the number on a drumblock, the faster events will follow one another.
2. The numbers on drumblocks represent durations that are proportional to one another; for example, a 2-block goes twice as fast as a 4-block; a 6-block goes twice as slow as a 3-block.

Thus, the 12-block in Voice 2 produces a beat that goes twice as slow as the beat produced by the 6-block in Voice 3. This is a 2:1 relationship. Similarly, the beat produced by the 6-block goes twice as slow as the beat produced by the 3-block in Voice 4—again a 2:1 relationship.

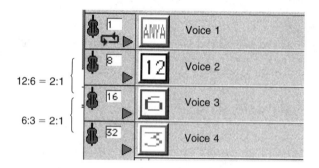

| EXPLORATIONS 1 | **Duple and Triple Meter** |

In working on these explorations, you will be moving back and forth between sounds, your actions, and descriptions in several media. These experiences will help develop your intuitive sense of a pulse, your feel for temporal organization, and especially your understanding of the important differences in the structures of duple and triple meters.

Building Duple Meter

To focus your attention on the relationships that characterize duple meter, turn off Voice 4, the fastest beat, and listen to just the relations between the slowest beat in Voice 2 and the tactus in Voice 3. As you listen, watch the continuously moving pointer in the graphics window. The pointer represents the continuous flow of time, while the static lines represent the marking off of that flow by the regularly recurring drum sounds—the beat. Can you hear that the beats made by the 12-block are going twice as slow as the tactus beat made by the 6-block? Or putting it another way, can you hear that two tactus beats are going by for each of the slowest beats? This temporal relationship is also represented by the spatial relations of the graphics: while one line is going by at the slowest (top) level, two lines are going by at the middle (tactus) level.

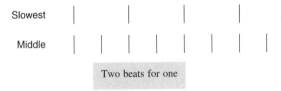

The slowest beat has the effect of grouping the tactus beats in twos. To reflect this grouping function, we will call the slower beat the *grouper beat.*

While you can see that the tactus and grouper beats are going along, each at a steady rate, you may have had a somewhat different impression as you listened. Instead of hearing two steady beats, each going along at its own rate with a 2:1 relationship between them, you may have heard a *"tick-tock"* effect—a kind of "on-off" effect, or alternation, as shown in the following figure.

What creates this effect? When the tactus beat and the grouper beat arrive together, they sound like one stronger beat (*tick*); the lone tactus beat (*tock*) falls in between. At the moments when tactus and grouper beats occur simultaneously, they reinforce one another to generate a regularly occurring *accent.* If you focus your attention just on the tactus beat, you can hear that tactus beats alternate between accented and unaccented beats. This is usually described as an alternation between *strong* and *weak* beats. Try clapping along with the tactus, marking this alternation between strong and weak beats. This regular alternation is the central characteristic of what we call *duple meter.* The term *duple* refers to the "two-ness" of this metric hierarchy.*

*Experiment with the instrumentation to make the grouper and tactus beats more distinct.

Turn off Voice 2 (the slowest beat) and turn on Voice 4 (the fastest beat). Listening just to the relations between the beats in Voices 3 and 4, you hear that the fastest beat is moving along twice as fast as the tactus—again a 2:1 relationship. Taking the tactus as point of reference, the fastest beat divides the duration of the tactus in half. We will call this fastest beat the *divider beat*.

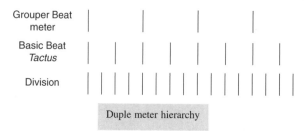

Duple meter hierarchy

Turn Voice 1 and Voice 2 on again and listen once more to "Anya" accompanied by all three percussion instruments. As you listen, shift your listening focus from one level to another. Can you clap each level in turn? Using both hands, try to tap out the beats at two different levels simultaneously. Can you hear and feel the 2:1 proportional relationship between the rates of beats at each of the three levels? It is this grouping of the tactus beats in twos that characterizes "Anya" as being in duple meter. You can see this duple structure represented in several ways: in numbers (12-6-3), in space-for-time graphics, and by following the continuously moving pointer. And most of all you can hear the duple meter structure and feel it by clapping the beats and by listening carefully.

From your experiments thus far, you can conclude that duple meter is created by the interactions among:

- the 2:1 relationship between the rates of the tactus beat and the grouper beat.
- the grouping of tactus beats in twos.
- the alternation between strong and weak tactus beats.

Using the Principles of Duple Meter

Given these underlying structures, it should be clear that the essence of duple meter is the relations among the beat durations generated by the piece, not any particular absolute durations. To demonstrate this principle, you can, for instance, create duple meter with other beat durations, as long as you keep the proportional relationships among them the same. For example, if we start with a 4-beat as the tactus, then 8 will be the grouper beat and 2 the divider beat.

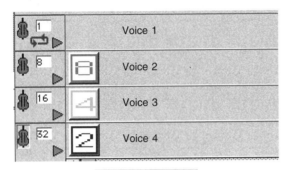

Another duple meter

Try it: To clear all the blocks from the Playroom, pull down the Edit menu and select Clear Voices. Now drag the 8, 4, and 2 blocks into the Playroom as shown in the example above. Click Play and listen. The beats certainly have the same proportional relations. What is the same and what is different between this duple meter hierarchy and the previous one?

Will this accompaniment fit with "Anya"? Try it: Drag the ANYA tuneblock into Voice 1 and click Play. The percussion accompaniment obviously conflicts with "Anya," but it actually sounds more interesting. What is generating this conflict, what makes it more interesting, and how can the conflict be resolved?

To get an idea, use the magnifying glass cursor to open the ANYA block. Look at the durations in the Duration box.

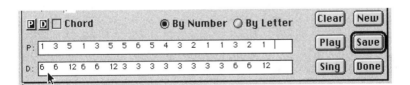

Can you change the durations for "Anya" so that the new metric hierarchy (8-4-2) will fit? *Hint:* Keep the proportional relations of "Anya" 's durations the same!

6 6 12 6 6 12... -----➤ 4 4 8 4 4 8.....

When you have made the changes in durations, click New, then Done. This will take you back to the main window and give you a new ANYA block in the Blocks area. Replace the ANYA block that's in the Playroom with this new one and click Play. Does the new accompaniment fit the new "Anya"? If so, what will happen if you replace this new ANYA block with the original ANYA block? Will the accompaniment and the tune conflict?

Think about this little experiment and make some notes in your log to explain what has happened here.

Revisiting Sousa and Lanner

Go back now and listen to Sousa's "Stars and Stripes Forever" and Lanner's "Styrian Dance" (Listening Examples 2.5 and 2.4). Listen several times to "Stars and Stripes Forever," each time clapping one level of beats. Listen once more and this time try to clap and tap two levels of beats at the same time. Can you hear that there is a 2:1 relationship between the levels? If so, your clapping "tells" you that "Stars and Stripes Forever," like "Anya," is in duple meter.

Now listen several times to the Lanner dance. Listen for and and clap along with each of the three levels of beats in this piece. Listen again and try to clap and tap the tactus and the grouper beat at the same time. What is the relationship between the tactus and the grouper beat? Can you hear that, unlike "Stars and Stripes Forever" and "Anya," there is a 3:1 relationship between grouper beat and tactus in Lanner's dance?

This 3:1 relationship between tactus and grouper beats makes the difference between duple meter and *triple meter.* And this difference between the duple meter of Sousa's march and the triple meter of Lanner's dance also exemplifies the fundamental difference between a march and a waltz: Marches are organized in duple meter, waltzes in triple meter. The following explorations will give you an opportunity to work with this difference.

Building Triple Meter

The triple meter hierarchy differs from the duple meter hierarchy only in the relation between the grouper beat and the tactus. In triple meter, there are three tactus beats for each grouper beat—a ratio of 3:1 instead of 2:1. Thus, the slowest beat groups the tactus beat in threes instead of twos. But notice that the fastest beat still divides the tactus in twos, just as in duple meter.

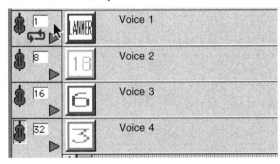

Grouper Beat meter					Grouper Beat meter			
Basic Beat Tactus							Basic Beat Tactus						
Division													Division											
Duple Meter					Triple Meter			

Using the Principles of Triple Meter

To experiment with triple meter, double-click METER in the Tunes Catalog, and when prompted to save changes, click No. Then drag the ANYA tuneblock in Voice 1 into the Trash and replace it with the LANNER tuneblock. Drag the 12-block in Voice 2 into the Trash and replace it with an 18-block. Click Play.

| Voice 1 |
| Voice 2 |
| Voice 3 |
| Voice 4 |

LANNER in Voice 1; 18-block in Voice 2

Notice, first of all, how "stilted" the dance sounds when played by the unbending computer instruments, as compared with the Viennese live performance. However, listening to the "exact" computer synthesized version, you can more easily shift your listening focus from one level of the hierarchy to another and clap each level in turn. Notice, too, that there are not enough beats in the percussion parts to accompany all of the Lanner melody. Make the necessary changes in the Repeat boxes so that the percussion instruments "fill up" the whole tune.

Turn off Voices 1 and 4. Listen to the relations between the tactus and grouper beats. Is the 3:1 relationship between grouper beat and tactus more evident now? Can you hear that three tactus beats go by for each grouper beat—18:6 = 3:1? The "three-ness" of a triple meter hierarchy has an interesting effect: Instead of hearing a symmetrical alternation between strong and weak tactus beats as in duple meter, you hear a strong beat always followed by two weak beats—an *oom-pah-pah* effect.

Duple Meter   Triple Meter

This difference between duple and triple meters is reflected in the differences between marching (in duple meter) and waltzing (in triple meter). Being two-legged creatures, we march well to the duple meter alternation of strong and weak beats—*left*-right, *left*-right. When we dance to a waltz, the feeling is more like smoothly gliding. Why? Probably because in waltzing we are always moving through two weak beats for every strong beat. And maybe more important, we must alternate between our two feet on the accent or downbeat: *left*-right-left, *right*-left-right. Imagine marching to a waltz!

Turn off Voice 2, turn on Voice 4, and click Play. As mentioned before, there is the new 3:1 relation between the tactus and the grouper beat, but there is still a 2:1 relation between the tactus and the divider beat. Thus, the "three-ness" of triple meter refers only to the grouping of the tactus, not to the division of the tactus. Of course, the tactus beat could be divided in other ways, and we will return to that in a bit.

Change the grouper beat to make the meter duple. Turn all the voices back on. Trash the 18-block in Voice 2 and replace it with the 12-block, making the meter again duple. Does this duple meter accompaniment change the effect or the structure of Lanner's melody? Can you describe the difference?

Experiment with making a triple meter hierarchy using other durations. For example, use a 4-block as the tactus again and change the grouper beat to make triple meter. Try the new triple meter accompaniment with LANNER. What is the difference between this conflict and the conflict when you tried a duple meter accompaniment?

Experiment with different percussion instruments to make the beat levels more distinct. To change the percussion instrument that is playing, pull down the Instruments menu for any voice, select an instrument, and listen to how the effect changes.

Instruments $\rightarrow$
menu

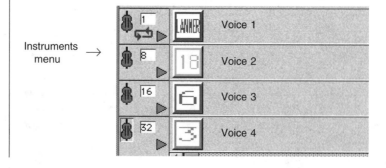

Revisiting "Bhimpalasi" and Hindemith

Finally, go back and listen again to Examples 2.1 and 2.2. Try to keep time as you listen—that is, clap a beat that fits with the music. Can you hear more clearly now the passages that generate a beat, in contrast to those that do not? And can you also hear the difference in effect between these passages? What about speculating on what sorts of temporal relations in the music create a beat, in contrast to relations that do not create a beat? We will return to this question in Project 2.4.

Intuitions and Notations: Can You Say What You Can Do?

EXPLORATIONS 2

It is eminently clear from the previous explorations that the metric hierarchy is an embodiment of temporal ratios—duple meter as fundamentally 2:1 and triple meter as fundamentally 3:1. But to be able to say that is really to start backward. The remarkable thing is that everyone can intuitively make these proportional relations in action—we can *do* them quite well without being able to say what it is we know how to do. And we can differentiate and recognize these temporal ratios in action when they are embodied in a melody. Moreover, composers can creatively elaborate these ratios through the varied durations they give to pitches or non-pitch percussion sounds.

For instance, given some reasonable beat (going, let's say, about as fast as we normally walk), most of us can clap another beat that goes twice as fast or twice as slow. That ability seems to be a natural development from the innate capacity to make a single beat, to "pulse," with which babies are born. But to describe the result of what we are able to do in action requires a major shift. We must move outside of ourselves—we must look at the results of our actions and grasp their relations. In short, we need to quantify, to invoke numbers. But as soon as we quantify, we get a particular proportional relationship—6:3, 12:6.

We know how to enact simple ratios; we can make them in all different sizes while keeping the internal proportions the same. We can start with any beat and intuitively clap twice as fast or twice as slow; three times as fast or three times as slow. But this seems rather far removed from quantifying relations.

Descriptions of actions are fated to deform our experience of them. So why should you try to say what you know how to do?

There are at least three reasons:

1. What we do in sound or in action instantly disappears; if we can say what we do, we can hold action and time still, and we can look at them and think about them.
2. If we have a notation to describe what we can do, we can use that notation to learn—to build, to develop, to elaborate on, and to understand in new ways what we know how to do in action.
3. If we can describe our actions, we can teach another person (and even a machine) how to do what we did.

Mini-Explorations: From Action to Description

Can you get a synthesizer drum to do what you do in action? Try the following:

- Clear all voices. (Pull down the Edit menu and select Clear Voices.)
- Put an 8-block in Voice 2 in the Playroom and enter 10 in the Repeat box.
- Click Play and listen to the beat while you clap another beat that goes twice as fast.
- Click Play and clap a beat that goes twice as slow.
- Make the synthesizer drum play each of the beats that you just clapped.

    Try another!

- Use a 6-block as your starting beat.
- Clap two times slower. (That's easy, because you just clap on every other 6-beat.)
- How about 3 times faster? (That's harder. Why?)
- Listen to the 6-beat and clap the slower and then the faster beats.
- Make the synthesizer drums play both of the beats that you just clapped.
- Listen to the result carefully.

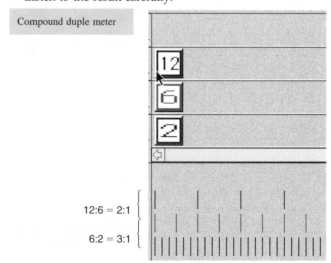

Compound duple meter

$$12:6 = 2:1$$
$$6:2 = 3:1$$

The basic beat you just started with (the 6-beat) is grouped in twos by the 12-beat. But it is also divided into threes by the 2-beat. This is probably a relationship among beats you wouldn't make so spontaneously. It's called *compound duple meter* because of the combination of duple meter (twos) at the grouper level and triple meter (threes) at the division level. Compound duple meter turns out to have interesting possibilities, which composers have exploited in various ways from the sixteenth century until the present. You will hear some examples when you work on Project 2.3.

Fast and Slow

The easy feeling we have for music moving faster or moving slower is actually created by a fascinating and varied mix of musical relations and dimensions. Most literally, fast and slow have to do with *tempo*. Tempo refers to the rate of the underlying beat or tactus. For instance, with your example of compound duple meter in the Playroom, click the right arrow under Speed in the Tools area—that is, speed up the tempo. As you listen, watch the moving pointer in the graphic. Now slow down the tempo by clicking the left arrow under Speed. Now listen and watch the moving pointer. What stays the same? What changes?

Another sense of moving faster or slower has to do with the particular durations of events that are being performed. Specifically, a piece moves faster if there are more notes played in the same period of time—or more notes per beat. For instance, in "Hot Cross Buns," the middle part goes faster than the beginning and ending parts because there are more notes per beat:*

---

*Did you notice that the rhythm of "Hot Cross Buns" is exactly the same as the rhythm of "Anya"?

"faster"

"Hot Cross Buns"

The difference between these two senses of "faster" can be heard quite easily by making the following little experiment: If you increase the tempo (click the right arrow), you see the moving pointer go faster and hear all the percussion instruments playing faster. But at the same time, the spatial relations in the graphics stay the same, and so do the relative durations among the three levels of the metric hierarchy. This comparison reflects the difference between *tempo* (rate of the underlying beat) and *relative duration* (the number of events per beat).

Fast and Slow Structures: Revisiting Beethoven, Haydn, and Vivaldi

Composers also use our intuitive experiences of fast and slow in structural ways. For instance, listen again to the excerpt from Beethoven's Symphony #9 (Example 1.2). Focus on the change from the Theme to Variation 1. Recall that in moving from the Theme to Variation 1, the number of instruments participating increases and the texture becomes more active. The bassoon plays a countermelody that weaves in and around the melody of the theme, played by the violas and cellos. We have the experience of moving faster for two reasons: First, the bassoon plays faster—more notes per beat (shorter durations) compared with the cellos and basses in the theme. Second, the texture changes from unison in the theme to increased inner activity created by the bassoon's rhythmically independent and competing countermelody. And all of this happens while the tempo remains the same.

For a somewhat more complex example of moving faster, listen again to the beginning of the Minuet movement from Haydn's Symphony #99 (Example 1.4). Recall the opening antecedent-consequent phrases with their internal contrasts in pitch movement and texture. Within each of these phrases, there is contrast between conjunct and disjunct movement, and between thin unison texture and thicker rhythmic unison texture. As the piece continues, notice again how Haydn fragments these opening phrases. Using only the beginning fragment of each phrase, Haydn makes two new phrases, each of which is half as long as the initial ones. In the process, the internal contrasts in pitch motion and texture are maintained, but the rate of change increases. As the phrases are fragmented, the time between these contrasts becomes twice as fast. Thus, even though the tempo and the durations of performed events stay just the same, the result is a feeling of speeding up.

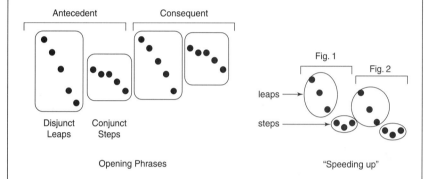

Opening Phrases   "Speeding up"

This structural sense of speeding up is wonderfully illustrated by Vivaldi. Listening again to the opening of "Winter" (Example 1.5), you can hear that Vivaldi establishes a clear beat by asking the instruments simply to play that steady beat together. The first contrast occurs when the solo violin enters. The violinist creates the feeling of getting faster by playing faster notes—that is, he plays more notes in relation to the steady beat.

With the return of the full orchestra and the opening steady beat, the tempo stays just the same but the piece seems to slow down again, helping to mark the boundary of this first solo, sequential passage. In the next solo passage Vivaldi plays with our sense of getting faster through new structural means. The violinist is playing more notes (the quick, repeated notes), but there is a more subtle difference, as well; can you hear that the time span of the sequentially repeated figure is much shorter? The result is that the moves from one iteration of the sequential figure to the next occur much faster.

This whole passage is a perfect example of how a composer can use change in structural rhythm to create contrast and excitement. A given sequential figure creates a structural beat that is equal to the time span of that figure. In the Vivaldi example, the first sequential figure is relatively long, including three inner figures plus a reminder of the orchestra's steady beat pattern—sixteen beats in all. This whole three-part figure is repeated three times, followed by an orchestral interlude.

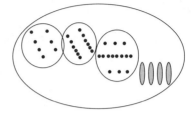

Three inner figures plus
a steady beat

After the orchestra's interlude, the solo violinist comes in with the next sequential passage. The total time span of this sequential figure is exactly half of the first—eight beats in all. Thus we have the feeling of the piece speeding up, not only because of the faster notes played by the violin soloist, but also because the structural rhythm is faster—that is, the beat implicitly generated by the sequential repetitions of the shorter figure creates a feeling of speeding up.

Listen to the Vivaldi excerpt several times, shifting your focus of attention among all these dimensions. As these dimensions interact with one another, they form a complex network of inner relationships; these relationships contribute to the almost magical experience of changes in the rate of motion even though the tempo remains the same throughout.

Project 2.2

Exploring Rhythm Notations

1. Understand and make multiple representations of temporal relations.

2. Consider the kinds of features captured by different representations and determine when each is useful.

3. Revisit the distinctions between figural and metric entities.

THE TASKS

You have seen two kinds of rhythm representations so far: space-for-time graphics (rhythm bars) and Impromptu number notation (drumblocks). For this project you will be looking at, comparing, and reflecting on these representations, along with others including conventional rhythm notation (CRN). The primary questions will be:

- What kinds of features and relations does each representation capture?
- What difference do the differences make?
- Under what circumstances is each representation useful?

Representations for rhythm, like representations for things that are in motion (wheels turning, swings swinging, balls bouncing, drummers drumming), make it possible to hold still that which is always "going on." With the rhythm held still to be looked at all at one time, like frames on motion picture film, we can see and describe how moving things work—

their changing internal structures. Conventional rhythm notation, like a map or an engineer's blueprint, also provides directions—directions for performing what a composer intends.

But static representations re-present experience in particular, sometimes peculiar ways. As mentioned before, we don't usually measure time relations as we listen—and yet we need to do just that in order to notate the relations we hear. And to read these static notated rhythms to perform these notations, we have to learn how to re-animate them. A notation, then, is an intermediary between what you know how to do in real time/motion, and what you want to help someone else do. But it's never just the same—the reader/player must reinvent your rhythm as he or she makes it. All of this depends ultimately on our internal ability to pulse, and our ability to turn this action know-how into units outside ourselves that we can count and measure.

To prepare for counting and measuring, we need a more precise description of the term *duration*. In the performance of a musical sound, its duration is taken to be the time from the start (the attack) of the sound to the start of the next sound. However, with regard to drum sounds, the duration of the sound itself is usually brief; thus the differences in duration among drummed events depend mostly on the duration of the silence, the "gap," between attacks of successive events. The single duration number on drumblocks, then, includes a "package" made up of the brief sound itself together with the silence between attacks. You may have noticed, in this regard, that you need at least *two* percussion events to hear the duration of *one*. This is another kind of boundary issue.

Multiple Representations

There are two basic principles that relate most Impromptu notations to conventional rhythm notation (CRN). Moving from Impromptu number notation (the numbers on drum blocks) to CRN is easy once these principles are kept in mind:

• Impromptu numbers and the symbols of CRN tell you the rate at which events are to be played relative to one another.
• Both conventional rhythm notation symbols and the numbers on drumblocks represent proportional duration values.

Due to the long and sometimes circuitous evolution of rhythm notation as we know it today, CRN symbols for durations are labeled as pro-

portional fractions—a quarter note is twice as long as an eighth note, a
half note is twice as long as a quarter note, and so on.

Impromptu drumblock numbers are not absolutely correlated with any
particular notational symbol in CRN, even though the whole numbers that
represent durations in Impromptu notation and the fractions that represent durations in CRN are proportional to one another. However, once
you assign a drumblock number to a CRN symbol, the mapping between
all other drumblock numbers and CRN symbols will follow. For example:

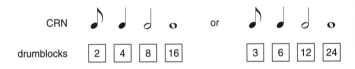

Mapping CRN and drum-
blocks

As the table shows, if a 6-block is represented as a *quarter note* (♩), then
a 12-block, which is twice as long, will be represented as a *half note* (𝅗𝅥)—
the same 2:1 relationship. In turn, a 3-block would be represented as an
eighth note (♪). But if we should choose instead to represent a 4-block as
a quarter note (♩), then an 8-block would be represented as a half note (𝅗𝅥)
and a 2-block would be represented as an eighth note (♪).

These mappings can be seen quite clearly if we compare Impromptu
notation for "Anya"'s duple meter hierarchy with conventional notation
for this same duple meter hierarchy. In Project 2.1 we used a 6-block for
the tactus:

Impromptu notation:
"Anya"'s duple meter
hierarchy

If we represent the Impromptu 6-block (tactus) as a quarter note (♩), and
follow the mapping shown in the illustration labeled "Mapping CRN and

drumblocks," the same duple meter hierarchy would look like this in CRN:

Conventional notation:
duple meter hierarchy

A triple meter hierarchy might look like this in Impromptu notation:

Impromptu notation:
triple meter hierarchy

Grouper beat	12
Basic beat Tactus	4
Divider beat	2

And if we choose to represent the Impromptu 4-block as a quarter note (♩), the triple meter hierarchy would look like this in CRN:

Conventional notation:
triple meter hierarchy

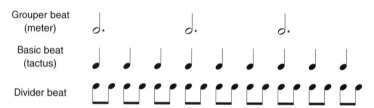

(*Question:* Why is the same 12-block mapped to a half note in the duple meter example and to a dotted half note in the triple meter example?)

For more information on the symbols of standard rhythm notation, see the section titled "Some Basics: Conventional Rhythm Notation" at the end of Part 2.

CRN has an additional notational convention called the bar line. Bar lines are a graphic sign that shows you the relationship between the tactus beat and the slower grouper beat. In duple meter, where there is a 2:1 relation between grouper beat and tactus, the bar line marks off two tactus beats per measure.* The specified number of tactus beats enclosed by bar lines is called a *measure.*

---

*While triple meter and duple meter are clearly distinct, the "two-ness" of duple meter generalizes to include a 4:1 relationship between grouper beat and tactus, as well.

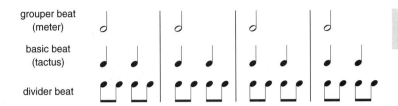

Duple meter: four measures

In triple meter, where there is a 3:1 relation between grouper beat and tactus, the bar line marks off three tactus beats per measure.

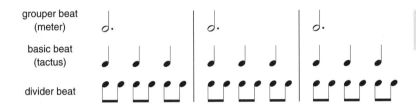

Triple meter: three measures

As pointed out earlier, when grouper beats and tactus beats coincide, they reinforce one another to generate an *accent* or *downbeat*. The conventions for counting in duple and triple meter reflect the arrival and departure of these downbeats. The procedure is as follows: Call the downbeat "1," then count up, giving each tactus beat one count, until you come to the next downbeat; then start over again with "1."

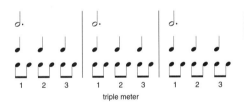

Counting beats

Using the Tactus to Measure Varied Durations

So far you have been working mostly with notations for beats and their internal proportional relations. What about the varied durations of melodies? Spatial graphics, such as those for "Anya" shown in the following figure, come close to representing the intuitive feel of performing a rhythm. Indeed, if you clap the rhythm of "Anya," you will find that the relative spaces standing for varied durations roughly correspond to the relative distances between your hands as you clap the varied durations.

ANYA | | | | | | ||||||| | | | *Spatial graphics*

But what about showing how much longer or shorter events are in relation to one another? How can you measure and thus notate these varied durations? To do that, you need to compare events not just to one another but to the tactus beat. The trick in notating the rhythm of a melody, then, is to make a concordance between the beat and the particular durations of the melody, and that is not always so easy. As someone once said: "You can't put the melody *on* the beat, you have to find the beat *in* the melody." But once found, the beat can function as a temporal ruler. *Using the tactus as a basic time unit for measuring varied durations is the principle behind most representations of rhythm.* Understanding this principle will help you to translate from one representation to another. Moreover, the process of using and comparing representations will help you better understand the principles they share.

The following table shows you the rhythm of "Anya" in a series of notational transformations: spatial graphics, Impromptu number notation, CRN, and finally CRN with added bar lines. Each notation is useful depending on when and for what you want to use it. When you compare these representations with one another, you can see that each one gives you a different kind of information and even a different feeling for the rhythm. Think about these differences as you explore the common principles they all share.

Multiple representations. Note that the sign 2/4 is *not* a fraction! The bottom number, 4, indicates that a quarter note represents the tactus. The top number, 2, means that there are two tactus beats in a measure. For more on standard rhythm notation, see the section titled "Some Basics: Conventional Rhythm Notation" at the end of Part 2.

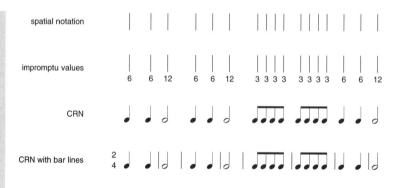

Spatial graphics (rhythm bars) give you a general picture of the proportional time relations of a melody. As such, these space-for-time graphics can serve as a model illustrating the underlying principle involved in representing rhythms in other notations. For example, the spatial unit representing the tactus beat can be given a numeric value in relation to which we can measure the varied durations of a melody. If we assign a value of 6 to this spatial unit, we can translate the proportional spatial relations into Impromptu number notation.

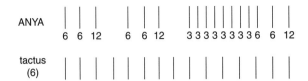

And once we have translated spatial relations into numeric values, it is easy to translate the numeric values into CRN symbols using the following table:

$$\boxed{12} = \quad \boxed{6} = \quad \boxed{3} =$$

With 6 = ♩, the rhythm of "Anya" in CRN looks like this:

"Anya": Conventional rhythm notation

Given a grouper beat of 12 or ♩, you can put in the bar lines, too:

Putting in the bar lines

Bar Lines and Beams

While bar lines and beams look quite different, they have a similar notational status but at different levels of the hierarchy. Horizontal beams join together faster notes whose values together equal the mid-level tactus.

Notes beamed together equal the tactus

Similarly, bar lines "box together" notes whose values together equal the top-level grouper beat.

| Notes "boxed together" equal the grouper beat |

Thus, with the tactus as reference beat, beams and bar lines are notational symbols that indicate the respective relations of the top and bottom levels of the metric hierarchy to the mid-level tactus.

But there is also an important difference in the musical status of bar lines and beams: Horizontal beams tell performers exactly what they are to do—how fast they must play the beamed notes (their duration value). Vertical bar lines tell the performer about the metric structure, but not explicitly what to play.*

Bar lines have another useful function for performers: Like mileage markers on a map, they can be used to point to a particular location on the "map" of the piece—that is, the printed score. For instance, in rehearsing a work, a group of performers often need to focus on a particular passage somewhere in the middle of a piece. To facilitate finding the passage to be worked on, measures are counted up and the cumulative numbers (usually every ten measures) are printed on the score. (Note that in the Beethoven excerpts reproduced in the section titled "Some Basics: Texture and Instrumentation" at the end of Part 1, measure numbers are printed every ten measures.)

In rehearsing, then, one of the performers or the conductor of an orchestra will say, "Please begin at measure 44." The members of the quartet or the orchestra will look for measure 40 marked in the score, count up four measures from there, and begin to play the passage at that location. (See the section titled "Some Basics: Conventional Rhythm Notation" at the end of Part 2 for more on counting and on rhythm notation.)

Tempo

Finally, what about tempo? Tempo refers most simply to the rate of the underlying beat or tactus. For instance, in clicking the right arrow for Speed, you increased the rate of the tactus and, relative to it, the rate of all the other events. But in doing so, the proportional relations among du-

---

*Novice performers sometimes do "play" the bar line: In an effort to play the notated rhythm correctly, they will mark the beginning of every measure (every downbeat) by playing it louder. This has the effect of stopping or breaking up the figural motion toward structural goals. (See also the following discussion of figural and metric entities.)

rations remained the same; everything went proportionately faster. In terms of the computer, when you speed up the tempo by clicking the right arrow, Impromptu sends a message to the computer clock to appropriately decrease the value that the computer clock is giving to Impromptu's basic time unit.

In conventional notation, tempo is often indicated in a general way by various terms borrowed from Italian, such as *allegro* (fast and lively), *andante* (moderately slow), and *vivace* (fast and brisk).* But composers most accurately indicate tempo by reference to a clocklike device called a *metronome*. The rate of the underlying beat, or tempo, is shown in relation to this outside fixed reference, which measures beats per minute. For instance, if ♩ represents the tactus or reference beat, and a composer indicates the tempo of a piece as ♩ = 60, then the performer's tactus beat will go along at a rate that coincides with the seconds of a clock. Similarly, if ♩ represents the tactus, and the composer changes the tempo so that ♩ = 120, then the performer will adjust the tempo such that the underlying beat will be moving along twice as fast as seconds on a clock and twice as fast as before.

But there is an important difference between Impromptu notation and the symbols of conventional notation: While both notations tell you about the durations of events relative to one another, the symbols of CRN do not tell you anything about the absolute duration of events. For instance, if we listen to the rhythm figure [2 2 4] and to the figure [3 3 6], the absolute values of the two figures are obviously different: The [2 2 4] figure is clearly faster—each of its events is shorter and the whole figure also takes less time. However, just listening to the two figures, we might notate both of them the same in CRN—only the tempo would differ:

The distinction helps to differentiate between tempo, which affects all durations, and internal duration values, which are relative only to each other. So, a piece might "speed up" in the sense that the tempo increases, or a piece might speed up in that the note values change from quarters to eighths. For instance, repetition of a 3-block will go twice as fast as repetitions of a 6-block, irrespective of a change in tempo. And eighth notes (♪) will go twice as fast as quarter notes (♩) regardless of change in tempo. Changes in tempo will change the relative rate of *all* events. Thus, the relations among durations in the duple meter hierarchy shown in CRN in

---

*See the section titled "Some Basics: Conventional Rhythm Notation" at the end of Part 2 for more on these terms.

the preceding figure would continue to sound the same internally, even if the tempo changed from ♩ = 60 to ♩ = 120.

Figural Groupings and Metric Units

With these notational issues in mind, we need to return to a question that harks back to the projects in Part 1: What is the relationship between the metric entities that have been the focus in Part 2, and the figural entities (such as tuneblocks) that were the focus in Part 1? Indeed, the question is an occasion to look back at the spectrum of multiple representations that have been accumulating and their implications for moving up and down the ladder of musical structure. Consider these representations for "Hot Cross Buns":*

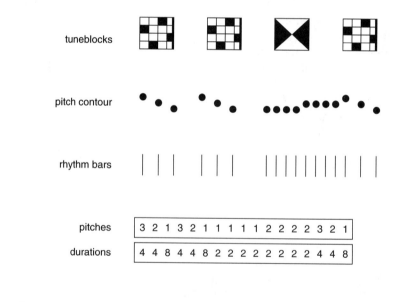

standard music notation

---

*Notice that the rhythm of "Hot Cross Buns" is the same as the rhythm of "Anya"—only the pitches differ.

You began by reconstructing "Hot Cross Buns" with tuneblocks—a task that was immediately obvious for most. But the act of construction simultaneously became a process of constructive analysis. As you looked at the completed sequence of blocks on the screen and listened to it again, the larger structural relations of the tune emerged: two repeated figures (A), contrast (B), and return (A').

Repeated figures   Contrast   Return

Structural relations

While you were reconstructing "Hot Cross Buns," you could choose to see either pitch contour graphics or rhythm bars in the graphics window. Each of these more fine-grained representations conformed to the larger relations shown by the blocks. However, comparing the representations reveals distinctions that are hidden in the more aggregated blocks representation.

Pitch Contour   Rhythm Bars

Revealing distinctions

For instance, the return to the opening figure after the contrasting middle is perfectly clear in the tuneblocks representation, and it is also perfectly clear in the pitch contour representation: The same three-note descending configuration stands out both at the beginning and at the end of the tune. But looking at the rhythm bars, the return is strangely obscured. Specifically, the boundary between the contrasting middle figure and the return seems to have disappeared—the tune seems to end with just two events instead of three.

The 3-note return is clear   Just 2 events; the return has
                                                        disappeared

Indeed, if you clap just the rhythm of the tune, or play just the rhythm using an Impromptu drum, you hear the same effect—two events at the end—and the boundary between contrast and return seems in the wrong place. Why?

The boundary is obscured because when only temporal relations are represented, the faster events of the middle figure run right on into the return; there is no change to generate a boundary. Looking again now at the pitch contour graphics, where pitch relations stand out, it becomes clear that the pitch dimension is critical in creating and accounting for the perceived boundary—temporal relations alone will not succeed.

It should be clear, now, that there is a critical distinction between metric units and the melodic gestural elements we have called figures or phrases. Figures, of course, are not "units" in the metric sense, if only because they vary in their time spans. But there are other, more general differences, which are also reflected in the distinctions between tuneblocks and drumblocks:

- A tuneblock is a structural element of a melody that represents and plays a group of notes (pitches and durations) which together compose a meaningful structural entity—a segment of a tune.
- A drumblock represents and plays a single sound that, in itself, has no structural meaning. However, when drumblocks are repeated, the invariant, measured time units become structurally meaningful by generating a pulse or beat.

It is particularly important for the performer, especially the beginning reader of conventional music notation (CMN), to distinguish between these two kinds of entities. The figural groupings embodied by tuneblocks are not represented at all by the symbols of CMN. While various kinds of markings may be overlaid on the score to show figural groupings, there is no consistent notational symbol indicating these structural entities. In contrast, metric units, as you have seen, are clearly marked by the symbolic conventions of CMN. (Recall the analogy with Leonardo's spatial grid in contrast to his elegant shapes.)

Beginning readers are often tempted to read the graphics of metric notation, which show durational equivalents, as if these beams and bars were indicating figural groupings. For example, notes that are graphically beamed together will often be seen as "going together" to form a small figural group.

Beams show metric equivalents

But, as you have seen, the graphic beam is a metric symbol and as such refers to an entity that is different in kind from a figural element. The beam is meant to indicate notes that "go together" in relation to the tactus—that is, notes that together are equal to the tactus. Similarly, the bar line, as a prominent graphic sign, may also seem to be marking off figural groups. As a result, the novice performer is often tempted to "perform" the bar line. The result may be to interrupt or break up the figural gesture, since the bar line may occur in the middle of a figure. In doing so, the performer is again confusing a graphic symbol that refers to metric entities with figural entities, which are, in fact, not clearly represented by the symbols of CMN at all.

For instance, the tune "Austrian" is in triple meter. If we mark the boundaries of figural groups (tuneblocks) with brackets, and mark the boundaries of the three-beat metric groups with bar lines, you can see that figural groups entirely overlap metric groups.

"Austrian"

This presents another interesting paradox: While figural groupings seem to be the groupings that we intuitively attend to as listeners in following the motion of a melody toward structural goals, performers learning to play a piece are faced with the problem of quite literally constructing these groupings. This leaves performers with a sometimes difficult but essential task: To create what we would call a "musical performance" when given only the metric units shown in the score, the performer must first develop an appropriate hearing of a piece. This includes listening for, experimenting with, and making decisions concerning possible boundaries of figural groupings. At the same time, each performer must develop means for projecting these perceived elements that are appropriate for his or her instrument—what is often called *shaping a phrase.*

Sometimes composers themselves, or editors who help prepare published scores, add markings to CMN to help performers with the task of hearing and projecting figural groupings—or what performers often call *phrasing.* For example, here is a copy of an excerpt from Bach's original manuscript for the Gigue from the Partita #2 for Solo Violin (Example 1.6).

From the original manuscript of "Gigue" from Bach's Partita #2 for Solo Violin.

Notice the long *slur* that Bach adds in measure 16 to show the pitches that are to be grouped together to form a figure. Notice, particularly, that the figural grouping goes across the notated metric units. And later in the excerpt, notice that slurs mark grouping in threes that again override the metric units.

Listen again to Example 1.6 and try to follow the figural groupings that Bach has marked in his manuscript.

As you go on to Project 2.3, these issues will take on practical importance for you. Specifically, as you make your own percussion accompaniments to tunes, you will need to take into account both the metric and the figural structure generated by each tune.

Project 2.3

Composing Percussion Accompaniments for Tunes

IN THE INTRODUCTION TO PART 2, IT WAS SUGGESTED THAT ONCE A METRIC hierarchy is established, it creates expectations for continuation. Indeed, it is only when the metric framework is established by the events in a composition that deviations from it can be surprising. This is another example of making complexity by elaborating and confounding what we take to be "norms."

For example, listen again to the "Ode to Joy" melody from Beethoven's Ninth Symphony (Example 1.1). Listen closely to the moment when the opening tune returns after the contrasting passage in the B section. Having solidly established the metric framework, Beethoven animates this joint between the middle section and the return by deviating from what he has led us to expect. Beethoven anticipates the moment of return, arriving at an accent just ahead of when we expect it. In turn, the expected accent comes after the return has already begun. "Breaking the mold" gives a fresh start to the return of familiar material.

Going on to variation 1 (Example 1.2), we hear that the rhythm of the bassoon's solo melody is in friendly competition with the metric structure of the theme, played by the violas. Specifically, there is often a stress on normally unaccented or weak beats. This kind of conflict, where accents occur on unaccented beats and where expected accents are anticipated or delayed, is called *syncopation*. Go back and listen to the theme and the three variations to get a feel for how Beethoven develops rhythmic conflict and complexity.

There are four tasks for Project 2.3, each of which involves making your own percussion accompaniments to tunes. The three tunes you will be working with are:

- EARLY
- LANNER
- TYROL

For each of the tunes, do the following four tasks:

THE TASKS

1. Make a percussion accompaniment that plays the metric hierarchy generated by the tune.
2. Compose a percussion accompaniment using varied durations (in contrast to steady beats). This accompaniment should reinforce the metric hierarchy found in Task 1.
3. Compose a percussion accompaniment that includes conflict with the metric hierarchy found in Task 1.
4. Write out the rhythm of each tune in Impromptu number notation and translate it into CRN.

The Metric Hierarchy as Accompaniment

INFO BOX
Starting Project 2.3
· In the Playrooms
  menu, select
  Drummer
· In the Tunes
  Catalog, select DAN
· In the Graphics
  menu, select
  Rhythm Bars

Building the metric hierarchy as an accompaniment for a tune is primarily preparation for composing more interesting accompaniments—you need to know the metric structure of a tune in order to build an accompaniment that reinforces it. Similarly, to compose conflicting accompaniments you will need to know what your rhythm patterns are conflicting with.

A Practice Session

Building up the metric hierarchy using percussion instruments should be quite straightforward, since you are already familiar with the general procedure from Project 2.1. We will use the tune "Dan" as an example. Follow these steps:

- Drag the tuneblock DAN into Voice 1. As you listen to it, clap the tactus beat.

- Listen again and count the number of tactus beats you clap.
- Enter that number in the Repeat box.
- Experiment with drumblocks in Voice 3 until you find one that matches your clapped tactus beat.*
- Listen for and clap a slower beat (grouper beat). Experiment with drumblocks in Voice 2 until you find one that matches the beat you just clapped. Enter an appropriate number of repetitions for Voice 2.
- To complete the metric hierarchy, clap a faster beat (divider beat), put a drumblock in Voice 4 that matches it, and add an appropriate number in the Repeat box.

A hierarchy for the beginning of "Dan" is shown here:†

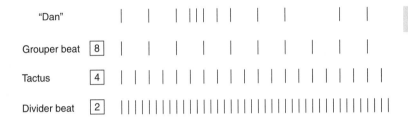

"Dan": Metric hierarchy

Following the general procedure described here, go on to build up the metric hierarchies for "Early," "Lanner," and "Tyrol." "Tyrol" is particularly interesting: Students often disagree on its meter and sometimes they hear the meter shifting.

Transcribing the Rhythm of the Tune

When you have finished building up the metric hierarchy for each tune, translate the rhythm bar graphics for the melodies into Impromptu number notation. With the metric hierarchy for "Dan" still in the PlayRoom, we will use it as an example of the procedure. Follow these steps:

1. Listen to the melody; while clapping the tactus, focus on the rhythm (the varied durations) of the melody.
2. Listen again; this time tap the tactus with one hand and the rhythm of the tune with the other.

---

*Keep in mind that the duration values used in programming the tune determine the duration value of the tactus. For instance, in programming "Dan," 4 was chosen as the tactus, so the drumblock that matches your clapping is also a 4-block.

†Of course, you may have selected a different value for the tactus (for example, 8) but the proportions among the levels should still be those that create a duple meter structure like this one.

3. Using the tactus beat (4) in Voice 3 as a unit of measure and following the space-for-time graphics, estimate the varied durations of the melody.

Duration of tune events

"Dan" | 8 | 8 | 4 | 2 | 2 | 4 | 4 |

4 | | | | | | | | |

4. To test your guess, build up the rhythm using a percussion instrument.
   a. In the Edit menu, select Improvise → Rhythm.
   b. Type your estimated durations for the melody into the Duration box in the Improvise window.
   c. Click the Play button in the Improvise window to listen to your rhythm.

The Improvise window

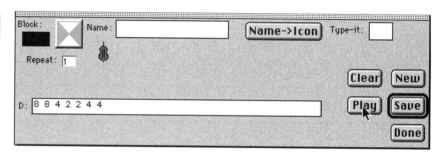

   d. When you have finished (or when you have a good start), click New to make a new block in the Blocks area.
   e. Drag your new block into Voice 2 and listen to your rhythm with the rhythm of "Dan" in Voice 1. (You can do this without closing the Improvise window.)
   f. When the Impromptu numbers match the rhythm of "Dan," translate the Impromptu numbers into conventional rhythm notation (see Project 2.2 for help if you need it).
   g. Write out both the Impromptu numbers and CRN in your log.

Composing Accompaniment Patterns That Reinforce the Metric Hierarchy

You have already listened to several examples of accompaniments that reinforce the metric hierarchy of a piece. For instance, Sousa, in his "Stars and Stripes Forever" (Example 2.5) composes an accompaniment that clearly supports and reinforces the duple meter hierarchy of the melody. And Lanner's melody in his "Styrian Dance" (Example 2.4) is carried along by the supporting triple meter (*oom-pah-pah*) accompaniment played by the lower strings. Listen again to these two examples. Go back to Haydn's Minuet (Example 1.2) and listen to how Haydn helps to create a feeling of stability in the closing passage of the A section by introducing a clear melody and accompaniment. The accompaniment, again the triple meter *oom-pah-pah*, strongly supports the meter of the melody.

For this task, your accompaniments can be modeled after rhythm figures, such as those you heard in the Listening Examples. These rhythm figures or patterns are usually made up of varied durations, in contrast to the steady beats you have been working with so far. The patterns you compose for each tune should reinforce the metric hierarchy that you made in the first task. (See Explorations 2 for more on rhythm figures.)

For instance, if you found that the meter of a tune was duple, you will want to make patterns of varied durations that also generate duple meter. And if you found that the value of the tactus was 4, you might try patterns that include multiples or divisions of 4 as a first experiment. While this kind of calculation is useful to begin with, the interesting work comes in listening to what you have made and then playing with it more intuitively. And when you make modifications as you go along, the resulting surprises will again be moments for potential innovation.

To begin your experiments, select the tune you want to work with in the Tunes Catalog and follow these steps:

- Drag the tuneblock (EARLY, LANNER, or TYROL) into Voice 1 and listen to it. (It may be more convenient to start with just the first part (FP) of the tune.) Try first to improvise (by clapping or drumming) some accompaniment figures that seem to "fit" with the tune. Short, repeated figures are the easiest to remember and to work with.

- Using what you already know about the metric structure of the tune, jot down your best guess at the durations of the accompaniment figure you have improvised.

- Experimenting with drumblocks, try to match the figure you clapped.

Listen closely to your experiments. What you hear may yield discoveries that are more interesting than patterns you planned or patterns you have clapped. Go on to experiment with figures for the other percussion instruments that enhance the first accompaniment you made. Keep in mind that your choice of percussion instruments in each voice can make a big difference in the effect of your accompaniments. Also, be sure to keep track in your log of what you try, what works, and what doesn't, and also try to account for the success of the accompaniments you like best.

For help, complete the following practice session.

A Practice Session

We will use the tune "Russian" to illustrate rhythm patterns that reinforce the metric hierarchy as well as patterns that conflict. In the Tunes Catalog, select RUSSIAN. Listen to the melody of "Russian" by itself. Did you notice that the rhythm is the same as for "Anya" and for "Hot Cross Buns"? Listen for the difference in effect created by the difference in pitch relations.

To establish the framework, recall the metric hierarchy for "Anya": The meter is duple—the tactus a 6-block, the grouper beat a 12-block, and the divider beat a 3-block. Build the metric hierarchy as an accompaniment and listen to it.

ANYA and RUSSIAN:
Metric hierarchy

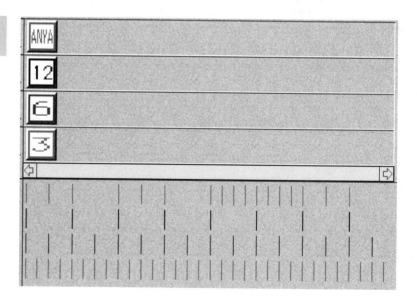

Now, select RUSS.FIT in the Tunes Catalog. This is an example of an accompaniment with a pattern of varied durations that reinforces the metric hierarchy. Why does the accompaniment reinforce the meter of "Russian"?

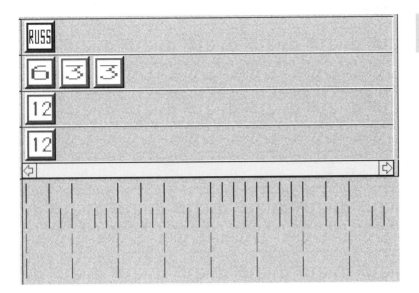

RUSS.FIT: An accompaniment

The 12-blocks in Voices 3 and 4 obviously mark the grouper beat or "measure." And, as the graphics show, it is clear that the repeated drum pattern in Voice 2 [6 3 3] also has a total time span of 12, which matches the duration of the grouper beat. Moreover, the faster durations in the accompaniment pattern [3 3] coincide with the divider beat. The accompaniment is clearly "in sync" with the metric hierarchy—it fits.

But what about the effect? Listening once more to the accompaniment, we hear that the faster durations in Voice 2 provide a bit of motion during the longer durations of the rather dragging melody, but the plodding beat in Voices 3 and 4 don't contribute much. How can we make this dull beat more interesting? We could compose a more varied accompaniment in Voice 3 or Voice 4, but there are other possibilities to explore, as well. These are discussed in the following exploration.

Delayed Entrances

EXPLORATIONS 1

In the examples so far, all the instruments have come in together at the beginning of the tune. What if these entrances could be staggered? For instance, what if the 12-beat in Voice 3 were to come in after the other instruments? But how much after? If composers want performers to come in at the right moment after the piece begins, they must tell a player how many beats to count before coming in. So players in a real orchestra who don't start playing right at the beginning of a piece must count beats from the start so they will know when to come in. In the same way, you must tell the instrument in Voice 3 exactly how long to wait before coming in.

Let's say we want the instrument in Voice 3 to wait for one beat before coming in—that is, the drummer should begin playing only on the second beat of the tune. Since the tactus beat has a value of 6, the Impromptu drummer for Voice 3 should begin playing after a "rest" of duration 6. This can be done with a tool called Wait Times, found in the Options menu:*

- In the Options menu, select Wait Times.
- Type 6 in Voice 3. (This inserts a rest of duration 6 at the beginning of Voice 3.)

Select Wait Times for each Voice:

Voice 1: `0`

Voice 2: `0`

Voice 3: `6`

Voice 4: `0`

Inserting a rest of duration 6 in Voice 3

- Click OK, then PLAY, and listen.

Can you hear the difference? Inserting a rest of duration 6 in Voice 3 has the effect of sliding the 12-block one beat over. The result is to create an alternation effect between Voices 3 and 4.

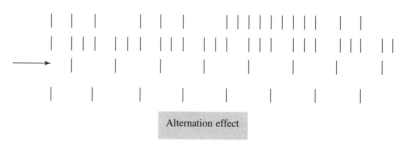

Alternation effect

Now try sliding the pattern in Voice 2 over by inserting a rest of duration 3. In the Options menu, select Wait Times and enter 3 in Voice 2.

---

*Inserting a rest in the percussion accompaniment is particularly useful when the tune itself begins before the first downbeat. This is called beginning with an *upbeat* or *pickup*. Keep this in mind as you work on the next task.

Voice 2 shifted over by a duration of 3

This makes the accompaniment a bit more interesting. Why? Turn off Voices 3 and 4. Notice that as the repeated pattern in Voice 2 goes along, its intersections with the melody occur at different places. Does this influence the way you hear the melody, as well? For instance, notice how the accent in the melody seems to shift, creating a bit of syncopation. Changing the instrumentation for the melody can also influence the effect. Try the xylophone or the kalimba for the melody if you have them on your synth.

These are the kinds of experiments you should make in composing your accompaniments. In fact, if we had saved each of these examples, we would have a little theme and variations. And if we also switched between "Anya," "Hot Cross Buns," and "Russian," all of which have the same rhythm, we would have a large set of variations.

RUSS.FIT1, RUSS.FIT2, and RUSS.FIT3 are other examples of accompaniments that match the metric hierarchy of "Russian." To try them, select them in the Tunes Catalog. If you are using MIDI, try the following percussion instruments:

> Voice 2: Castanets
>
> Voice 3: Bongo1
>
> Voice 4: Cowbell

Notice that RUSS.FIT2 is more lively than RUSS.FIT1. In fact, the accompaniment in RUSS.FIT2 verges on creating conflict with the metric hierarchy of "Russian." To hear what is generating this potential conflict, try turning off Voice 4. Then turn off Voice 2 and listen to the tune with only Voice 3 as accompaniment. Play with turning voices off and on and experiment with percussion instruments to make the differences sharper. Look at the graphics and duration patterns. Can you hear what is happening? Think about this example when you listen to Stravinsky's accompaniment to Lanner's waltz in the next group of Listening Examples. Why does

RUSS.FIT1 generate less conflict? RUSS.FIT3 is a variation on RUSS.FIT2.

Using these accompaniments for "Russian" as examples, go on to build accompaniment patterns that reinforce the hierarchies for "Early," "Lanner," and "Tyrol." As you work, pay attention to the following and jot down your thoughts in your log:

- Strategies you used in designing and implementing your accompaniments.
- Experiments you made and surprises you encountered: what you expected, what you got, an accounting of the differences, and how you used these surprises
- A description of the structure of your completed accompaniment—for example, how it reinforces the metric hierarchy of the tune; how it influences your "hearing" of the tune; what you like about it

When you have finished composing your accompaniments, remember to write out the rhythm of each tune in Impromptu drum block notation and in CRN.

Saving Your Work

Be sure to save each tune and your accompaniments so they can be played for others. To save your work on a floppy disk, to be turned in with your paper, follow these steps:

1. Insert your floppy disk in the disk drive.
2. In the File menu, select Save As.
3. Select Desktop and double-click the icon for your floppy disk.
4. Delete "#0" and type in your name.
5. Click Save.
6. Remove your floppy disk by dragging the floppy disk icon to the Trash.

LISTENING EXAMPLES: RHYTHMIC CONFLICT

Example 2.4: Lanner, "Styrian Dances" (1840)
Example 2.6: Stravinsky, *Petrouchka* (excerpt) (1911)
Example 2.7: Mozart, Concerto for Piano (K. 467) (1785)

Example 2.8: "Bulerias" (flamenco)

Example 2.3: Porter, "Night and Day" (Billie Holiday, vocal) (1937)

In preparation for composing more complex percussion accompaniments that conflict with the metric hierarchies of tunes, it will be helpful to listen to some musical examples in which the accompaniment conflicts rhythmically with the melody. The examples in this section are again drawn from different musical cultures and from different time periods, so it is not surprising that rhythmic conflict is created through different means and thus with different effect. However, Examples 2.4, 2.6, and 2.8 all share an important commonality—they are all dance music. Indeed, even the jazz example, Cole Porter's "Night and Day," might be associated with dancing. What, then, are the musical means that make each example different from the others?

Example 2.4: Lanner, "Styrian Dances" (1840)

Before listening to Example 2.6, the first example of rhythmic conflict, listen again to Lanner's waltz (Example 2.4). Recall that the Lanner dance, like all waltzes, marks a triple meter that is clearly reinforced by the *oom-pah-pah* accompaniment.

Example 2.6: Stravinsky, *Petrouchka* (excerpt) (1911)

Listening now to Example 2.6, an excerpt from Stravinsky's music for the ballet *Petrouchka,* you will immediately hear that Stravinsky has borrowed his melody from Lanner's dance. But it is just as obvious that Stravinsky is playing games with Lanner's melody. Composing music for a ballet about a circus and a clown named Petrouchka, Stravinsky takes Lanner's Viennese café music and turns it into merry-go-round music. How does he do that?

Stravinsky's use of instrumentation is clearly an important factor. Listening again to both pieces, you will hear that the Lanner waltz is played by a string orchestra (violins, violas, cellos, basses), with the violins playing the melody. Stravinsky ingeniously orchestrates his music to imitate the music box sound of the merry-go-round. He gives the accompaniment to the bassoon in the lower register while the trumpet plays Lanner's melody.

But it is Stravinsky's accompaniment that introduces imaginative rhythmic conflict against Lanner's melody. Listen once more to both examples, this time paying particular attention to the two accompaniment figures. Lanner's accompaniment, played by the lower strings, is the typical triple meter, *oom-pah-pah* figure that almost defines the waltz. In contrast and in conflict with Lanner's triple meter melody, Stravinsky's bassoon figure organizes itself into compound duple meter.

Recall the previous discussion of the compound duple meter hierarchy (see Mini-Exploration I in Project 2.1):

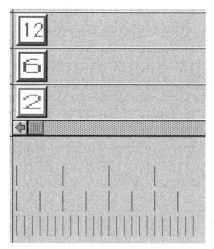

Compound duple meter:
12:6 = 2:1; 6:2 = 3:1

In that example, the mid-level beat (6-beat) is grouped in twos by the grouper beat at the top level (12-beat). But the mid-level beat is divided into threes (2-beat). This configuration of relationships is called compound duple meter because of the mix of metric groupings.

The following illustration shows you in CRN a comparison between the triple meter hierarchy of Lanner's accompaniment and the compound duple meter hierarchy of Stravinsky's accompaniment. Notice that either of the accompaniments can work because the rate of beats at the top and bottom levels of the hierarchy is the same. Thus the differences between them occurs at the mid-level.

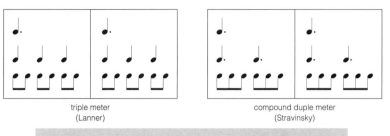

Triple meter hierarchy and compound duple meter hierarchy compared

Mini-Explorations: Mixing Meters

To hear the games Stravinsky is playing, begin by clicking Play and listening to a synthesized version of the Lanner melody with a triple meter waltz accompaniment (*oom-pah-pah*—the *oom* is in Voice 3, the *pah-pah* in Voice 2). Tap the grouper beat while you count and tap the tactus beats.

<table>
<tr><td>INFO BOX
Mixing Meters
· In the Playrooms menu, select 4-voices
· In the Tunes Catalog, select Lanner</td></tr>
</table>

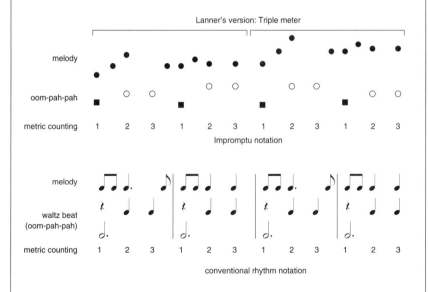

Now turn off the waltz accompaniment (Voices 2 and 3) and drag the Stravinsky accompaniment block (STRAV) into Voice 4. The accents generated by Stravinsky's accompaniment are shown as black boxes in the following figure.

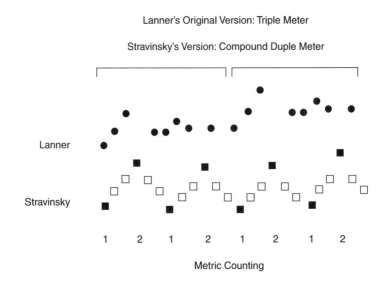

Lanner's Original Version: Triple Meter

Stravinsky's Version: Compound Duple Meter

Metric Counting

Turn off Voice 1 (Lanner's melody) and listen just to Stravinsky's accompaniment. As you listen, clap all the notes of the accompaniment with one hand, and with the other clap just the accented notes. Notice that the shape of the accompaniment figure creates these accents. Since all the notes are of equal duration, the accents are generated when the pitch contour reverses direction—that is, on the highest and lowest pitches. Try clapping again, and this time count the meter as shown in the preceding figure.

Turn Voice 1 back on and listen again to Lanner's melody along with Stravinsky's compound duple meter accompaniment.

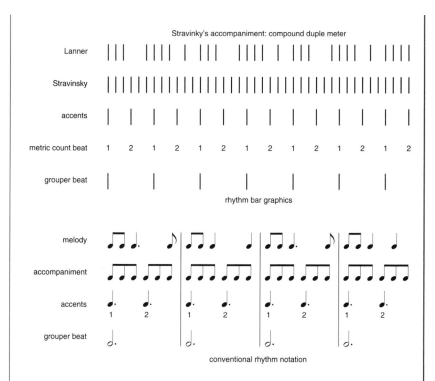

Play around with the two accompaniments by turning Voices 2, 3, and 4 off and on. Can you hear how the accompaniments differ? Can you hear how Stravinsky's accompaniment builds a new relationship with Lanner's melody, changing the character of that same melody? Finally, turn all the voices on and listen to both accompaniments together. Notice that the *oom* of the waltz accompaniment also fits with Stravinsky's accompaniment. Why? How does it work?

To get a feel for the shift from compound duple to triple meter, select Drummer in the PlayRooms menu and then select MIX in the Tunes Catalog. Click Play to hear just percussion instruments playing the shift from compound duple meter to triple meter. Listen several times and try to clap along with the shift in the middle voices.

For a more lively version of this shift, listen to MIX1, which was made by a professional drummer.

Coming back to the initial comparison between Lanner and Stravinsky and back to the 4-Voices PlayRoom, it should be clear now that both accompaniments work because they share the same slowest beat and the same fastest beat, despite the differences in grouping and accents.

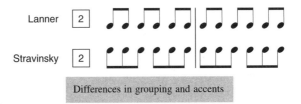

Differences in grouping and accents

It should also be clear that the conflict between the two accompaniments occurs at the mid-level of their hierarchies: Lanner's mid-level beat (4-block) and Stravinsky's mid-level beat (6-block) create a conflict: 3 beats against 2 beats, but both sharing the same grouper beat and thus fitting into the same measure (12-block).

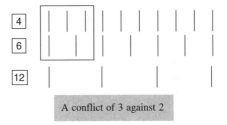

A conflict of 3 against 2

Finally, just to make for greater confusion, the conventional representations of triple meter and compound duple meter differ with respect to the level of the hierarchy that is symbolically used to represent the tactus.

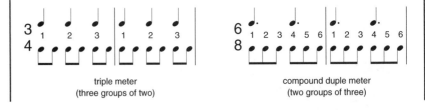

triple meter
(three groups of two)

compound duple meter
(two groups of three)

Triple meter (waltz time) is notated as 3/4—where 3 stands for the three beats per measure (the beat you "count on"), and 4 stands for the quarter note as the symbol representing that beat. In contrast, compound duple meter is notated as 6/8. Here, the divider is treated as the beat you "count on." Thus, the 6 in 6/8 stands for the six faster beats per measure and the 8 stands for the eighth note as the symbol representing that faster beat. The difference in the symbolic representation blurs the fact that both 3/4 meter and 6/8 meter include the same six faster beats per measure even though they are grouped differently: 3/4 is made up of three groups of two faster beats (3 × 2); 6/8 is made up of two groups of three faster beats (2 × 3).

We started these explorations with a question: How does Stravinsky take Lanner's Viennese café music and turn it into merry-go-round circus music? Go back now and listen to the two pieces as their composers intended them to be played. Have the explorations helped you hear the answer to that question?

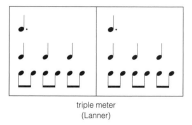

triple meter
(Lanner)

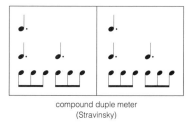

compound duple meter
(Stravinsky)

Example 2.7: Mozart, Concerto for Piano (K. 467) (1785)

This is an excerpt from the slow movement of one of the many concertos Mozart wrote for a solo instrument and orchestra—in this case, piano and orchestra. In it, Mozart puts "two against three" but creates quite a different effect from the Stravinsky example. Much of the difference derives from the level of the hierarchy at which the metric mix appears. Indeed, *where* the conflict occurs in moving up and down the metric ladder makes a significant difference in the intensity of conflict. In this example, Mozart is making the two-against-three mix at the lowest level of the hierarchy—the divider beat. Listen!

The excerpt begins after an orchestral introduction, as the piano soloist enters. You will hear that the meter is duple (4/4) with the tactus beat divided into threes by the accompaniment figure. The piano, moving slowly above it, divides the tactus beat in twos. The effect is a beautiful melody that seems to float or hover above its accompaniment.

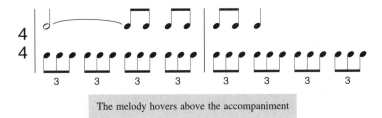

The melody hovers above the accompaniment

Now, to move from the sublime to the banal, let's briefly revisit Impromptu. Go back to RUSS.FIT1 in the Drummer PlayRoom and compare it with these musical examples of metric mix.

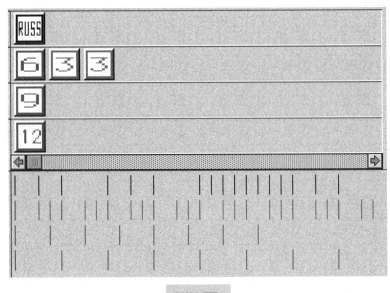

RUSS.FIT1

Focusing on the accompaniment in Voices 3 and 4, what are the similarities and differences between the 9-block and the 12-block in RUSS.FIT1, Stravinsky's accompaniment to Lanner's waltz, and Mozart's accompaniment to the piano melody?

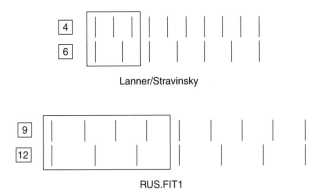

Lanner/Stravinsky

RUS.FIT1

Example 2.8: "*Bulerias*" (flamenco)

Example 2.8, like Stravinsky's *Petrouchka*, is music to be danced. But unlike the ballet with its stars, brilliant choreographers, and composers, flamenco is popular music played, sung, and danced by the people of Spain. As in this example, it is typically performed by one or more guitar players along with hand clapping and heel stomping, all of which accompany singing and dancing. Listen to the excerpt straight through just to enjoy its excitement. Then go back and try to hear what rhythmic characteristics generate the inescapable energy.

The effect is quite different from any of the previous examples. You will notice, for instance, that hand clapping generates a fast, steady beat accompanying the relatively slow-moving melody. But this beat is "attacked" by irregular accents interspersed by both the clapping and by the guitar. Is there a slower beat that groups the fast clapping? Or is this an example of beat without the framing of a slower beat—that is, without meter?

Example 2.3: Porter, "Night and Day" (Billie Holiday, vocal) (1937)

Revisiting Billie Holiday's wonderful performance of Cole Porter's tune "Night and Day," you will appreciate not only Billie's willowy bending of the beat, always carrying us along on the figural gestures of the melody, but also the remarkable rhythms of the instrumentalists playing with her.

To hear the complexity of these rhythms, you will need to practice "listening through the texture." This means selectively focusing your attention on each instrument or group of instrumentalists, respectively, as they work with and against the basic beat of the rhythm section. As the rhythm section (percussion and bass) play the beat, the brass is often marking the slower grouper beat. Listen particularly to the piano as Joe Sullivan plays against, in between, and all around the steady beat. He does that in a different, complementary way to Billie's expressive "give" in shaping the melody rhythm. The two are magically and freely responsive to one another. Perhaps it is only when temporal framing of beat and grouper beat are so alive and so present that such guileless freedom becomes possible.

It is unlikely that you and the computer can come anywhere near to what these composers and live musicians with their particular genius have made. However, the ideas of metric mix and of syncopation, which is so closely associated with jazz, are ideas that you may be able to learn from and use. Syncopation is pushing, bothering the beat by avoiding events that play on the beat and emphasizing, accenting moments *between* the underlying beat and/or the downbeats. In "Night and Day" the piano in particular makes these "off-beat" events that, going *against* beat and meter, make both come alive. Listen again to the flamenco piece for examples of syncopation of another sort. With these examples in mind and ear, go on to the next task—composing percussion accompaniments that conflict with the metric hierarchy of tunes.

Accompaniments That Conflict

The trick in working on this task is to make an accompaniment that conflicts with the metric hierarchy generated by a tune, but one that is still coherent! This means, for instance, that just some random, arbitrary durations will not do. The puzzle becomes, how do you create rhythmic conflict without creating chaos?

The pieces you have just listened to are good examples. They illustrate, for instance, how you can generate conflict at different levels of the metric hierarchy—at the grouper beat level (Stravinsky and Lanner), at the tactus level (syncopation, as in "Night and Day"), or at the divider beat level (Mozart). Which level you choose can make a big difference in the intensity of conflict that you feel.

Experimenting with Rhythmic Conflict

Again, we will use "Russian" as an example. Select RUSS.CON1 in the Tunes Catalog. Click Play and listen closely. What relationships in the accompaniment are generating conflict with the metric structure of "Russian"? To explore that question, here are some general possibilities.

- Listen to each voice separately and then in various combinations.
- Substitute some different durations and listen to the difference.
- Experiment with the wait time.
- Experiment with tempo and with instrumentation.

Using RUSS.CON1 as an example of rhythmic conflict, try some experiments. Consider the questions asked, jot down your impressions, and try to explain what changes make significant differences. As you work, keep in mind the metric hierarchy you initially built for "Russian."

- Listen just to the melody and Voice 4—that is, turn off Voices 2 and 3. Do you hear any conflict? How does the 18-beat relate to the regular grouper beat of 12? For instance, when and where does the 18-beat coincide with events in the tune? What does this suggest about the metric level at which conflict is being generated?
- Trash the 18-block in Voice 4 and substitute a 12-block. Does the conflict disappear? If so, why?
- Turn Voice 2 back on. Does this increase or decrease the conflict? Why?
- Trash the 12-block in Voice 4 and put the 18-block back. Why does this reduce conflict? Or does it? Notice the proportional relations between [6 3] in Voice 2 and [18] in Voice 4.
- Turn Voice 3 back on. Can you predict how this will change the effect of conflict?
- Other things to try: Play with wait times in Voice 1 and then in other voices. Put the 12-block back in Voice 4. Play with tempo and instrumentation.

For other examples of conflicting accompaniments, select RUSS.CON2 and RUSS.CON3 in the Tunes Catalog. For RUSS.CON2, try castanets in Voice 2 if you have it on your synth. Notice that the shorter durations in Voice 2 [4 2] seem to conflict with the normal divider beat [3]. How does conflict at this level compare with conflict at the tactus or grouper beat levels?

RUSS.CON2

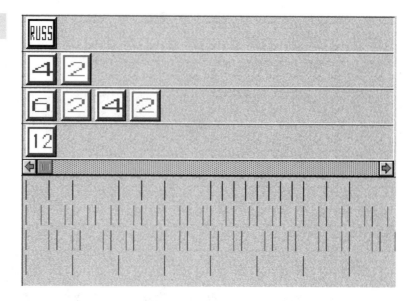

Compare RUSS.CON2 with RUSS.CON3. (Try woodblock in Voice 3 for a better effect.) What generates the differences between RUSS.CON2 and RUSS.CON3, especially with respect to intensity of conflict?

Go on now to compose your own percussion accompaniments for "Early," "Lanner," and "Tyrol." Remember that these accompaniments should generate conflict with the metric structures of the tunes, but they must still be coherent. Indeed, we have some big questions to think about:

• What do we mean by *coherence*?
• What creates coherence in the midst of conflict?
• What relations are necessary to create a sense of organized structure, and when do accompaniments slide into chaos?

EXPLORATIONS 2

Figural Grouping Boundaries

In the introduction to Part 2, two questions were raised:

• What kinds of temporal relations generate the boundaries of rhythm figures?
• How do rhythm figures differ from and also relate to metric units?

The experiments that follow will help you explore these two questions.

Experiment 1

- In the Edit menu, select Clear Voices.
- Put drumblocks [3 3 6] in Voice 2.
- Repeat this figure six times.
- Before you click Play, clap the pattern you expect to hear.
- Click Play.

The repeated figure that you heard, short-short-long, probably matched what you expected.

But sometimes perceived figures surprisingly differ from what you would expect.

Experiment 2

- In the Edit menu, select Clear Voices.
- Put drumblocks [6 3 3] in Voice 2.
- Repeat this figure six times.
- Before you click Play, clap the pattern you expect to hear.
- Click Play.

Did you hear what you expected to hear? Did your hearing match the pattern you clapped? Did your hearing match the repeated pattern represented by the numbers [6 3 3]—that is, long-short-short?

Groupings predicted by numbers

Or did you hear the groupings as shown in the next figure—that is, short-short-long?

Perceived groupings?

You may have heard either [6 3 3] or [3 3 6] as the repeated pattern, but people most often hear the second option. That is, instead of groupings of [6 3 3] as the numbers would suggest, they hear groupings of [3 3 6]—the same as in the first experiment! But how can this be?

The difference between the number pattern that the computer was "told" to execute and the figures we actually hear is good evidence that our hearings are, in fact, constructed. But what generates these perceived figures? What are the internalized "rules" that guide the particular constructions we seem intuitively to make? Recall the first experiment: Repetitions of the durations [3 3 6] generated no surprises; you heard repetitions of the pattern [3 3 6]. Notice that the shorter 3's *go to* the longer 6's. The longer duration, 6, in turn, generates a boundary "bundling up" the shorter durations to form the repeated figure [3 3 6]. Similarly, in the second experiment, where we used the number pattern [6 3 3], we also can hear the shorter 3's *going to* the longer 6's. As a result, the given pattern of durations, [6 3 3], may create a kind of "wraparound" effect: the "tail" of the given pattern, [3 3], attaches itself to the "head" [6] of its next repetition. We hear a solitary first sound (a 6-block) followed by repetitions of the [3 3 6] figure, with the final [3 3] sounding like it ends up "in the air."

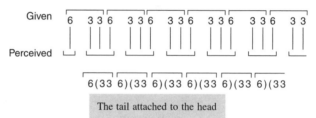

The tail attached to the head

If this is what you hear, as many listeners do, your internal mental organizers regroup the number patterns, shaping your hearing on the principle that shorts attach themselves to longs, and longs generate boundaries. Given no other features (for example, pitch), this commonly shared "mental rule" guides the way we group individual temporal events to form larger events or figures. And, interestingly, the visual grouping of lines that we see in the spatial graphics (rhythm bars) corresponds with what we hear as temporal groupings: Just as a longer time between events forms heard boundaries, larger spaces between lines form *visual* boundaries.

Visual grouping boundaries

Go on to Project 2.4, where you will find new ways to make use of what you have learned so far.

Project 2.4

Composing Percussion Pieces: Some Challenges

Compose five percussion pieces that do the following:

1. Generate duple meter.
2. Generate triple meter.
3. Generate a beat but shifting meter.
4. Generate a beat but no meter.
5. Do not generate a beat.

In preparation for these tasks, listen to the following Listening Examples, which embody some of the structures you will be asked to compose.

LISTENING EXAMPLES: RHYTHMIC COMPLEXITY

Example 2.9: Ziporyn, "What She Saw There" (excerpt) (1990)

Example 2.10: Haydn, String Quartet, Op. 76, #5 (Minuet) (1797)

Example 2.11: *Music from the Forests of Riau,* "Balai Pusing"

Example 2.12: Stravinsky, "Dance of the Adolescents" (excerpt) (1913)

Example 2.9: Ziporyn, "What She Saw There" (excerpt) (1990)

Example 2.9 illustrates a steady beat but shifting meter—that is, an example of Task 3. This brief excerpt from Ziporyn's "What She Saw There" is the beginning of a long composition for marimba and bass clarinet. The marimba is played by two players, four hands on one instrument; the composer plays the clarinet solo.

The pieces you listened to for Project 2.3 demonstrated rhythmic conflict between and among instruments. In this piece, Ziporyn creates shifting meter within a single rhythm line performed by the two marimba players in rhythmic unison (same rhythm, different pitches). As you listen to the opening, clap along with the grouper beat and try to hold it steady. What has Ziporyn done with the durations to so quickly disrupt the grouper beat—that is, the meter?

The piece begins with a brief alternation between just two pitch clusters, creating a strong tactus beat that groups in twos—duple meter. This is immediately followed by a long-short rhythm pattern that establishes the duple meter as compound duple or 6/8—that is, six beats in two groups of three:

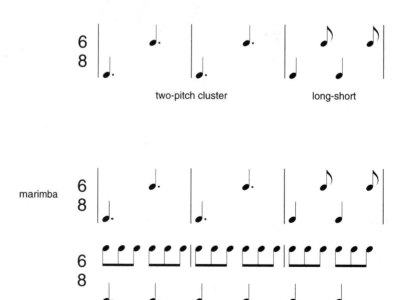

But after we hear the long-short pattern three times, there is a kind of hiccup, a feeling of arriving too soon at the downbeat—we have lost a moment in time. What is going on?

Ziporyn makes this jump by *truncating* the long-short figure—the figure loses one eighth note. The result is a shift in meter from 6/8 to 5/8, and we tumble into the downbeat before we are ready. The whole pattern then returns.

compound duple   truncated   return

The effect is a feeling of speeding up, rushing to a precipitous arrival of the downbeat and to the return of the beginning pattern. Compare this rushed arrival with the moment of return in the B section of Beethoven's "Ode to Joy" theme. There is, of course, no shift of meter in Beethoven's melody; the downbeat arrives when it is expected. But recall that in "Ode," the moment of return is also anticipated; the large melodic leap going to the accented pitch that begins the return occurs just before the downbeat and just before we expect the return.

As the piece goes on, Ziporyn plays with the norms he has set up; the rate of change increases, creating an increase in complexity as well. And just as the music becomes most intense, Ziporyn takes us to an almost literal repeat of the whole opening, now played more softly. The repetition is followed by the entrance of the bass clarinet playing a free-roving melody over the marimba's continuing repeated patterns. The clarinet's entrance signals the beginning of a long story, which we unfortunately have to leave just as it begins.

Example 2.10: Haydn, String Quartet, Op. 76, #5, (Minuet) (1797)

In Example 2.10, Haydn also creates a clear beat, but with a shift in meter. And, like Ziporyn, he creates the shift by shortening a recurring rhythmic motive. However, Haydn takes more time in establishing the beat and meter before introducing the shift.

Like all minuet movements, this one is organized in the familiar A B A' form. A coda is added at the end of the A' section to close the movement.* In the first section of the Minuet (A), Haydn creates the clear triple meter we associate with minuet movements. It

---

Coda is the Italian word for "tail." It is used in musical terminology to describe a closing section of a piece that is, so to speak, appended to the body of the piece.

is only in the next section (B) that Haydn causes the meter to shift. As stated earlier, like Ziporyn, he creates this contrast and complexity by abbreviating his motivic material—that is, by truncating a figure that he has set up. At the beginning of the B section, Haydn takes the three-beat closing figure that ends the A section and removes its "head." In this way he makes a three-beat figure become a two-beat figure.

Repetitions of this abbreviated, "headless" figure, with its pattern of shorts attaching themselves to longs, effectively shifts the meter from triple to duple.

This shift to duple meter gives the feeling of the music speeding up. Why? As a result of the figural grouping, downbeats seem to occur more frequently—on every two tactus beats instead of on every three tactus beats.

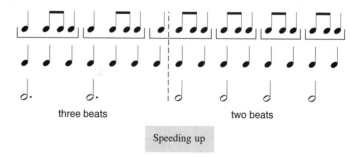

Haydn then fragments the figure further by removing the last note, the "tail," of the previous figure. This leaves only faster notes (eighth notes), all of equal duration. Again there is a feeling of going faster, but now because all the notes being played are actually going faster—that is, there are more notes per beat. At the same time, with all the notes of equal duration, for the moment the meter becomes quite ambiguous.

 Ambiguous meter

With the return of the opening material, Haydn, like Ziporyn, once again clearly establishes the meter. And with the return (A') the previous tension and intensity subsides. The return is followed by a Coda, where the fragmenting process and the shift to duple meter occurs once again. The 2-beat, headless figure is played this time by the cello. The movement ends with a new transformation of the little closing figure. Repeated statements of the transformed closing figure in its triple meter form brings the Minuet to a solid and stable close.

Example 2.11: *Music from the Forests of Riau,* **"Balai Pusing"**
Example 2.12: Stravinsky, **"Dance of the Adolescents" (excerpt) (1913)**

Examples 2.11 and 2.12 illustrate beat without meter—an example of Task 4. This means that a steady beat is clearly established, but there is no regular grouping of that beat to form a slower pulse or meter.

Example 2.11, "Balai Pusing," is music from the forests of Riau in eastern Sumatra. It is played by two drummers. Example 2.12, "Dance of the Adolescents" from Stravinsky's *Le Sacre du Printemps,* was composed in Paris and is played by a full modern orchestra. Both pieces are music to be danced: The first accompanies a sacred healing ritual; the second, like *Petroushka,* was written for the Ballet russe in collaboration with the choreographer Diaghiliev. In the midst of these enormous differences, listening closely to these two examples—one, music of the Indonesian forest, the other, music of cosmopolitan Paris—you will hear a striking similarity in the means used to create energy and excitement. What are these means and what are the dimensions of rhythmic conflict?

Listening closely to "Balai Pusing," you hear first one drum called the *penyelalu* and then a second drum called the *peningka.* They differ noticeably in their functions. The *penyelalu* player, the primary drummer, plays an uninterrupted stream of steady beats; the *peningka* player, making a kind of disruptive counterrhythm, plays continually varied durations that become more and more complex in their relation to the *penyelalu* as the piece goes on. While the *peningka* drummer begins with a few rather tentative sounds, the effect as he continues is one of dropping sharp, irregular accents into the steady stream of the *penyelalu*. Using our terms for describing the metric hierarchy, the first drummer, the *penyelalu* player, creates a clear tactus beat that is interrupted by the irregularly occurring accents of the *peningka* player. Thus we hear a clear, steady tactus beat, but no regularly recurring grouper beat, and thus no meter.

Rhythm and rhythmic complexity play a central role in much of Stravinsky's music, and "Dance of the Adolescents" is no exception. As in "Balai Pusing," you hear a marked and steady beat throughout, and also like the Indonesian piece, accents occur quite irregularly and unexpectedly. Of course, regular accents would not be unexpected if Stravinsky did not first set up some initial expectations.

In this regard, Stravinsky's dance differs from "Balai Pusing." At the beginning of the excerpt we have a clear sense of duple meter generated by alternations of repeating pitches, as in Ziporyn's piece. But with the entrance of the low, driving repeated notes, sharp irregularly occurring sounds are introduced that, as in the Indonesian dance, drop disrupting accents into the steady stream of the underlying pulse. The result is to disrupt any sense of a regular grouping of the tactus. In this case, the accents interrupt and confound the initial duple meter; the contrast between moments of regularity of meter and moments of ambiguity of meter, heard in relation to the strong underlying pulse, helps give both pieces their intense energy.

With these examples in mind, go on to the five tasks for Project 2.4. Remember, as always, to keep a log of your work. Pay special attention to instances where what you hear is not what you expected. For Tasks 1 and 2, this might include instances where you expected to hear a clear duple or triple meter, but that's not what happens. Or perhaps you hear the downbeat in a different place from where you expected it. For Tasks 4 and 5, you might be surprised to hear a beat and/or meter even though the durations you picked didn't predict that. When these surprises happen, ask yourself:

- What reasons did I have to expect that my durations would create a certain pattern (triple meter, no beat, and so on)?
- How would I describe what I did hear?
- What does this tell me about the relation between notation and perception?
- In the light of all of the above, how can I change things so as to hear what I expect/want to hear?

Explorations: Drummer Playgrounds

Drummer Playgrounds are environments for creating your own percussion pieces in new ways. Playgrounds include three different kinds of blocks: tuneblocks, drumblocks, and in addition *pattern blocks.*

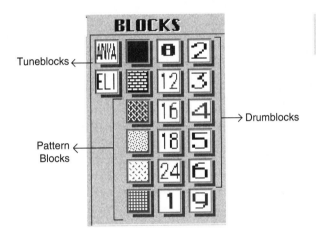

ELI: Three kinds of blocks

For example, the sound file ELI includes the following:

1. *Tuneblocks:* ANYA and ELI. These are tunes you can use if you want to make your percussion pieces into accompaniments.
2. *Drumblocks:* These are the familiar drumblocks, each block playing a single duration with the value of the number on its icon face. You can use them in the following ways:
   - Make new pattern blocks.
   - Practice reconstructing the given pattern blocks at the individual duration level.
   - Mix them with the pattern blocks in a single voice.
   - Create just an underlying pulse in one voice when you have patterns in others.
3. *Pattern Blocks:* These are small precomposed rhythm patterns/figures. You can play with the pattern blocks in several ways:
   - Arrange several blocks in one voice to make a longer percussion piece.
   - Arrange several blocks in more than one voice to make a multivoice percussion piece.

- Try to reconstruct pattern blocks using individual drumblocks. (Put a pattern block in one voice and try to match it by putting individual drumblocks in another voice.)
- Open a pattern block and find out what is in it or edit it to make a new block.
- Use Block-It to join two or more pattern blocks to make a single, bigger block.

The examples you will find in the Drummer catalog include the following:

- CLEMENTINE: The tune "Clementine" with an *oom-pah-pah* accompaniment, along with a somewhat conflicting inner part.
- DRUM: Here there are only three drumblocks called T, S, and L for Tiny, Short, and Long. Each block is just a single duration with each related to the next longer block by a ratio of 2:1. With just these three percussion blocks, you can make remarkably interesting percussion accompaniments. DRUM includes a sample accompaniment for the tune "Lightly Row."
- DRUM1: DRUM1 includes the T, S, and L blocks and also two pattern blocks that play a pattern of varied durations. In this example, the pattern blocks are used to create a somewhat more lively accompaniment to "Lightly Row" than in DRUM. Try to hear what is going on with the pattern blocks, and then use the magnifying glass cursor to open them.
- YANKEE.D: A variety of pattern blocks make a kind of military band accompaniment for "Yankee Doodle."
- ELI: An accompaniment made up of pattern blocks that makes use of the Wait Times option. These pattern blocks are particularly interesting because, like the examples of figural regrouping, they seem to transform before your very ears.
    Try experimenting with the pattern blocks in ELI:
  - In the Edit menu, select Clear Voices.
  - Put the wait times back to 0 in each voice.
  - Try repeating some of the pattern blocks by themselves.

For example, listen to the first pattern block in the Blocks area. It is playing durations of [4 2 2 6 2]. Looking at the duration numbers and the graphics, you might expect to hear a figure that starts with long-short-short-long. But what you hear instead is a figure that "wraps around" itself. That is, it starts with the last 2 and comes around to make an accent on the 4: [2 4 2 2 6]—short-*long*-short-short-long. The pattern generates a clear duple meter, but the figural grouping crosses over the perceived bar line.

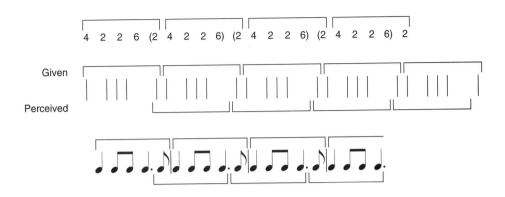

A Pause

This might be a good moment to ask yourself: What have I learned about rhythm so far? What can I say about what I know? What can I do with it? Think about the following possibilities:

- Performing music sets sound in motion while marking off time into regularly recurring impulses/beats—the temporal scaffolding of our musical experience.
- Beats are continuously generated in real time: you can make a beat by yourself (clapping, tapping, drumming) or you can follow a beat, feeling it out as you listen to a tune or a drum pattern.
- Once a beat gets going in a piece, the ongoing music is heard in some relation to it.
- The beat becomes a living unit, continuously regenerated by the relations among performed events. There is "give" in this living unit: It is not only played *by* performers, it is also played *with* by performers.
- The beat also creates a "living ruler," which can be used to measure the varied durations of the piece that generates it. This is the principle behind most notations for musical time.
- There is an important difference between figural and metric entities. We listen most intuitively to figures and their motion toward structural goals. But metric entities call up our innate, intuitive abilities to pulse, to regularly mark off the continuousness of time. A big question to consider further: What are the meaningful intersections, the shared dependencies, between metric and figural entities? What are the intersections between Leonardo's grids and the elegant shapes he draws?

Some Basics:
Conventional
Rhythm Notation

THIS IS A SUMMARY OF THE INFORMATION ON CONVENTIONAL RHYTHM NOTATION (CRN) discussed earlier. As you will recall, CRN is based on a set of symbols that stand for the duration of an event as measured against a given time unit, or beat. The ability to read CRN assumes the ability to hear a set of varied durations in relation to this unvarying beat.

The Basic Symbols

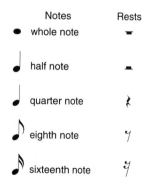

	Notes	Rests
●	whole note	▬
♩	half note	▬
♩	quarter note	𝄽
♪	eighth note	𝄾
♪	sixteenth note	𝄿

Durational symbols are proportional to each other, related in multiples of two:

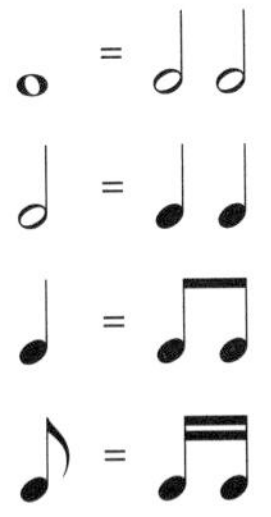

$$\mathbf{o} \; = \; \text{𝅗𝅥} \; \text{𝅗𝅥}$$

$$\text{𝅗𝅥} \; = \; \text{♩} \; \text{♩}$$

$$\text{♩} \; = \; \text{♫}$$

$$\text{♪} \; = \; \text{𝅘𝅥𝅯𝅘𝅥𝅯}$$

This notation may be confusing at first because the whole note, from which the other symbols derive their names and values, is rarely used in modern notation as the symbol for the beat. The most common notation for the underlying beat is probably the quarter note. Thus if you are keeping time to a piece (as in the projects in Part 2), the beat that you are clapping is most often (but certainly not always) written as a quarter note. In turn, the varied durations of a melody are written as multiples or divisions of that basic quarter-note beat.

Other Conventions

The duple relationship among the symbols representing durations can be altered when needed. For instance, a beamed group of notes with a 3 annexed to it tells the performer to play three notes in the time usually taken by two notes of the same value. Thus, three eighth notes beamed together, as shown in the following figure, are to be played in the same time as two eighth notes or one quarter note:

$$\overset{3}{\text{♫♪}} \; = \; \text{♫} \; = \; \text{♩}$$

A *dot* after a note increases its length by one-half its value:

$$\text{♩.} \; = \; \text{♩} \; + \; \text{♪}$$

A *tie* connects two notes together indicating that the second note should not be sounded, but that the duration of that note should be "tied" to the first:

$$\text{♩}\underset{\smile}{\text{♩}} \; = \; \text{𝅗𝅥}$$

A tie is often used over a bar line where syncopation occurs. That is, the event that usually marks the downbeat at the beginning of a measure is not played, because it is tied to the last note of the previous measure and is thus silent. The limitations of the notation make it impossible to write a single note of the desired duration over the bar line, but the tie also shows the performer that syncopation will occur.

Time Signatures

The *time signature* placed at the beginning of a score tells us two things: (1) the number of beats that group together to form the meter, and (2) the durational unit of notation that will represent one beat. Thus in 2/4 meter, the upper number, 2, means that the piece will be in duple meter—that is, beats will be grouped in twos, a 2:1 relation between grouper beat and tactus. This grouping is reflected by the bar lines marking *measures*, each of which will be two beats in total duration. The lower number, 4, means that the basic beat will be notated as a quarter note. Similarly, 3/4 meter indicates triple meter—that is, there will be the equivalent of three beats in each measure and the beat will be notated as a quarter note.

duple meter   triple meter

There are a number of other meter designations, but the principle is always the same. For instance, 4/4 is also a duple meter. While the quarter note is still representing the tactus, there are four quarter notes rather than only two in each measure. Following the same principle, the compound duple meter, 6/8, means that the eighth note is the tactus and there are six of them in each measure. (For a lengthy discussion comparing 3/4 meter with 6/8 meter, see the section titled "Listening Examples: Rhythmic Conflict" in Project 2.3.)

Tempo Designation

As you know, the notation system depends on measuring time in relation to some given unit, but the symbols of CRN tell you nothing about the *rate* of this beat—that is, the *tempo*. The *metronome* provides the only precise method for fixing the rate for the beat (see the discussion of tempo,

the differences between CRN and Impromptu notation, and the uses of
the metronome in Project 2.2).

Tempo is also indicated by more general, but also quite vague terms,
and here Italian words again predominate:

largo	very slow ("broadly")
andante	moderately slow ("walking")
adagio	slow
moderato	moderate
allegretto	moderately fast
allegro	fast ("cheerful")
vivace	fast ("lively")
presto	very fast

Part 3

The dove, representing the Holy Spirit, whispers chant melodies to Pope Gregory while he dictates to a scribe. (Image: Bayerische Staatsbibliothek, Munich)

Pitch Relations

Introduction: Looking Back and Moving On

As you worked with the projects in Parts 1 and 2, your musical intuitions served you well as a source for making sense of melodies and rhythms. But in that process, your intuitions were a target for inquiry, as well. Thinking back to your tune building projects in Part 1, recall that you were able quite intuitively to create melodies that made sense both to you and to others. You found, for instance, that you had a good feeling for the functions of blocks—which blocks could work as beginnings, and which blocks sounded like endings. By experimenting you were able to hear how blocks might follow one another, and you were able to create longer sequences of blocks that together made up structurally coherent tunes. These experiences suggested that you have an intuitive model of a sensible tune and that this mental model is guiding your compositional decisions. Indeed, even without your intentionally meaning to, your tunes often embodied many of the same structural principles found in the tunes you reconstructed and also in the more complex compositions included in the Listening Examples. We call these principles *simples* or *generative primitives* because they form a common scaffolding shared by much of the music in Western culture.

In working with rhythms you reflected on your feel for and ability to keep time with the beats generated by the rhythms of tunes. Metric structures were made more explicit through Impromptu's spatial and numeric representations, which, in turn, mapped quite easily onto the proportional symbols of conventional rhythm notation. Each notation said particular things about a rhythm, and each had uses that another did not. In composing percussion accompaniments to tunes and in composing your own drum pieces, simples such as metric structure became generative primitives with which to build and elaborate on what you knew already.

But now we need to ask, what are the more specific musical relations that constitute melodic simples? What could be the constituents of our shared intuitions? What, for instance, are the specific pitch relations that generate what you intuitively hear as an ending? Or, as one student put it at the end of her paper on Project 1.2: "A big question in my mind: what makes a certain sequence of notes, blocks—sound like an ending? We see that most people agree on what things have ending sounds, so what makes it that way?" You may already have some tentative answers to this student's questions. But it is important to test these hunches. In Part 3, we will delve deeper into these relationships to help account for your musical intuitions while also helping you to go beyond them.

More specifically, in Project 3.1, you will explore the organization of pitch in music and how it relates to the conventions of music notation. In doing so, you will need to think critically about the kinds of elements captured by our pitch notations, our units of description, and how these may differ from more intuitive units of perception. Why do the conventional symbols for representing pitch, like those for representing rhythm, sometimes inform and sometimes confound intuitive hearings?

But we will also keep larger questions in mind: How do commonly shared pitch and time relations give shape, coherence, and meaning to melodies? How are these organizing principles elaborated in the structuring of larger, multidimensional complex compositions? And how are composers able to make use of a relatively small set of shared elements and relations and still compose pieces each of which is unique? Finally, as you learn to shift your focus of attention among these organizing principles, how will this change what you hear and perhaps also what you like?

Pitch Notations and Their Uses

In most of the world's music cultures, there is no written music notation. In these cultures, a young musician listens to and watches more experienced musicians, often learning through individual guidance and practice in a close master-student relationship. As in our own jazz tradition, learning to participate with others in playing music is also an important part of learning to be a musician. Learning to improvise with others, for example, means internalizing shared underlying musical structures upon which improvisations are based, while also developing the ability to creatively elaborate on them using musical gestures that are indigenous to the particular cultures.

In contrast to these aural, improvised traditions, written notations have been a part of most Western music practices for many centuries. Indeed, music notation has had considerable influence on the evolution of Western music, and that is a fascinating, complex story in itself.* The notations we use today evolved through a long, slow

---

*The remarks that follow concerning this evolutionary process are much simplified; they are intended only to give some summary background that might be useful for an understanding of modern music notation.

process. The evolutionary paths are often difficult to follow and account for, largely because evolution and change was rarely the result of specific or intentional design. Rather, these changes in ways of representing pitch were a collective response to the practical needs of performers and composers at different times in this history, coupled with the changing role of music in society.

For example, early in this history, graphic shapes or squiggles called *neumes* were sometimes written above the text of the Church liturgy.

Music notation made its first appearance around the ninth century in the form of signs added above the words of liturgical texts. These signs, called *neumes*, acted as graphic mnemonic devices.

The neumes represented short, melodic figures that were segments of longer melodies—rather similar to the figures played by tuneblocks. These squiggles were useful primarily as mnemonics to remind singers of melodic figures they already knew.* Over time, in response to the changing role of music in society and the needs of musicians, symbols evolved that represented specific and discrete pitches and durations. The emergence of these notations was due in part to the Church's desire to "standardize" the singing of the service in distanced communities, and in part motivated by the rise of individual composers and their music. For instance, instead of a body of music that was shared and well known by a community, unique compositions were being composed. If an individual composer, call him composer X, wrote a new piece and he wanted performer Y to play it exactly as he composed it, composer X needed to find some consistent way of "telling" performer Y exactly what notes to play, without having to play the composition for him first.

Despite their differences, the evolution of modern systems for representing pitch depended on identifying a basic collection of pitches and organizing these collections

---

*Similar squiggles are still present in the Hebrew Talmud. Called *cantillations*, they are used to remind those who are saying or singing prayers how the conventional melodies go.

in some systematic way. As Isaac Rosenfield, author of *The Invention of Memory*, has said, "we perceive the world without labels, and we can label it only when we have decided how its features should be organized." Particular collections of pitches have, in general, been derived from the body of music that happened to be current at different periods in music history. To label pitches, derived collections were usually organized in a low-high series—a "ladder" of pitches. And once ordered low-high, pitches can be named according to their position in the low-high ordering. Names for elements of these "ladders" of pitches have typically been borrowed from common symbols that represent other ordered series—primarily, but not only, letters and numbers. Practical need, then, along with the need for conceptual coherence, has led to the close connection between our notation systems and the structures we call scales.

Note, however, that there are also other systems for representing pitch relations based on different principles. For instance, the guitar notation found in popular-music scores (originally called *tablature* and used by lute players) pictures the neck of the instrument, including the *frets,* which mark off the neck of the instrument. Dots written into these pictured frets show performers where to put their fingers on the strings. This notation is, of course, instrument-specific, unlike other notations that can be applied to any instrument.

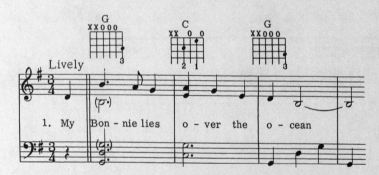

Guitar tablature: Three chords notated as tablature, shown above the staff, harmonize the first phrase of "My Bonnie Lies over the Ocean."

The selection of pitches drawn from melodies that are familiar today when reordered from low to high form the *major and minor scales.** For example, most of the melodies you have worked with so far used pitches that, if reordered from low to high, would form a major scale. However, "Anya"'s pitches, if reordered, would form

---

*The word *scale* comes from the Italian word *scala,* which means "ladder."

a *minor* scale. And the Portals blocks, which sounded less familiar, made use of a larger collection of pitches, which if reordered would form a *chromatic* scale.*

It is important to emphasize that the structure of these scales and the elements we label are not given as entities beforehand. Rather they are structures that have been abstracted and organized from pitch materials already present in common melodies. To make this point quite clear, you will actually build up the major scale from a melody with which you are certainly familiar. The melody is "America," which you may know as "My Country, 'Tis of Thee" (or, in some places, "God Save the Queen"). But first a brief introduction will help you move comfortably from pitch contour graphics to traditional staff notation.

Pitch contour graphics or piano roll graphics, with which you are already familiar, have been useful in giving you a general feel for pitch motion and for the general shape of a melody. Like a graph, the vertical axis of the graphics shows you pitch movement going up and down by leap or by step, while the horizontal axis shows you movement through time.† For instance, if you compare the graphic notation for "America" with traditional staff notation for "America," you can see that both notations work in a similar way: Pitch motion up and down lies on the vertical axis and movement through time lies on the horizontal axis. (For more information on staff notation, see the section titled "Some Basics: Conventional Pitch Notation" at the end of Part 3.)

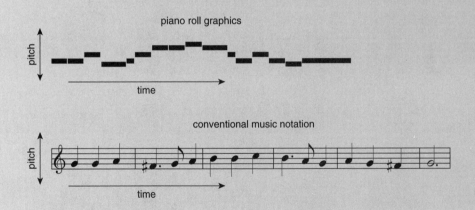

---

*For more on the differences between major, minor, and chromatic scales, see Project 3.3 and also the section titled "Some Basics: Conventional Pitch Notation" at the end of Part 3.
†Pitch contour graphics actually assume that pitches have already been ordered from low to high. The terms *high* and *low,* or *up* and *down,* are metaphors borrowed from objects that occupy real space, which sounding tones obviously do not. Sounding tones occupy space only when they are embodied by an instrument (for example, a keyboard). Then, the ordering of tones makes up the geography of the instrument. When submitted to a notation, tones also come to occupy "virtual" space—paper space.

However, staff notation includes both more specific and also different kinds of information. In addition to showing you the general pitch shape of the melody and the relative position and duration of notes, staff notation tells you exactly which pitch to play and also the duration of each pitch in relation to a constant unit.* Thus, each note symbol in staff notation includes two properties—a pitch and its duration.

The pitches to which note symbols refer are made explicit by the five lines that divide up the symbolic paper space to form the *staff*. Each line of the staff and each space between the lines is associated with a specific pitch. For instance, if you compare pitch contour graphics for "America" with staff notation, you can probably see that the first section of "America" begins and ends with the same pitch. But in staff notation, you can also identify that pitch as G (on the second line of the staff).

But notice that while staff notation gains in specificity and in its level of detail, it does not include aspects of the melody that you found most immediately accessible in listening—namely, larger structural entities such as the figures or phrases represented by tuneblocks. Recall that you met with a similar issue in comparing representations for rhythm: Spatial graphics more easily show figural groupings, while conventional notation for rhythm shows only metric information—information that is necessary as instructions for performance.

In fact, all notations are partial, and they are so in two senses: Each notation captures certain features but ignores others, and each is partial to, or favors, certain kinds of features and relations. Thus, different notations are useful for different purposes; the trick is to be able to choose effectively among multiple notations, depending on what job you want the notation to do for you. If you want to learn to play a piece that you have never heard before, staff notation is clearly most useful because it tells you exactly which notes to play. But staff notation may be confounding at first, precisely because its discrete notes do not reflect the boundaries that group the sequence of notes into figures and phrases.

And here is that paradox again: In listening to music, we focus most naturally on larger structural entities; in learning to play a piece from staff notation, we must necessarily begin by focusing on the smallest entities—recognizing and playing each note. This leaves the performer with the problem and the work of learning to hear, of actually making figures and phrases—the very aspect of a piece with which we begin, as listeners, in making sense of a piece. As pointed out earlier, these disjunctions between

*The moves from pitch contour graphics to staff notation can be roughly compared with the historical change from neumes to staff notation.

the focus of our intuitive sense-making and the focus assumed by our notations help account for why conventional notation may be confounding when novices initially try to use and make sense of it. But by moving back and forth between multiple representations, along with listening, playing, and practicing with notations, each can enrich and inform the other.

Project 3.1

Deriving the Major Scale from "America"

THE TASKS

1. Reconstruct "America" using tuneblocks.
2. Derive the major scale from "America."
3. Construct the model of a major scale.
4. Derive the skeleton structure ($\hat{1}$ $\hat{5}$ $\hat{1}$) from common melodies.

INFO BOX
Starting Project 3.1
· In the Playrooms
  menu, select
  Tuneblocks
· In the Tunes
  Catalog, select
  AMERICA

In Project 3.1, you will derive the major scale from the familiar tune "America." In the process, you will also be taking critical steps down the structural ladder of music to the detail level of single pitches. In turn, you will be shifting contexts—plucking pitches out of their more intuitive context, embedded in the chronological ordering of a melody, to put them into the more formal context of pitches ordered from low to high.

It will be helpful to start once again at the more familiar middle level of the structural ladder—that is, with the melody's motivic and phrase structures and their functions. To do so, reconstruct the tune just as you reconstructed the tunes in Project 1.1. Listen to the whole melody (click the AMER block), paying attention to how you might chunk it into tuneblocks and into larger sections. Then listen to the given blocks and compare them with your chunking. Now go ahead and reconstruct the whole tune.

A First Look at "America"

In reconstructing "America," you may have noticed that it has some unusual structural aspects. Unlike the tunes you reconstructed in Project 1.1, there is no literal repetition—each block is used only once. However, there is rhythmic repetition, but these repetitions go largely unnoticed until you focus on them directly. In fact, the rhythm pattern with which the melody begins occurs four times in four different blocks. Looking at the rhythm bar graphics, we can see the repetitions quite clearly. Why do these repetitions remain hidden until they are explicitly pointed out? We will return to this question in the Explorations sections.

With respect to the melody's general pitch motion, looking at the pitch contour graphics, you can see that, like Beethoven's "Ode," the melody is very conjunct—it moves in small steps and avoids large leaps. (This makes it easier to sing.)

Pitch contour graphics: The melody moves in small steps

The most obvious leap occurs between the two large sections of the melody (marked A and B in the preceding illustration). Indeed, as in "Ode," this large leap helps mark the boundaries of these two large sections. The grouping of blocks is also unusual: The melody does not begin with an antecedent-consequent pair, and there is no contrasting middle section and no return. And despite the fact that the blocks/figures are equal in total time (6 beats), the two large groupings, A and B, are not—B is clearly longer than A.

What are the actual pitch relations within the tune that help generate these structural relations and the coherence we hear? For instance, why can you intuitively hear which motives or phrases come to rest (sound ended), and which do not? What generates the boundaries of the inner figures as well as the two large sections? Understanding the relations between the scale and your intuitive perceptions will help answer some of these questions.

As a first step, focus your hearing on stability in contrast to instability. Listen to "America" again, and this time listen for just those moments that sound most at rest. Following the preceding picture of the pitch contour graphics, circle each of the dots representing pitches that sound most stable—that function to resolve the onward motion of the melody.

You certainly circled the final pitch in the melody and probably also the pitch that ends the first section (A), as well. Following along the horizontal line drawn in the next illustration, you can see that the same pitch both resolves the first section and also completes the tune.

The same pitch resolves both the A and B sections

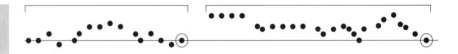

This single pitch in a melody that emerges as the most stable, most at rest, is called the *tonic*. But, thinking back to the student's "big question," why is there only one pitch that can serve this function? To deal with this question we need to give names to pitches so that we can refer to them. And to do that, we need to look at our notational conventions.

Deriving the Major Scale

With "America" shown in staff notation, we now can identify and give names to the collection of pitches that, in this example, the tune includes.* There are only seven different pitches in this collection. The asterisks in the following illustration mark the first occurrence of each of these seven pitches.†

First instance of each pitch in the collection

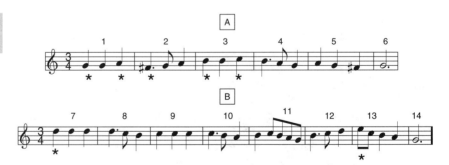

---

*For this example, we have arbitrarily chosen to write "America" using the particular collection of pitches that generate G as the tonic. As you will see later, other pitches would work just as well as long as the relations among them stay the same. For more on that, see Project 3.2.
†The numbers above the score mark the measures.

Notice that while five of the pitches are introduced in the first three measures of the A section, the remaining two pitches are introduced in measures seven and thirteen in the subsequent B section. This late entrance of the two last pitches plays a significant role in the structure and effect of the melody.

If we now reorder these seven pitches from the lowest pitch in the tune (in measure 2) to the highest (in measure 13), the result is the sequence of pitches shown in the following illustration:

Ordering the pitches from lowest to highest

To hear this reordered pitch collection, click the L-H tuneblock and follow the ordering as shown.

We will now reorder the same pitch material of "America," this time beginning with the tonic, G, in recognition of its primary position.* With this reordering of the pitch material, starting now from the tonic, G, we have derived the pitch collection and the low-high ordering of the G-major scale. The G-major scale is shown in the next illustration.

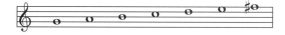

Pitches reordered from the tonic, creating the G-major scale

Calling the tonic, as starting pitch, the *first degree* of the scale and going up from there, we can assign consecutive *scale degree numbers* to the consecutive ordering of the pitches.† Scale degree numbers can be indicated in shorthand by numbers with "hats": $\hat{1}$, $\hat{2}$, $\hat{3}$, and so forth. The following illustration shows you the pitches of the G-major scale in staff notation together with the letter names of the pitches and their scale degrees. To hear the G-major scale, click the SCALE block. Sing along with the G-major scale and also play it on the keyboard.

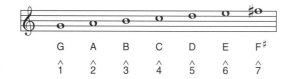

G-major scale in staff notation with letter names and scale degrees

*Notice that by beginning with the tonic, G, the F# that was the first pitch in the initial ordering must be moved up an *octave*. The phenomenon of the octave is explained in the section titled "Some Basics: Conventional Pitch Notation" at the end of Part 3.

†The term *degree* is used in music terminology to denote "a note's classification regarding its position in the scale" (*Oxford Dictionary of Music*).

You undoubtedly heard that the last pitch in the series, the seventh degree or $\hat{7}$ (F#), is highly unstable. Sing the scale up to the seventh degree; what pitch will resolve this instability, and what does this tell you?

First, given the G-major collection of pitches, it is obviously the next pitch in the series that resolves the cliff-hanging F#—the G an *octave* above the starting G. Thus, in general, given this collection of pitches, a G in any register (an octave lower or higher) will acquire a tonic function.

Second, starting with the tonic (G) and going up the seven pitches of the major scale, you arrive at a pitch with the same name but one octave above the starting pitch. And continuing down from the starting pitch, the previous pitches and their names are also repeated an octave lower.* Pitches that are related by an octave are described as belonging to the same *pitch class.* Higher or lower pitches that belong to the same pitch class are described as in a higher or lower *register.*† Thus, the major scale divides each octave into eight different pitches or seven different pitch classes as shown in the following illustration. The relationship among these eight pitches will be discussed in a moment.

The major scale divides each octave into seven different pitch classes

!G   !A   !B   C   D   E   F♯   G   A   B   C   D!   E!   F♯!   G!   A!

Third, when you add the higher G to the series of seven pitches, the result sounds like a familiar tune with a beginning and an end. But it is important to remember that we have derived this ascending scale from the pitches as they occurred in a melody. While a "scale tune" sometimes occurs in a piece of music (for example, the beginning of "Joy to the World" is a descending series), a scale is not, in itself, a melody. Rather it is an abstraction, a derived structure, constructed from the pitch material of actual melodies.

---

*In Impromptu, an ! *following* a pitch name or a scale degree number means that it is in the octave above the octave *above* middle C. An ! *preceding* a pitch name or scale degree means that it is in the octave below the octave *below* middle C. For instance, E! is in the octave above the octave *above* middle C and !E is in the octave below the octave *below* middle C. There are a number of other conventions for designating the register of a pitch.

†For more on pitch class and register, see the section titled "Some Basics: Conventional Pitch Notation" at the end of Part 3.

Structure of the Major Scale

We began by deriving a particular major scale, the G-major scale, from the melody "America." But, in fact, the major scale is a generalizable structure—that is, a major scale can be built starting on any pitch. The specific structure of the major scale depends on the sequence of its internal *intervals*—that is, the pitch distance between one pitch and the next in the ordered series. The smallest interval between any two pitches found in most of our familiar music is called a *half step.* The smallest interval between any two immediately adjacent piano keys is also a half step. Half steps on the keyboard include adjacent white to black and black to white keys and also adjacent white to white keys. The next larger interval is called a *whole step.* There is a whole step between adjacent white keys that have a black key in between, a whole step between adjacent black keys that have one white key in between, and a whole step between a white key and a black key where there is another white key between.

With these relationships in mind, the easiest way to see the interval structure of the major scale is to use the G-major scale as model, and see how it lies on the piano keyboard. In the picture of the piano keyboard, the piano keys of the G-major scale in the middle octave are marked with an asterisk (*).

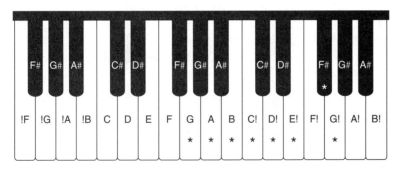

G-major scale

Degree	1^	2^	3^	4^	5^	6^	7^	8^
Pitch:	G	A	B	C	D	E	F#	G
Interval:		1	1	1/2	1	1	1	1/2

G-major scale: sequence of whole and half steps

The picture of the keyboard shows you that the intervals from G to A and from A to B are whole steps—there is a black key between each pair.

But B to C and F# to G are half steps—there is no black key between B and C, and F# is immediately next to G. The diagram shows the names of the pitches of the G-major scale, along with the sequence of whole- and half-step intervals within it.

While the series of whole and half steps may appear to be asymmetrical, there is an important symmetry in the structure. The same sequence of intervals appears at both the bottom half and the top half of the series: Scale degrees $\hat{1}$–$\hat{4}$ and scale degrees $\hat{5}$–$\hat{8}$ form two identical groups of intervals (1 1 $\frac{1}{2}$), with the two groups of intervals separated by a whole step. The two groups of four identically related pitches are called *tetrachords*. Scale degrees $\hat{1}$–$\hat{4}$ make up the lower tetrachord, and scale degrees $\hat{5}$–$\hat{8}$ make up the upper tetrachord.

Tetrachords: Two identical sets of intervals

$\hat{1}$	$\hat{2}$	$\hat{3}$	$\hat{4}$	$\hat{5}$	$\hat{6}$	$\hat{7}$	$\hat{8}$
G	A	B	C	D	E	F#	G

| 1 | 1 | 1/2 | 1 | 1 | 1 | 1/2 |

Lower tetrachord   Upper tetrachord

Another critical feature of the major scale structure is the relationship between the first and fifth scale degrees—the scale degrees that mark the start of the lower and upper tetrachords. The fifth degree of the scale, through the various quirks of music history, is called the *dominant*. As you will see, this relationship between the tonic and dominant scale degrees, together with the likeness between the bottom and top tetrachords of the major scale, is an important feature in the shared structures that help create the coherence of common melodies.

Having derived the major scale and described its internal structure, we are now able to do the following:

- Give consistent number names to pitches within the context of a particular pitch collection and its ordering
- Use the names of pitches in the series to indicate the position and function of pitches in relation to the tonic
- Use the model of a major scale to build other major scales
- Move further in accounting for intuitive hearings and our model of a sensible tune

The Tonic Function: An Internal Affair

In deriving the major scale from the pitches of "America," we started with an intuitive hearing of the pitch that sounded most stable—the tonic. But notice, in looking at the notation for the melody, that you can see other instances of this tonic pitch (on the same line in staff notation), which you do not hear as equally at rest, or indeed, probably not even as the same.

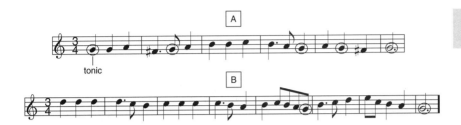

Tonic pitches are not equally stable

Why? Listening to "America" once again, or better, singing it, notice that the tonic pitches that sound stable and thus function as endings occur on strong beats and with a longer duration. The tonic pitches that occur on weak beats or with a shorter duration cause them to move onward rhythmically. Thus, the extent to which a pitch sounds stable may also be influenced by its position in relation to the metric hierarchy and by its duration.

But despite all these differences, there is still only one pitch class in this melody that sounds stable, really at rest. How can we explain this tonic function, which seems so immediately intuitive? While theorists have argued about answers to this question, most agree that for listeners who have grown up in Western musical culture, the stable function of the tonic derives primarily from its relation to the other pitches that surround it. Thus, the tonic function that a pitch acquires is entirely an internal affair: a pitch acquires a tonic function through its contact with a specific collection of pitches, and the particular ordering and rhythmic orientation of this collection as each melody unfolds through time.

"America," as well as most of the tunes you worked with in Projects 1.1 and 1.2, reaches a conclusion because the last notes of the tune have acquired a tonic function through their association with the previous pitches. Just as the function of a tuneblock depends on the context in which it occurs in the unfolding of a melody, so the function or "meaning" of a pitch also depends on the context of pitches in which it occurs. And, as you might expect, the same pitch that sounds so stable in one collection of pitches may sound quite unstable when embedded in a new collection of pitches. In turn, this new context will result in some other pitch acquiring a stable function.

We might compare this phenomenon of context generating meaning with the way the same shape can change its meaning when embedded in different contexts. For instance, look at the changing meaning of the same 90° angle when embedded in these two different contexts: The 90° angle forms the corners of a square in one context and the joining of arms or legs in the other context.

90° angles with different meanings

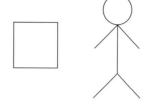

But it needs to be emphasized that to hear, even to make, these relationships between tension and stability, to hear certain pitches as needing to move on while others generate resolution, is something we learn through everyday experience in listening to the music of our own culture. This becomes clear in listening to the music of cultures with which we are unfamiliar (India, Indonesia), where relationships between moving on and coming to rest are generated in quite different ways. People who have grown up with music that differs from Western music will not hear the relationships that seem so obvious to us, just as we will not hear relationships between tension and resolution in their music. So that you can experience these differences yourself, examples of music from other cultures have been included in the Listening Examples.

We can now add that your model of a sensible tune most probably includes this property of generating a focal pitch or tonic as a necessary means of creating coherence. Indeed, this property of tunes—to generate a central pitch toward which all the others gravitate—is another one of the simples or generative primitives shared by all our familiar melodies, as well as more complex pieces composed over the long period in the history of music beginning from about 1650. However, in more recent times, some composers have abandoned this means of generating comprehensibility while continuing to include some of the other generative primitives from the past. Indeed, the lack of a tonal center accounts for one of the primary reasons why the Portals blocks you worked with in Project 1.2 sounded strange. The Listening Examples include compositions by several other twentieth-century composers, for instance, Example 3.5 by Robert Helps, composed in 1974; Example 5.10 by Bela Bartok, written in 1938; and Example 2.9 by Evan Ziporyn, composed in 1990.

EXPLORATIONS

Revisiting "America"

Beginning with your intuitive hearing of the tonic function in "America," we derived the major scale and described its structure in terms of that tonic. How can this help you understand and hear the structure of "America" in new ways, and also help you account for its particular coherence? Consider just the first section (A) of the tune:

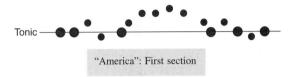

"America": First section

Looking again at the general shape of the melody, with the tonic function shown as larger dots, it becomes clear that the first section is organized entirely around the starting tonic pitch—it begins there; moves below, above, and through it; and finally comes to rest on it.

The beginning of the second section (B) is marked by a leap:

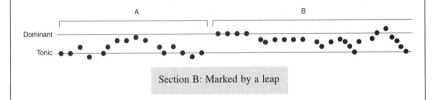

Section B: Marked by a leap

This leap goes up to the fifth degree of the scale, the dominant—which you will recall is introduced in the tune for the first time here. Looking at the picture of the graphics for the B section with tonic and dominant pitches marked, you can see that repetitions of the dominant pitch emphatically move the melody out and beyond the tonic area with which the melody begins, creating a distinct contrast to the first section.

The repeated dominants of the B section form the beginning of sequentially repeated figures, the second repetition beginning one step lower on the fourth degree. The sequential figures are followed by a downward rush, lightly touching the tonic then turning around to climb quickly back up to the dominant. A brief closing gesture, momentarily going above the dominant, rapidly moves down through the whole pitch space, coming to rest once again on the tonic.

Looking back, you can see and hear that the pitch motion of "America" on the most global level is formed by the moves from tonic to dominant and back to tonic. This is the skeleton structure created by pitch events that get the most emphasis rhythmically and by the contrasts in pitch motion. The tonic, G, is the focus of the first section; the focus of the second section shifts to the dominant. The shift is created by the leap to the dominant, D, and its extension through repetition, both of which create tension and contrast. The B section continues by winding back down inconclusively to the tonic, then revisiting the dominant, and once more returning to the tonic, now with emphasis. The return to the tonic resolves the tension created by the leap to the dominant, bringing the melody to a close with a sense of completion.

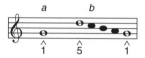

Indeed, this $\hat{1}$-$\hat{5}$-$\hat{1}$ skeleton, even the leap to the dominant and the filling in of this pitch space, also forms the skeleton structure of many other familiar tunes, as well as the underlying structure of more extended relations in longer, more complex compositions.

A Generic Tune

The clearest, most basic, bare-bones example of this structure is found in the common tune "Twinkle, Twinkle, Little Star." Before going on to elaborations of this basic structure and the complexities spawned in more fully developed compositions, pause to look at and listen to this tune more closely. If you wish to listen to it, you will find it in the Tunes Catalog under the name STAR.

"Twinkle, Twinkle, Little Star"

There are two balanced phrases marked *a* and *b* in the notated version shown in the preceding figure. The *a* phrase makes the leap from $\hat{1}$ to $\hat{5}$, with $\hat{5}$ extended by the little push up above it and back. The *b* phrase fills in that pitch space, moving down stepwise back to the tonic—$\hat{1}$-$\hat{5}$-$\hat{1}$.*

*While the skeleton of "Star" looks just the same as the skeleton for "America," the way in which that skeleton is fleshed out makes all the difference.

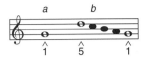

Basic pitch movement

Notice that in the sketch, G and D delimit the functional pitch space of the tune. Now it is the reciprocal interaction between the two pitches G and D that gives meaning to both. That is, we apprehend and attribute functional meaning to both pitches only insofar as each one determines the function of the other, and the particular reciprocal relations between these two pitches create the setting for the rest of the tune. It is because we have learned and internalized the "rules" that generate these reciprocities that we can also perceptually assign particular and different functional meanings to the pitch events that follow.

For example, with this setting established, we hear the first phrase, *a*, move away from stability toward tension at its boundary. In turn, we hear the second phrase, *b* as moving back down stepwise, filling in the gap left by the leap in *a*, to arrive at stability and the release of tension generated at the end of *b*. Indeed, it is only after we have apprehended these reciprocal relations that we can assign the names $\hat{1}$ and $\hat{5}$, or tonic and dominant, to these tune events.

Once assigned, we can say that scale degrees $\hat{1}$ and $\hat{5}$ function as points of orientation around and between which the other secondary pitches move. The secondary pitches either embellish or fill in the moves between these fundamental skeleton pitches. In the following sketch labeled "Primary and secondary pitches," the goals of pitch motion are shown as white dots, and the secondary, "fill in" pitches are shown as black dots. Within *a*, the diagram shows that the initial move to $\hat{5}$ is embellished or prolonged by the stepwise move up away from it and back down again (on the words "little star"). The effect is much like a rubber band held still, stretched, and snapped back again.

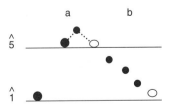

Primary and secondary pitches

Within *b*, the secondary pitches are shown as filling in the gap between the dangling $\hat{5}$ at the end of *a* and the return to the tonic at the end of *b*. The bare skeleton pitches are shown in the following illustration:

Bare skeleton

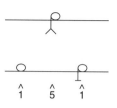

This mark ⌄ stands for an incomplete ending;
This mark ⊥ stands for an arrival at stability.

Finally, notice that the two figures are balanced or symmetrical in two senses. First, they are equal in their total duration—each has the same number of beats; second, they are complementary in that the first (*a*) generates an essential tension, while the second (*b*) resolves this tension. And since the two figures are equal in their time spans, the move toward tension and the subsequent move toward the resolution of that tension are also balanced in their temporal unfolding.

All of these features and relations of "Star" conspire together to generate a fully defined and complete mini-structure. The notion of a fully defined and complete mini-structure and the pitch relations that characterize "Star" as such become more starkly clear if we compare the structures within this section of "Star" with the structures within the beginning section of "Hot Cross Buns," where these critical relations are noticeably impoverished.

"Hot Cross Buns"

Looking at the notation for "Hot Cross Buns," notice that the whole tune moves only between scale degrees 1̂ and 3̂, never making it to the dominant, 5̂. Moreover, the repetition of the single figure *a* precludes the complementarity that is such a critical feature in the relations between the two inner figures of "Star," *a* and *b*. "Hot Cross Buns" is, of course, a street vendor's chant. Without the reciprocity generated by the moves between tonic and dominant, the tune remains more of a shout than a song.

Looking back at the tunes you reconstructed in Project 1.1, you will find that "Susanna," "Lassie," and "Early" are all built around the 1̂-5̂-1̂ structure, each elaborating it in a unique and particular way. Indeed, this 1̂-5̂-1̂ progression and its myriad elaborations in the music of Western culture is so pervasive that it can be added to our collection of simples—those generative primitives that, through experience, we have learned to associate with, even to expect in, the music that we intuitively hear as making sense.

"America" 's Puzzles Once More

Finally, can all of this help to account for the puzzle raised earlier: Why are the repetitions of the opening rhythm pattern in "America" obscured? Answering that question takes you down into the greatest detail, makes use of much of what you have learned thus far, and also uses these generative primitives to account for the complexity inherent even in this tune. For instance, while the three blocks that compose section A all revolve around the tonic, they do so in quite different ways. Most important, the first block is heard as relatively onward-moving; the second block is more stable, and the third block, of course, brings the section to a close.

What creates these differences in structural functions? They are generated particularly by the pitches that are accented—that is, the tune events that have longer durations and coincide with the grouper beat on the first beat of the measure. Accent and direction of pitch motion within these blocks join with the structural functions of pitches to generate complexity that elaborates and goes beyond the bare simples embodied by "Star."

For example, compare the first and second blocks, which have the same rhythm pattern. Notice that in the first block it is the highly unstable seventh degree (F#) that is accented. Passing quickly through the tonic to move up to the second degree (A), the block is still in need of resolution.

Block 1
seventh degree accented

Block 2
third degree accented

The second block places the accent on the more stable third degree (B), then falls to the tonic but on a weak beat. Thus, the accent and pitch boundaries of Block 1 are formed by the tension of onward- and upward-moving scale degrees, $\hat{7}$ to $\hat{2}$, while the more settled and downward-moving scale degrees, $\hat{3}$ to $\hat{1}$, form the accent and pitch boundaries of Block 2.

While you surely could not have described these features before, differences in accent, direction, and ultimately functions of pitches included in the two blocks loom large in an accounting for your intuitive hearing, while also contributing to the relative complexity of "America." Of course, once noticed, the rhythmic repetition is quite clear; yet when you are "just listening," these contrasting pitch functions tend to take precedence over and obscure your hearing of the literally repeated rhythmic patterns.

Going On

These explorations have answered some questions, but they raise more. The gap between your intuitive hearings, on one hand, and the conventions with which we traditionally describe and analyze music, on the other, has been confronted and to some extent bridged. For instance, deriving the major scale from your hearing of "America" was an effort to help you relate your intuitive hearings with the making of the major scale—the abstract structure derived from the tune's pitch collection. And with this structure in place, it was possible to name and to refer to pitches as they are represented in traditional notations. Close analysis of "Star" revealed some of the generative primitives that, when elaborated, create complexity and that we depend on for making sense of this complexity. In this process, you have hopefully gained insights that further the quest toward accounting for your seemingly spontaneous (but learned) abilities to make sense of the music you listen to every day, perhaps coming to hear this music in new ways as well.

But questions remain: How can you use the model of a major scale to build major scales starting on any pitch? How are scales related to the *key* of a piece, and how is one key related to another? How is the key of a piece represented in standard notation? How are these key relationships played out in larger pieces? These are some of the questions you will explore in Project 3.2.

Project 3.2

The Logic in Our Musical Intuitions

THE TASKS

1. Listen to familiar melodies changing key.
2. Describe melodies as made up of particular sets of intervals.
3. Build major scales starting on any pitch.
4. Interleave scales to make modulations.

The pitch relations that you have been exploring thus far—the Î-5̂-Î structure within melodies, the model of a major scale, the generating of a tonal center as an "internal affair"—are small samples of a whole network of interrelations called *tonality*. Tonality and its internal logic frame the coherence among pitch relations in the music with which you are most familiar, much as the metric hierarchy frames the coherence of time relations. But both the metric hierarchy and tonality are descriptions of these underlying structures—we don't listen to them as things in themselves. Rather, we have learned to use these structures as principles lurking behind and organizing the events that we *do* listen to.

For instance, to derive the model of a major scale from an ordered set of pitches that are the constituents of a melody, we started with your intuitive sense of the pitch that sounded most stable. From there we went on to try to account for that intuition. We described your hearing of the tonic function as an internal affair: You hear a pitch acquiring a tonic function through its contact with a specific collection of pitches, their particular arrangement, and their rhythmic orientation as each melody unfolds through time.

The notion of the *key* of a piece takes us one step further toward broadening these relations. Put most simply, *key* refers to the tonic pitch generated by a scale or by a melody. Thus, if the tonic of a scale or of a melody is G, we say that the melody is in the key of G major.* We also use the term *tonality* to refer to this structure of organized pitch relations—the tonality of the piece is G major. But each of these terms has much broader implications. In particular, "tonality" is actually about the network of pitch relations that we are responding to when we hear a piece as sounding familiar—when we, so to speak, know what to do with it.

This system of relations that we call tonality can be represented in multiple ways, and Impromptu provides several working environments for exploring them. Like multiple representations for temporal and pitch relations, each of these environments includes different kinds of elements at different levels of structure. Thus each suggests a somewhat different view.

You will be working with two of these—the Set Key environment and the Practice Scales environment. The Set Key environment provides a relatively global representation—an overview. The Practice Scales environment brings you into more immediate, hands-on contact with the collections of pitches that generate a single key.

The vitality, even the presence, of these organizing structures becomes most evident when they are disrupted; for it is at these moments that we become more aware of what we have been taking for granted in our hearing of coherence. Much as when we wander from a familiar path and lose our way, these are moments when the familiar path of a piece wanders off and our orientation becomes tenuous, stretching the limits of our coherence-making.

For instance, we seem to lose our bearings when pitches are reorganizing around the stability of a new tonic, making us more aware of the important presence of a tonic as the point of orientation. In the following explorations, you will investigate the kinds of pitch relations that are effective in "overthrowing" an established tonic, as well as relations that succeed in making us hear a new pitch taking over as the new tonic. You will also ask whether some disruptions are more disturbing and also more exciting than others.

While you will be given some guidance in navigating these working environments and their respective representations, your own curiosity and willingness to play will be most important in developing new insights.

---

*The tonic G can also be the tonic of the key of G minor. See the section titled "Some Basics: Conventional Pitch Notation" for more information.

"America" Migrating

In this first exploration, you will use Impromptu's Set Key environment, in which you will hear a melody moving from one tonality to another in a rather dramatic fashion. The first part (FP) of "America" will be used now as a movable melody. To watch and hear FP jump (migrate) from one key to another, follow these steps:

- Put the FP block for "America" in the PlayRoom.
- In the Options menu, select Set Key. The Set Key window opens.

INFO BOX
Starting Explorations 1
· In the Playrooms
  menu, select
  Tuneblocks
· In the Tunes
  Catalog, select
  AMERICA

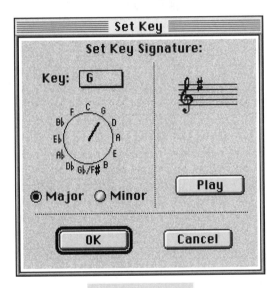

The Set Key window

The key is set to G, and the dial hand points to G as well. This means that FP is currently playing in the key of G; thus, the pitch you hear as most stable is G, the tonic. The staff to the right shows the *key signature* for G. The F# in the key signature indicates that to generate G as tonic, the collection of pitches must include one sharp, F# (as you know).

- Click Play in the Set Key window and listen to FP in the key of G major.
- Sing the last pitch of FP—the tonic, G.
- Select D in the Key menu in the Set Key window, or click the letter D, the next letter clockwise after G, on the dial.

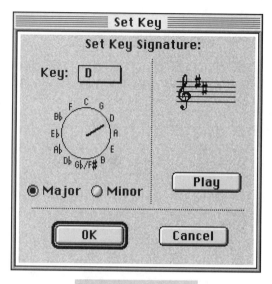

Set the key to D

The dial hand moves to D, and the key changes to D, as well. This means that FP is now going to play in the key of D; the pitch you will hear as most stable will be D, the new tonic. The staff to the right shows the key signature for D. C# has been added to the F# in the key signature, which indicates that to generate D as the tonic, the collection of pitches must include two sharps, F# and C#.

- Click Play in the Set Key window. Watch the graphics jump down and listen to FP in D.*
- Sing the last pitch of FP—the new tonic, D.
- Go back and click the letter G to compare again.
- Click Play, listen, and watch the pitches jump up as Impromptu moves FP from D back to G and plays it.
- Sing the last pitch of FP—the tonic is G again.

Notice the following:

- The pitch contour of the FP block kept its shape, maintained its integrity, throughout the moves.

---

*"Jumping down" in the context of changing key should not be confused with simply changing octaves, as in men and women singing the same tune with the same pitches but in different octaves.

- You could clearly recognize the tune as "America" in either key.
- But you could see and hear that the actual pitches playing the melody were different in each key.

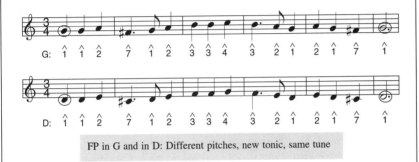

FP in G and in D: Different pitches, new tonic, same tune

- You could hear that a new tonic was established with each move; the final pitch, the pitch that sounded most stable, changed from G to D.

What can you conclude from these observations? Did you have a sense of disorientation with the moves from one key to the other? Most probably not; you were able to quickly adjust! How is it, then, that almost instantly you are able to adjust to a new context of pitches—to hear instantly, for example, the changing functions of G and D in each context? What are you paying attention to in order to make G sound stable at one moment and D at the next? What stays the same? What changes?

Recall that in the previous project we proposed that hearing a pitch as stable, specifically as the tonic, is an internal affair:

- A pitch acquires a stable function as the result of the interaction between that pitch and the collection of pitches that surround it.
- The same pitch that sounds so stable in one collection of pitches will sound quite unstable when embedded in a new collection of pitches.
- A new context of pitches will result in a new pitch acquiring a stable function.

These proposals now come alive in the light of the experience with "America" migrating. Once you clearly heard one pitch, G, as the stable point of arrival, it was enough only to hear the first little figure of "America" (the pitches and durations for "My country, 'tis of thee") to adjust to the new tonic, to construct the whole new framework within which the tune was now functioning.

How do we do that? Once again, we use our acquired ability to turn pitch and time relations into heard structural functions. Focusing our attention on the motion toward melodic goals, we adjust our perception of arrivals and departures in response to the pitch events that have become, by association with those around them, relatively stable or unstable. That sounds a little like going in circles, and indeed it is. Tonality is an internal affair.

A Closer Look

But we can now go further. We can ask, what is it that we know how to do when we recognize a tune as "that tune" even when it is played using a different collection of pitches? To pursue that question we need to step down the structural ladder and return to the model of the major scale.

Remember that the ordered set of pitches in any major scale includes a common sequence of intervals: [1 1 $\frac{1}{2}$ 1 1 1 $\frac{1}{2}$]. And recall that the sequence of pitches starting from the tonic is named by consecutive scale degree numbers. So, if we follow a particular sequence of scale degrees within the key of G major, and then the same sequence of scale degrees within the key of D major, we will necessarily hear the same sequence of intervals. Specifically, if we follow the sequence of scale degrees that plays "America" ($\hat{1}$ $\hat{1}$ $\hat{2}$!$\hat{7}$ $\hat{1}$ $\hat{2}$, and so on), whether in the key of G, D, or any other major key, we will hear different pitches, but the same sequence of intervals and thus the same tune.

$\hat{1}$ $\hat{1}$ $\hat{2}$!$\hat{7}$ $\hat{1}$ $\hat{2}$ $\hat{3}$ $\hat{3}$ $\hat{4}$ $\hat{3}$ $\hat{2}$ $\hat{1}$ $\hat{2}$ $\hat{1}$!$\hat{7}$ $\hat{1}$

Same sequence of scale degrees, same sequence of intervals, same tune

So when we recognize a tune, we recognize its internal relationships—the unfolding of a sequence of interval relationships coupled with a sequence of rhythmic relations.

A scale degree representation, then, is more general than a list of particular pitches, since it shows the internal relations among pitches. Further, for these same reasons, a scale degree representation comes closer to describing the critical features of our figural hearings. Recall that figural characteristics, which seemed most intuitive, emerged through a focus on relations internal to a melody—particularly groupings and structural functions within the context of these groupings.

Take some time now to explore and play with these ideas. Use the Tunes Catalog to select other tunes. Compare the differences in what you hear when you make various melodies migrate to keys that are both close and also more distant around the dial. For instance, try "Bonnie" and "Yankee Doodle." For each tune, put a block such as FP or SP into the PlayRoom, and then experiment in the Set Key environment.

As you go along, remember to keep careful notes in your log about what you discover in these explorations:

- What differences do you hear when moving between closely related keys, as compared with more distantly related keys?

- Does the particular tune make a difference—that is, do some tunes seem to move more comfortably between keys?

- Are you convinced by the description of what generates a tonal center? Do you have further ideas that you would like to explore?

Linking Scales and Emergent Tonics

Each key is itself a network of relations that can be represented in various ways—the ordering of pitch collections to form a major scale, the collection of intervals within that ordering, the significance of the interval of a fifth in establishing relative degrees of stability. This network of internal relations is repeated within each key, but is embodied each time by differing collections of pitches.

In the preceding exploration, Impromptu did the work of moving from one key to another—all in one fell swoop. Key areas were juxtaposed; you were simply in one key and then in another. But what about the process by which one tonal area and its tonic is deposed and another established—that is, how does one tonic become another?*

---

*The proper word for changing key is *modulation*. In the previous exploration, FP was made to *modulate* from G major to D major.

The repeated interval pattern in the model of a major scale is helpful and revealing:

Scale degrees	$\hat{1}$	$\hat{2}$	$\hat{3}$	$\hat{4}$	$\hat{5}$	$\hat{6}$	$\hat{7}$	$\hat{8}$
Intervals	1	1	$\frac{1}{2}$	1	1	1	$\frac{1}{2}$

Symmetry of the major scale

Recall that the lower half of the scale, called the lower tetrachord (scale degrees $\hat{1}$–$\hat{4}$), has the same interval structure as the upper tetrachord (scale degrees $\hat{5}$–$\hat{8}$). As a consequence, scales related by the interval of a fifth intersect very closely.* If one major scale begins on the dominant (fifth degree) of another, the top of the first forms the bottom of the second. For instance, the D-major scale begins on the dominant (fifth) of the G-major scale, so the pitches that form the top of the G scale (scale degrees $\hat{5}$–$\hat{8}$) are the same as those that form the bottom of the D scale (scale degrees $\hat{1}$–$\hat{4}$).

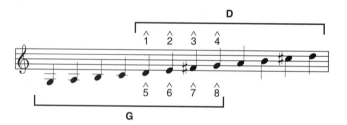

Moreover, all of the other pitches within these two scales are the same, except for one. The seventh degree of the D scale, C#, is the one new pitch needed to make the G-major scale become a D-major scale. This is reflected in the addition of C# in the key signature for D.

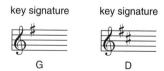

*Remember that in referring to pitch, an interval is the distance between two pitches. Within a major scale, the intervals between pitches are named according to the number of scale degrees they span. (See the section titled "Some Basics: Conventional Pitch Notation" at the end of Part 3 for more on intervals.)

The close relationship between keys related by a fifth, such as G and D, is critical to the network of relations that we call tonality. Moving up the structural ladder, consider again the dial that you saw represented in the Set Key window. It represents the fifth relations among all keys and is thus, not surprisingly, called the *circle of fifths*.

Circle of fifths

This circle represents graphically the whole network of closely and distantly related tonal regions. The letters representing keys that are closely related are adjacent around the circle (for example, G and D; F and B♭); those more distant around the circle (for example, D and E♭) are more distantly related.

As one goes clockwise around the circle of fifths, each of the adjacent tonics, like those of G and D, is related to the next by a fifth up—that is, tonics of closely related keys span an interval of an *ascending fifth*.

Intervals spanning an ascending fifth

As one goes counterclockwise around the circle, tonics of closely related keys span an interval of a *descending fifth*.*

---

*Notice that if you continue on around clockwise going up the left side of the circle, adjacent keys are again related by the interval of an ascending fifth. For more on intervals and specifically the relations between ascending and descending intervals, see the section titled "Some Basics" at the end of Part 3.

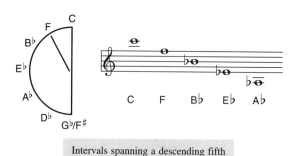

Intervals spanning a descending fifth

Just as the G-major and D-major scales are interleaved and have all but one pitch in common, so each of the other adjacent keys around the circle does so as well. Thus, just as $\hat{5}$ in the G scale becomes $\hat{1}$ in the D scale, so $\hat{5}$ in the D scale becomes $\hat{1}$ in the A scale. And just as the top of the G scale forms the bottom of the D scale, so the top of the D scale forms the bottom of the A scale.

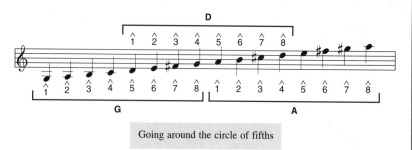

Going around the circle of fifths

But what will you hear if you actually play these interleaving scales? Will the tonic change as you go along—one tonic becoming the other? If so, when will it change, and will this give you a feeling of disorientation? You can use the virtual keyboard in the Practice Scales environment to explore these questions—to actually make and play these interleaved scales.*

---

*Of course, you can use a real piano keyboard to play these interleaved scales. The only advantage in using the virtual keyboard is that you can listen at least to the results of ascending scales as often as you like without playing the progression again yourself. Listening without playing gives you a certain distance that is often useful in thinking about what you are hearing.

The Practice Scales Environment

For these experiments you will be working in Impromptu's Practice Scales environment, which can be used to practice building scales starting on any pitch; this will be the focus in Project 3.3. But here you will be using the Practice Scales environment to pursue questions such as the following:

INFO BOX
Opening the Practice
Scales Environment
· In the Scales menu,
  select Practice
  Scales

• How are moves made among scales, and thus among keys?

• If hearings are organized around the stability of a single tonic, what circumstances cause us to lose our bearings?

• What kinds of pitch relations create this disorientation—this overthrowing of an established tonic?

• What generates a tonal center in the first place?

Before working on these experiments, take time to become familiar with the Practice Scales environment and to work through a practice session.

Building Scales: A Practice Session

You previously derived a major scale from a melody, "America," but now the process will be reversed—you will construct major scales starting from the model that you previously derived. You need to keep three things in mind as you begin:

1. The map of the keyboard—remember that letter names repeat each octave.

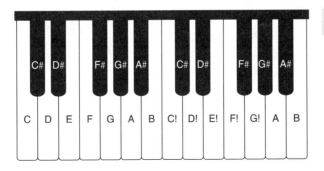

Map of the keyboard

2. The whole-step and half-step arrangement of the geography of the keyboard:

    Half steps: Immediately adjacent keys (white-white; black-white; white-black);

Whole steps: Keys with one key interposed (white [black] white; black [white] black; white [white] black; black [white] white).

3. The model of a major scale and its interval sequence: $1\ 1\ \frac{1}{2}\ 1\ 1\ 1\ \frac{1}{2}$

With the Practice Scales environment on your screen, notice that it includes two areas. The upper area is your workspace for building scales. The lower area is where you check your work and also where you set the key and the *Pitchset*. To build the D-major scale, follow these steps:

• In the lower area, set Pitchsets to Major and Key to D:

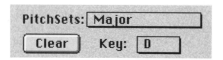

• In the upper area, select "by Letter."

Scale Pitches: ○ **by Number** ● **by Letter**

• Following the template of whole steps and half steps, complete the D-major scale by clicking the virtual keyboard keys.

Completing the D-major scale

click keys →

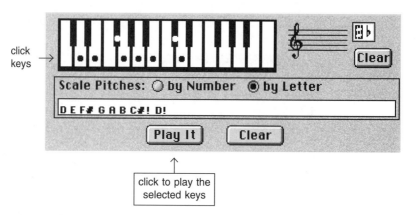

click to play the selected keys

• Click Play It to hear the whole scale played back.

• Click Clear; and this time type the letter names of the pitches for the D-major scale in the box below the virtual keyboard (see the following "Notices" box to learn how to type sharps).

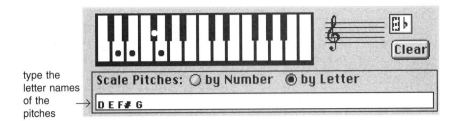

type the letter names of the pitches →

• In the lower part of the window, click Show Scale to check your work.

Notices
· To type a letter name with a sharp, hold down the Option key.
  Example: To type F#, hold down the Option key and type F. (Make sure Caps Lock is off!)
· To type a letter name with a flat, hold down the Control key.
  Example: To type A♭, hold down the Control key and type A.
· If you type or play a pitch that is not a member of the selected key, it shows up as a ?.
  Example: In the key of D major, if you play C instead of C#, Impromptu shows a ?.

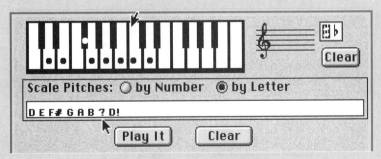

A pitch *not* in the selected key

· To correct an error on the keyboard, double-click the virtual keyboard key where you made the error.
· To correct an error in typing, use the Delete key.

Emerging New Keys

EXPLORATIONS 3

In these experiments you will be building interleaved scales so as to trace the process of moving from one key to another. As a first experiment, listen to what happens if you interleave the D-major scale and the A-major scale. Remember that two scales related by the interval of a fifth share a tetrachord. In this case, the top tetrachord of the D-major scale (A B C# D) is also the bottom tetrachord of the A-major scale. Try it.

With the D-major scale already built on the virtual keyboard, think of its upper tetrachord (A B C# D) as the lower tetrachord of the A-major scale and continue on to build the upper tetrachord of the A scale (E F# G# A):

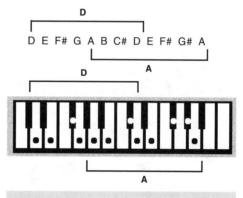

D-major and A-major scales on the virtual keyboard

Once built, listen to the whole thing (click Play It). Do you hear the tonic change? Listen several times, carefully. When does the tonic change and to what? Listen again, following the staff notation.

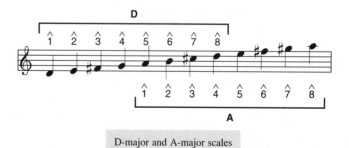

D-major and A-major scales

Did you hear that when you arrived at the D an octave above the starting D, D sounded clearly stable, at rest—the tonic? But when you arrive at the end, the A now sounds stable!

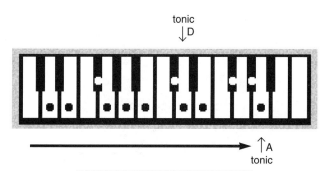

tonic
↓D

↑A
tonic

D is overthrown; A becomes the tonic

If your hearing matches that description, it seems to take very little to overthrow an established tonic—just one "foreign" pitch. In this case G# is a "stranger" in D major, but a necessary element in establishing A major. Just the process of going a half step from G# to A is enough for A to emerge as a new tonic. In conventional terminology, you have at least "proposed" a modulation from one key (D) to its dominant (A). To make this migration convincing, you would need to spend more time establishing the new key. Does this shift in context leave you a bit disoriented, perhaps dissatisfied? Or do you go gently into the new key? Listen to the progression several times.

Now listen to the same series of pitches *descending*—starting on A, go down to D.

- Click Clear.
- Starting at the upper A, play each note of the series going down on the virtual keyboard:

    A G# F# E D C# B A G (natural) F# E D

(The virtual keyboard can only play back ascending series. To hear the descending series, play each note of the series going down again.)

- Click Play to hear the ascending series again.

How does the descending series differ from the ascending series with regard to changing tonal centers? Consider the change in the function of the pitch A: Going up, the first A sounded as an unstable dominant; going down, that same lower A sounded as the stable tonic.

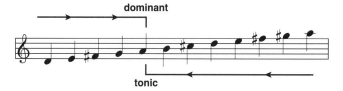

dominant

tonic

But by the time you continue on down to the lower D, D has once again taken over as the tonic.

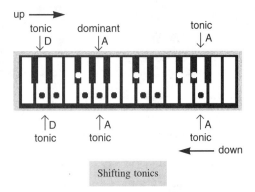

Shifting tonics

The G-natural, a foreign pitch in A, becomes the turning point on the way down to D. At the very moment when we hear the G-natural after the A, G-natural sounds like a disruption, a "cancellation." Only in retrospect does it come to belong. How can we hear "retrospectively"?

This demonstration should be convincing evidence of the powerful adaptability of our musical minds—our clever capacity to respond to changing pitch contexts and to reconstruct the shifting structural functions they create.

More Exploring

Make some more experiments. Try linking other closely related scales. For instance, try scales that are adjacent around the circle of fifths going counterclockwise. These scales are related by a fifth *down*, and the bottom half of one scale (scale degrees $\hat{1}$-$\hat{2}$-$\hat{3}$-$\hat{4}$) becomes the top half of the next scale around the circle (scale degrees $\hat{5}$-$\hat{6}$-$\hat{7}$-$\hat{8}$). For example, going counterclockwise, F major comes after C major.

F major comes after C major

The tonic of the F scale is the fourth degree of the C scale (called the *subdominant*).* So the *bottom* tetrachord of the C scale (degrees $\hat{4}$-$\hat{3}$-$\hat{2}$-$\hat{1}$) is the same as the *top* tetrachord of the F scale (degrees $\hat{8}$-$\hat{7}$-$\hat{6}$-$\hat{5}$).

---

*The fourth degree of the scale is an interval of a fifth *below* the tonic—thus the term *subdominant*, meaning "under dominant."

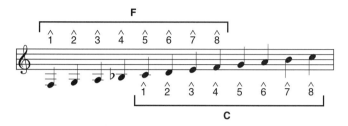

Bottom of C major becomes top of F major

Going to a key that starts on the fourth degree of a previous key is called going to the key of the subdominant. Use the virtual keyboard to play these linked scales. Can you predict what will happen to your sense of tonal center?

What about scales that are not so closely related—scales that are more distant around the circle of fifths and that therefore have fewer pitches in common? Will the sense of disruption, of disequilibrium, be more intense as the path through the pitches takes you further away from established territory? How about D major to A♭ major?

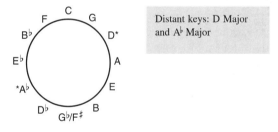

Distant keys: D Major and A♭ Major

What pitches do they have in common? Build the scales on the keyboard.

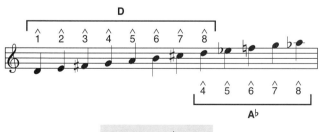

D Major and A♭ Major

Listening to the pitches progressing through the D and A♭ scales, how would you describe the effect? Keep track of your impressions in your log book. For instance:

- Where do you hear the tonal center changing?
- Does the junction (D–E♭) seem more abrupt as compared with the junction in the previous scales?
- Is A♭ a convincing tonic when you get to it?

Try playing on the keyboard the same series of pitches going down.

Going down

- Do you have the feeling of being in "tonal limbo" as you go along?
- When do you arrive at stability (or do you)?

These examples illustrate once again that it is perhaps only by disrupting, perturbing, intercepting, and intersecting present, welltrodden paths that we can become aware of both limitations and possibilities in what we take for granted. For example, think about the interval of a fifth and its ubiquitous presence. In Part 1, the fifth emerged as essential to the coherence we hear in common tunes. And now the fifth appears to be essential in effectively navigating the intersecting networks of the whole tonal terrain. The next explorations will reveal more.

EXPLORATIONS 4

Names, Notations, Functions, and Context

Key signatures have been referred to several times so far. But what is represented by the key signature associated with each key and what is represented by changes in key signatures? How do key signature representations relate to linked scales and to the circle of fifths? These questions will come alive as you go back again to the circle-of-fifths dial in the Set Key environment. In the Options menu, select Set Key.

Circle of fifths

Move the mouse around the circle, click the letters for keys, and watch the key signatures change. As you do so, think about the relations between these key signatures and the interleaving scales that you just built and listened to.

Once more the ubiquitous interval of a fifth comes forward. Notice that as you go around the circle clockwise, sharps in the key signatures cumulate in fifths, as well—F#, C#, G#, D#, A#. Consistent with the cumulating fifths, notice that the last sharp in each key signature (the newest one added in the series) is always the seventh degree of that scale. Thus, in the key signature for A major, G# is the last sharp and it is the seventh degree of the A-major scale. So an easy way to tell the key represented by a key signature is simply to take the last sharp and move up a half step. Try it.

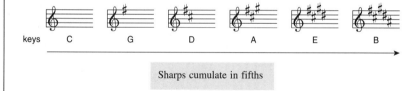

keys   C   G   D   A   E   B

Sharps cumulate in fifths

Going *counter*clockwise, *flats* also cumulate in fifths: B♭, E♭, A♭, D♭, G♭. Here, the last flat added is always the fourth degree of the scale. Consistent with flats being added in fifths, the penultimate flat in a key signature is always the tonic of that key. Thus, if E♭ is the last flat, B♭ is the key. Can you figure out how that works?

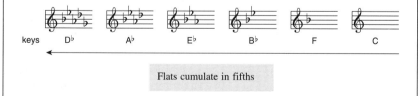

keys   D♭   A♭   E♭   B♭   F   C

Flats cumulate in fifths

Did you realize that the cumulating sharps and the cumulating flats make up the same set of pitches? But they are named differently and they cumulate in opposite directions.

Cumulating sharps and flats	sharp side ⟶

F♯   C♯   G♯   D♯   A♯

G♭   D♭   A♭   E♭   B♭

⟵ flat side

Why is this not immediately obvious? Probably because you would expect pitches that are named differently to sound differently. But the pitches G# and A♭, for instance, are played by the same key on the keyboard and thus sound identical. So why are the same pitches named with flats on one side of the circle and with sharps on the other?

This brings us again to structural functions and context. While G# and A♭ sound identical when played in isolation, notice the difference in their functions within their respective contexts—for instance, G# in the A-major scale and A♭ in the E♭-major scale:

Differences in function	A Major	A	B	C♯	D	E	F♯	G♯	A
		$\hat{1}$	$\hat{2}$	$\hat{3}$	$\hat{4}$	$\hat{5}$	$\hat{6}$	$\hat{7}$	$\hat{1}$!
	E♭ Major	E♭	F	G	A♭	B♭	C	D	E♭

Playing the A-major scale, G# functions as the seventh degree. Stopping on G#, you feel that it definitely is leading up to the tonic. Playing the E♭ scale, the same pitch, now called A♭, functions as the fourth degree. Stopping at A♭, you feel it tending to move downward toward the tonic.

It is this difference in function within each of the respective tonalities that is reflected in the different names. Indeed, while piano players are stuck with the fixed tuning of their piano strings, singers and also string players, who make pitches by placing their fingers on the instrument's strings, can finely control tuning. They can be responsive to differences in context and structural function—G# will be played and sung slightly differently from A♭. Specifically, when performing a piece in A major, G# will be a bit higher (leading upward), while when playing a piece in E♭ major, A♭ will be played a bit lower (leading downward).

Names for pitches are made consistent within keys to keep the exact pitch collection of a tonality distinct and to keep these functions unambiguous. This accounts for why scales are represented by a series of names that include one and only one of each of the seven different letters—there are no repeated letters and no letters are skipped. Thus A♭ cannot exist in the key of E major. It would involve skipping G and showing two kinds of A's—A$^\flat$ and A-natural.

An impossible representation of E major

Even though playing these notated pitches would sound like an E-major scale, experienced musicians on seeing it would momentarily be thrown into "tonal limbo." Performers expect the names (notations) for pitches to have functional meaning; seeing this notation, a performer might think, what could the composer be trying to say with this ambiguous notation?

In general, then, flats and sharps cannot live together inside the notation for a major scale pitch collection. While this may seem to be merely a notational convention, it reflects again the deep importance of context as generating functional meaning.

Project 3.3

Building Major and Minor Scales

1. Using the model of a major scale as a template, build major scales starting on any pitch.
2. Play the scales you construct on the keyboard and write them out in staff notation.

Project 3.3 is primarily a straightforward practice in building major scales in all keys. To more effectively explore the relationships among scales, work systematically through the circle of fifths. In the Practice Scales environment, click the Key menu for another representation of this set of fifth relationships.

For example, you can see that the key of D major comes after G, going up the circle of fifths. Going down, the key of C comes after G. Select keys using this menu. Following the steps in the practice session in Project 3.2, build scales for each key following the keys at least up to E and down to A♭.

A brief reminder of some the peculiarities of the Practice Scales environment.
· To type a letter name with a sharp, hold down the Option key.
  Example: To type F#, hold down the Option key and type F. (Make sure Caps Lock is off!)

· To type a letter name with a flat, hold down the Control key.
　　Example: To type A♭, hold down the Control key and type A.
· If you type or play a pitch that is not a member of the selected key, it
　shows up as a ?.
　　Example: In the key of D major, if you play C instead of C#, Im-
　promptu shows a ?.

A pitch not in the selected key

· To correct an error on the keyboard, double-click the virtual keyboard
　key where you made the error.
· To correct an error in typing, use the Delete Key.

After building each scale in Impromptu's Practice Scales environment,
do the following:

- Compare your virtual keyboard scale, the letter names, and the key sig-
  nature with those shown in the lower Show Scales area.
- Click Play It in the lower area and compare it with Play It in the upper
  area.
- Practice playing the scale on a real keyboard.
- Write out your scale in staff notation.

Minor Scales and Keys

EXPLORATIONS 1

The network of tonal relations would not be complete without introducing minor scales and keys. Every major key is closely related
to two minor keys. However, the relationship between major and
minor keys differs in each case. In one case, a tonic is shared by both
a major and a minor key; in the other case, a key signature is shared
by both a major and a minor key. For example, C major and c minor share the same tonic. In these cases where a major and minor

INFO BOX
Starting Explorations 1
· In the Playrooms
  menu, select
  Tuneblocks
· In the Tunes
  Catalog, select
  AMERICA

scale share a tonal center, the keys are called *parallel*. Thus, C major and c minor are parallel major/minor keys. In contrast, C major and a minor share the same key signature.* Major and minor scales that share the same key signature are called *relative*.

To hear the differences between C major and c minor, use "America" again.

Open the SCALE1 block using the magnifying glass cursor. In the Pitchset menu, select Harmonic Minor. Then click Play to hear a g minor scale.

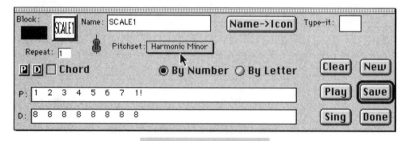

Selecting Harmonic Minor

Of the first five degrees of minor scales, only the third degree differs from the major scale that shares its tonic. The third degree is a half step lower in the minor scale than in the major scale. Or, putting it another way, the intervals between degrees $\hat{2}$-$\hat{3}$ and $\hat{3}$-$\hat{4}$ are reversed.

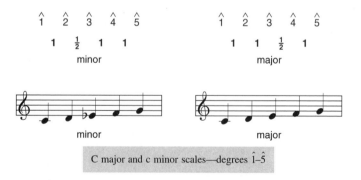

C major and c minor scales—degrees $\hat{1}$–$\hat{5}$

---

*Notice the convention of using uppercase letters for major keys and lowercase letters for minor keys.

The difference is easy to hear if you listen to "America" in G major and then in g minor. To do so, open the FP block with the magnifying glass cursor and click Play. Then select Harmonic Minor in the Pitchset menu and click PLAY again. Notice the rather remarkable change in mood or character.* But notice, too, that the scale degrees stay the same. Can you say why?

There are three forms of the the minor scale—*natural, melodic*, and *harmonic*. In each form, scale degrees $\hat{1}$ through $\hat{5}$ remain the same; the differences apply only to the top tetrachord. Specifically, scale degrees $\hat{6}$ and $\hat{7}$ vary, and thus the intervals between degrees $\hat{5}$-$\hat{6}$-$\hat{7}$-$\hat{8}$ also vary.

natural · harmonic

To hear the natural minor and the harmonic minor versions of the c minor scale, open the SCALE1 block again. In the Pitchsets menu, select Minor to hear the natural minor scale. Then select Harmonic Minor to hear that scale. The melodic minor scale is derived from the common forms that ascending and descending melodies often take in the minor mode. The top of the ascending form is exactly the same as the top of the major scale:

Melodic minor ascending

The descending form of the melodic minor is just the same as the natural minor:

Melodic minor descending

The relative minor of a major key shares the key signature of that key. A relative minor scale is built on the sixth degree of its relative major. The sixth degree of the C major scale is the pitch A. Thus, a minor is the relative minor of C major, sharing its key signature of

---

*For another melody in the minor mode, listen again to "Anya." "Sweden" (found in the Tunes Catalog) is also in the minor mode.

no sharps or flats. Or, going the other way, the third degree of a minor scale is the first degree (tonic) of its relative major.

This relationship between relative major and minor keys can be expressed through concentric circles of fifths—major keys on the inside, their relative minor keys on the outside. Thus d minor is the relative minor of F major; B major is the relative major of g minor, and so on.

Major keys inside, relative minor keys outside

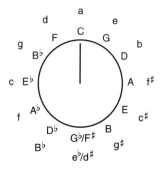

Practice building the different kinds of minor scales—natural, harmonic, melodic—starting on any pitch. You can use the virtual keyboard in the Practice Scales environment or a real keyboard. Write out the scales that you build in staff notation.

Putting It All Together: The Magic Square

The Magic Square captures in a single visual representation the whole intersecting network that you have been exploring and that we call tonality. This larger network defines the terrain that composers have been navigating for some 300 years.* We might compare the Magic Square representation of the tonal network to an aerial map of a large terrain, while the representations of linked scales are maps that show only local paths traversing that terrain. It is a surprising and sometimes discombobulating experience, when traveling along a familiar path through a terrain, to unexpectedly find yourself at an intersec-

*However, as you have already heard, some twentieth-century composers have developed different organizing principles that generate different terrains, and there will be more to say about that in a moment.

tion between two paths that you thought were in separate parts of the area—you had always traveled them separately. But these moments of surprise and confusion can also be moments of insight. For instance, seeing that it is possible for these two paths to meet one another could help you expand your separate, non-intersecting local maps into a larger, single map of the terrain—one that could represent your separate paths and also their intersections. Building such a single map of the tonal terrain, one that can hold all the local paths and their intersections, is the purpose of the Magic Square.

Magic Square

	C	Db / C#	D	Eb / D#	E	E# / F	Gb / F#	G	Ab / G#	A	Bb / A#	Cb / B
F#		x		x		▦	Φ		x		x	x
B		x		x	x		x		x		▦	Φ
E		x		▦	Φ		x		x	x		x
A		x	x		x		x		▦	Φ		x
D		▦	Φ		x		x	x		x		x
G	x		x		x		▦	Φ		x		x
C	Φ		x		x	x		x		x		x
F	x		x		x	Φ		x		x	▦	
Bb	x		x	▦		x		x		x	Φ	
Eb	x		x	Φ		x		x	▦		x	
Ab	x	▦		x		x		x	Φ		x	
Db	x	Φ		x		x	▦		x		x	
Gb		x		x		x	Φ		x		x	▦

Code

x   Pitch collection

Φ   Tonic

▦   New pitch

Spend some time studying the Magic Square; look for patterns and notice repeating figures. Pay attention to the code at the bottom of the square. For instance, what do you make of the parallel diagonals showing the trajectory of tonal centers (Φ)? How do these diagonals relate to the parallel diagonals showing the trajectory of new pitches added (▦) as you move up and down the tonal terrain? What is the connection between these diagonals and the multiple kinds of fifth relations involved in the network of linked scales and keys?

What about the letters going down the side of the square as compared with the letters going across the top? It may seem surprising, but the letters you see going across the top of the square refer to the same collection of keys as the letters going down the side. Here, the difference is not in the naming but in the ordering! Down the side, you see names for keys that are consistently related to one another by the familiar interval of a fifth. With the neutral C in the middle, the "sharp side" goes up the side from C, and the "flat side" goes down. Across the top, these same letters name keys that are also consistently related to one another, but here each is related to the next by a half step. Thus, both series include all of the twelve pitches found in Western music. While the vertical series represents tones that are distant on the keyboard, the top series matches keys on the keyboard, both black and white, that are in closest geographical proximity. And this raises, again, what we might mean by "near and far" as distances within the network we call tonality.

The upper sequence of pitches at the top of the square, ordered low to high and related by a half step, forms what is called the *chromatic scale.* Since both the chromatic scale and the circle of fifths include all of the twelve pitches generally found in Western music, the chromatic scale can be thought of as reordering from low to high the tonics all around the circle of fifths. Conversely, each major scale key is made up of only seven pitches; thus each scale is a particular subset of the chromatic scale. We can, then, describe the major scale model in terms of the chromatic scale, as well.

The next illustration shows the following:

1. Chromatic numbering for the chromatic scale (0 1 2 3 4 5 6 7 8 9 10 11 12).

2. The C-major scale numbered chromatically, where it can be seen as a particular subset derived from the full chromatic set (0 2 4 5 7 9 11 12).

3. The C-major scale with scale degree numbers.

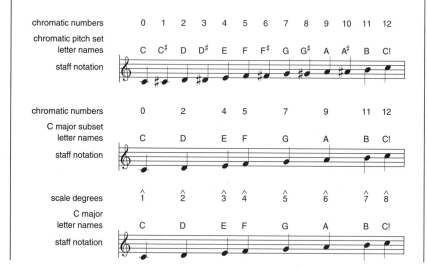

Notice that the chromatic numbers for the C-major scale also show you the structure of intervals that constitute the major scale. For more on these comparisons, see the section titled "Some Basics: Conventional Pitch Notation" at the end of Part 3.

It is interesting that when playing the chromatic scale, where all intervals between adjacent pitches are the same, every pitch is just as important as every other pitch: We no longer hear a tonic, no relative stability or instability. And this helps to explain why the "Portals" blocks were initially difficult for you to work with. The "Portals" blocks include all twelve pitches, and this is largely responsible for the fact that no pitch comes to the fore as the most stable, the tonic. Accustomed as we are in this culture to orienting ourselves around one central pitch generated by association with a particular subset of pitches, we can lose our way when thrust into a pitch terrain that provides no single point of orientation. But, as you found in successfully composing tunes with the Portals blocks, other means of comprehensibility can be created. These become centrally important for composers who also use the complete palette of twelve pitches in their compositions. We will return to some of these in the Listening Examples that follow.

LISTENING EXAMPLES: TONAL COHERENCE AND CONFLICT

The projects in Part 3 have focused your attention on tonal coherence, more generally on the whole framework we call tonality, and most specifically on the importance of the fifth relationship in our hearings of tonal centers. You have heard, for instance, how the function of a pitch may change depending on the context in which it is embedded: At one moment a certain pitch is heard as the central one around which we orient our hearing; at another moment that same pitch can be almost surreptitiously usurped as another takes on its central role.

How do composers exploit these possibilities? The following Listening Examples will illustrate, for instance, how composers artfully maneuver changes in key and in pitch function—sometimes simply juxtaposing key areas, sometimes creating passages that subtly evolve into new tonal contexts. And with these imaginative musical means, composers also create both contrasts and coherences as the larger structure of the piece unfolds in time.

Example 3.1: Bach, *Minuet in G* (1725)

Example 3.2: Bach, *March in D* (1725)

Example 3.3: Bach, *Minuet in G* (excerpt) (1725)

Example 1.3: Haydn, *Symphony #99, Minuet A* section (1793)

Example 1.4: Haydn, *Symphony #99, Minuet* (1793)

Example 3.4: Chopin, *Mazurka*, Op. 67, #2 (1849)

Example 1.7: Liszt, *Faust Symphony,* First Movement (1854)

Example 3.5: Helps, *Gossamer Noons,* #2 (Bethany Beardslee, vocal) (1974)

Notice that the examples are listed chronologically and that they span a period of nearly 250 years (1725–1974). Thus, while listening to the unique structural unfolding of each work, you will also find it interesting to trace the differences in the uses of tonality as compositional styles change over this relatively long time period in the history of music. Indeed, by the time we reach the twentieth century, tonality, the basic means of comprehensibility in the eighteenth and early nineteenth centuries is nearly abandoned. You will need to ask (as you did in working with the "Portals" blocks), without tonality, what musical means can composers invoke to provide coherence?

Examples 3.1 and 3.2 are taken from a collection of short keyboard pieces that J. S. Bach composed for his young wife, Anna Magdalena. These two compositions bring together in relatively compact form many of the compositional means you have been studying in Part 3. As you go on to revisit the Haydn Symphony Minuet (Example 1.3), you will focus on Haydn's continuing development of the motives with which he begins the movement, listening now to how he carries them through a maze of changing keys and out again to the return. In the later examples, including revisiting Liszt's Faust Symphony and a work that leaps into the twentieth century (Examples 1.7 and 3.5), tonal structures that we tend to take for granted will become more vivid as you listen to compositions in which tonality is no longer a given.

Example 3.1: Bach, *Minuet in G* (1725)
Example 3.2: Bach, *March in D* (1725)

Listening to these two short pieces, you will immediately recognize some of the structural simples that you have heard so often before, but now, as always, elaborated in unique ways. For instance, both pieces are organized into hierarchical structures such as those you worked with in building melodies in Part 1 (motives, phrases, sections). But having worked with the structures of tonality, you will also be able to hear that these structures are further elaborated by the moves among related keys. Listen to each of these small compositions, one after the other and jot down first impressions in your log book.

For instance:

- How does Bach use the various dimensions you have been studying to help create both unity and variety in the larger structural organization of each piece—metric structure, figural grouping, motivic transformation, key migration, and so on?
- Do you notice any significant differences between the two pieces, particularly with respect to the means used in shifting keys?
- Do the differences between the pieces influence the character or mood of each piece? If so, how?
- Does one piece sound more complex than the other? If so, can you say why?

Example 3.1: Bach, Minuet in G (1725)

As you know from Haydn's Minuets, the minuet is in triple meter. It was originally music to accompany dancing—the minuet being a particular kind of dance. Listen to Bach's Minuet (Example 3.1) again and follow the structural sketch shown here. Notice the ‖: :‖ symbols that indicate that the music between them is to be repeated. Thus section A is repeated and then section B, the transition, and section A′ are repeated.

Does your hearing agree with the hearing described by this sketch? For instance, do you hear the same structural boundaries? And does the labeling (A's and B's) correspond with your hearing of similarities and differences?

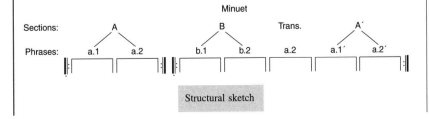

Structural sketch

Zooming in, the following illustration shows you more detailed structure:

- phrases within sections A and B (*a*.1 and *a*.2; *b*.1 and *b*.2);
- the small motives or tuneblocks within each phrase (1-2-3-4; 1′-2′-1x-5);
- the change of key that occurs in moving from Section A to Section B (G → D).

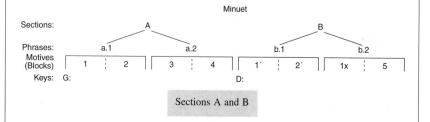

Example 3.3: Bach, Minuet in G (excerpt) (1725)

Listen now to just the sections labeled A and B (Example 3.3) while following the previous illustration. Can you hear why the motives are labeled as they are?

Bach actually presents all the motivic material for the entire piece in section A. Indeed, as the piece unfolds, he uses this material to make musical puns: Reusing the same motives in ever-new contexts, he plays with their possible meanings. For instance, the melody phrase *b*.1 is exactly the same as in phrase *a*.1, except that phrase *b*.1 is in a new key. Phrase *b*.2 is different from phrase *a*.2, but Bach is still playing with similarities. Can you hear them?

You will return to Bach's Minuet in Project 4.1, where you will work more actively with the details of this little minuet. Playing with the tuneblocks yourself, you will hear how Bach played with them in composing this minuet.

Example 3.2: Bach, March in D (1725)

Listen to Example 3.2, the Bach March, in the context of your deeper familiarity with the Minuet. The March is clearly in two large parts with each part repeated. But within these two parts, and even in their relations to one another, the March is considerably more complex than the Minuet.

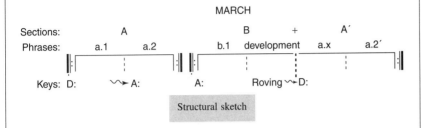

But what does it mean to be "more complex"? Thinking about complexity and comparing the Minuet with the March, consider the following as you listen again:

- The March feels more continuous—ongoing—rather than clearly sectional. The large boundaries of the two big sections of the March (A, B + A') are well defined, especially as each is repeated. But the "edges" of the phrases within these large sections are less clear.

- There is more rhythmic independence between upper and lower voices—that is, the texture becomes more active, with one voice moving forward while the other stands still or rests.

- Within the first big section, A, Bach already moves to the new key—again, the key of the dominant. Moreover, the change of key within this section happens relatively gradually—through evolution, in contrast to simple juxtaposition, as in the Minuet.

- The second section, B, begins, as in the Minuet, with a statement of the opening motive in the new key. However, this section continues on with a development—a sequential passage that is roving and ambiguous in its tonal center. Here, you probably do have a feeling of "losing your bearings"; there was nothing like this in the Minuet. The instability in this passage is generated most noticeably by the use of chromatic pitches, especially the chromatic bass melody—G, G#, A, A#, B. The roving progression works because the chromatic line and the sequential figures generate an implicit circle-of-fifths progression.

- There is no simple return to the opening motive, but rather a gradual resolution of instability. The March finally comes to rest only at the end with the return of the closing figure from section A with its stable, marchlike character.

Example 1.3: Haydn, Symphony #99, Minuet A section (1793)
Example 1.4: Haydn, Symphony #99, Minuet (1793)

After working on the projects in Part 3 and listening to the Bach Minuet and March, you will almost certainly hear Haydn's Minuet (from his Symphony #99) in new ways. For instance, looking back at the structural sketch of the Haydn Minuet, you can see that both the Haydn and the Bach March can be schematized by the familiar A B + A′. But Bach and Haydn each realize this structure in different ways and with unique means. The Haydn Minuet is obviously much more elaborate in its instrumentation, in its extended development of motives, and in its sheer length. Indeed, the differences tempt one to question the shared schematic diagram. And yet such top-level generalizations are sometimes useful in revealing the nature of differences.

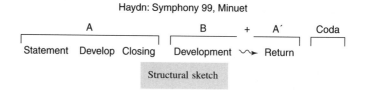

Haydn: Symphony 99, Minuet

A   B   +   A′   Coda

Statement   Develop   Closing   Development ⤳ Return

Structural sketch

Recalling the structural sketch of the Haydn Minuet, listen again just to the A section (Example 1.3). Pay special attention to the passage labeled "development: moving onward" in the diagram.

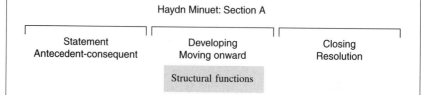

Haydn Minuet: Section A

Statement   Developing   Closing
Antecedent-consequent   Moving onward   Resolution

Structural functions

When you first listened to the Minuet in Part 1, you were focusing on motivic elaborations. There, the beginning of this "moving forward" passage was described as a more active, less stable "working out" of figures derived from the opening phrases. Focusing on these motivic transformations and on their rhythm in Part 2, we pointed out that Haydn has truncated the normative phrase length established by the two opening phrases, and as a result contrasts happen more quickly—the pace seems to speed up. Shift your focus now to the other ways that Haydn finds to intensify the feelings of moving forward. Does Haydn use any of the same means that Bach does?

For instance, in the Haydn passage:

- *The texture becomes more active.* Instrumental voices become independent of one another (as in Bach's March) but there is also imitation between them—that is, the same descending motive (taken from the opening) is played by both the upper and lower strings but out of phase, as if they are chasing one another.
- *There is a suggestion of a metric shift.* As a result of the figural grouping, the meter seems to momentarily shift from triple to duple.
- *There is a change of key.* Through a sequential passage (as in Bach's March), the tonality gradually evolves from B♭ major to the key of the dominant, F major.

Listening to the whole A section once more, notice that you can quite easily hear the stability at the outset of the Minuet, how it becomes increasingly unstable and onward moving, and then resolves into stability again in the closing section. But you are probably unaware of the changing key, except as it is contributing to the feeling of instability. Haydn maneuvers this change of key so elegantly that we are aware of arriving at stability in the closing section but unaware that in doing so, we also arrive at a new key. The original tonic has been deposed and its dominant has acquired primacy.

How does Haydn make the closing section sound so very stable? What makes it so?

- The active texture subsides into a clear melody with the familiar *oom-pah-pah* accompaniment.
- The phrases are repeated, their structure is clearly defined and balanced, and they all end on the pitch we now hear as the tonic.
- The bass instruments reiterate the tonic throughout the passage, solidly establishing the new key.

Listen to the whole Minuet again (Example 1.4). Focus on section B, an extended development section. Here, as Haydn really takes off, we must leave behind our comparison with the small keyboard pieces by Bach. As the term *development* suggests, Haydn uses section B to further explore and exploit the initial motivic material and the family of related keys. Beginning by reversing the direction of the opening motive—going up instead of down—Haydn takes us through a thicket of changing keys, traversing a circle of fifths where tonality is on the move. Then there is a gradual progression into a return to the opening material and to the original key.

But instead of repeating the initial A section and simply coming to a close, Haydn introduces a surprising cliffhanger; still in the same key, we are suspended on the dominant! Fully ready for resolution now, Haydn brings us down to the closing passage, this time sitting solidly on the tonic of the original key.

Example 3.4: Chopin, Mazurka, Op. 67, #2 (1849)

Like the Bach and Haydn minuets, Chopin's Mazurka is also written for the keyboard (specifically the piano) and it is also based on dance music in triple meter. However, the minuet and the mazurka belong to very different cultural backgrounds: The mazurka belongs to Polish folk culture, while the minuet comes from Austro-German culture. Like that of Haydn's Minuet, the structure of Chopin's Mazurka can be schematized as A B + A'. But here the similarities stop: If the differences between Bach and Haydn were striking, the differences between both of them and Chopin's Mazurka are even more so.

Instead of going into a detailed analysis of this moving work, just listen to the Mazurka several times and enjoy some of the following characteristics:

- The A B + A' structure is clearly heard. The contrast between the A and B sections is marked by the increase in tonal ambiguity in B. The return to A is strongly anticipated by a poignant, unaccompanied "waiting passage."

- Within A there are smooth shifts from the minor mode, with which the piece begins, to the relative major and back again to minor. The two larger sections within A could be described as a large antecedent-consequent pair, with the first section ending incompletely, and the second section beginning again like the first but ending completely on the tonic and in the minor mode.

- Chopin creates the ambiguity of the B section by twice traversing a clear circle of fifths. The second time around the passage gives way to a rather improvisatory solo melody, which, as a waiting passage, is made more poignant by its wispy chromaticism.

- The A' section is nearly identical to the opening A. However, influenced by the preceding ambiguity of B and the waiting passage, the effect is different: We are arriving, returning again into relative stability, familiarity, and calm resolution.

Example 1.7: Liszt, Faust Symphony, First Movement (1854)

Recall that you listened to the beginning of Liszt's Faust Symphony in Part 1, where it was one of several examples that illustrated sequential progressions. Revisiting it now with a focus on tonal relations and in the light of the previous examples, you will immediately hear that it differs from all the others in that it seems to be tonally ambiguous throughout. In the Bach, Haydn, and Chopin pieces there were certainly moments of tonal ambiguity, but these were moments of contrast that departed from but always resolved back into tonal stability. Liszt persistently resists settling into a clearly defined tonal center. And yet, while never quite achieving resolution, he seems to keep us on its edge, with tonal stability never far out of reach.

Tonal ambiguity, like metric ambiguity, can help bring into focus those simples, which are otherwise so familiar as to be invisible. To repeat: By moving away from what we know best and then looking back, we can often discover what it is we know so well. Listening to music that is tonally ambiguous, we can look *at*, and listen *to*, that which we usually just listen *through*.

You need to keep two questions in mind as you listen again to the Liszt excerpt: First, what creates coherence in the midst of this tonal ambiguity—what do we follow? Second, how does Liszt create this tonal ambiguity?

Listening again just to the opening of the Faust Symphony and considering the question of coherence, you will hear again that the four repetitions of the three-note motive, a descending sequence, form a path to follow. But, considering the second question, the three-note sequential figure itself confounds our sense of tonal center. Why? The three pitches of the sequential figure are equidistant from one another, three whole steps. Further, each iteration of the sequential motive moves down by a half step. The result, when the sequence as a whole is completed, is an accumulation of all twelve pitches of the chromatic collection. In composing this opening sequence, Liszt has not limited himself to that particular subset of pitches and relations that could define any one key. Instead, as the sequence unwinds downward, accumulating the whole chromatic pitch collection, we are left necessarily with tonal ambiguity.

Adding to this tonal ambiguity, Liszt varies the internal rhythm of the sequential figures while keeping their total time the same. Moreover, he inserts a rest so as to blur any regularly recurring accent. As a result, another structural simple, meter, is also obscured.

This leaves the time span of the sequential motive, which remains the same throughout, to function as the basic temporal unit.

Returning to our first question—what generates coherence in the midst of tonal ambiguity—it becomes clear that it is the figural aspect, the unique structural elements, that become central in guiding both rhythmic and melodic coherence.

As the excerpt continues, figural elements continue to be foremost. Still based on the same three-note motive, the descending melody suddenly expands upward. Covering two octaves in the same time it took to cover only half an octave previously, the whole melody seems to get faster—more pitch distance in less time. Reaching the top of the range, Liszt introduces new, very disjunct figural elements that create a slowly descending but still sequential melody. If we follow the path of these figural gestures, we can learn to suspend our dependence upon and our belief in tonal orientation as a necessary constituent for making coherence.

But ambiguity, especially when the structures of both meter and tonality are so nearby, strongly influences the feeling that Liszt is trying to evoke. The Faust Symphony is a musical depiction of a story whose central character, Faust, makes a pact with the Devil. How does Liszt evoke this diabolical, somewhat scary feeling that his title suggests? What is the relationship between the dramatic effect and the musical means? Consider that ambiguity and uncertainty in life situations often produce apprehension and fear. And then consider that against a backdrop of our dependence on tonality, tonal and rhythmic ambiguity create musical uncertainty—disorientation, lack of security. And musical uncertainty, just as the uncertainties in life situations, also evokes feelings of apprehension and fear. The conventional structures of musical organization are not just abstract constructs; they are means for creating the feelings and emotions that draw us into music.

Liszt also uses instrumentation to enhance these feelings generated by rhythm and pitch relations. He gives his melody to the limpid sound of the woodwinds playing in unison, without the support of any accompaniment. Then, at the highest point of the melody, the woodwinds hand off their pitch to the thin sound of the high strings, who continue with their large, empty, melodic leaps, again in unison. And as they wend their way slowly down through the whole range, the high strings give the melody over to the lower strings, who complete the descent of the still ambiguous melody into the lower regions.

To play with the opening motives yourself, select LISZT from the Tunes Catalog in the 4-Voices PlayRoom. Blocks 1–4 play each of the three-note motives but all with the same duration. This obviously creates a regularity that is not Liszt's. To hear the effect of the irregularities, substitute Blocks 2a and 4a, which include Liszt's varied durations, for Blocks 2 and 4. Then insert Block R between Blocks 2a and 3 for the rest that occurs between the pairs of motives. Notice the effect of these subtle differences, particularly as they contribute to enhancing the spooky character of the melody.

Example 3.5: Helps, *Gossamer Noons*, #2 (Bethany Beardslee, vocal) (1974)

With this last example, Gossamer Noons, the composer, Robert Helps, abandons tonality almost entirely. What, then, are we to pursue in seeking coherence? First of all, the text. In this song, the poetry to which the music is set is crucial—generating the mood and the mood changes, and also guiding the organizing structure of the whole song. Before listening to the song, read the poem closely, imagining what the music might be.

Gossamer Noons II

(From *The Running Sun*)

James Purdy

Wicked sounds haunt the glen tonight
voices from non-human throats
clear cries of splendid pain
and then after a bit
more cries again.

Can you for one moment dare to doubt that
frogs have echoes through the bog
and hear their own lovesongs
under lily pads
and imminent wet clouds.

Now, as you listen, pay attention to how Helps captures the mood and suggests the objects referred to in the poem—and even their sounds. Follow the text and notice how the music changes in response to the change of mood in the middle of the second stanza. What musical means does Helps use to project the textual sense of the poem?

The sounds of the poem are quite literally imitated in the music: The cellos' plucked strings provoke a steady beat while playing very disjunct, non-tonal pitches ("wicked sounds"). The cellos are inter-mittently but persistently interrupted by the "shrieks" of low brass and high woodwinds ("voices from non-human throats / clear cries of splendid pain"). The music expresses an uneasy, haunted feel—we follow the steady beat but with no meter to frame it, and no tonal center to which we can comfortably settle ourselves—musical ambiguity, uncertainty.

As the singer enters, the very tone of her voice is haunting above the orchestra, which continues on now as her accompaniment. We follow her consistently ascending melody line—evenly spaced in both pitch and time, making her own beat, gliding free of the cel-los' beat. As pitches rise, the pace of these events slightly quickens. But within each rising line, pitches remain equidistant from one an-other—each separated by a whole step. The evenly spaced whole-step progression, like the evenly spaced chromatic collection, defies any major scale with its particular sequence of whole and half steps. But the effect of the whole tone series, compared with Liszt's cu-mulating chromatic collection, is quite different—more opening up than intensifying.

Helps marks each line of text with a new whole tone series, each rising higher than the next, and each spanning an octave from bot-tom to top. The last, going twice as slow, culminates on the highest pitch, "clear cries of splendid pain."

As if to continue a reflection of this "pain," the persistent beat is taken over by the harsher brass in a short interlude. With the re-entry of the voice, "then after a bit," the singer begins again with the lower whole tone series, continuing on more slowly with "more cries again." The brass picks up the slowly rising whole tone line; the strings revert to keeping the beat; and then silence!

The beginning of the second stanza seems to almost fold back into the first—the steady beat interrupted by the shrieks of the woodwinds over which the voice enters again with the rising whole tone series. But now Helps breaks up the lines of the text: "Can you for one moment dare," then starting again and getting faster, "to doubt that / frogs have echoes." A brief interlude, then folding back, repeating, "have echoes through the bog."

In response to the changing mood of the text, now there is calm and contrast in every dimension. Signaled by the gossamer sound of the triangle, bowed strings (rather than plucked) play sustained slow notes together. Over them the voice floats in a touching melody that curves slowly upward, reaching its peak on "and hear their own lovesongs."

But the calm does not last. Returning to the relentless beat of the plucking strings, the melody line returns to the rising whole tone melody, "under lily pads, " and seeming almost to evaporate with the last line, "and imminent wet clouds."

Completing the song with just the orchestra, Helps gives the brass a rising melody that obscures tonality in still another way: a series of rising fifths. Going steadily upward instead of around the circle of fifths, each new pitch denies the tonal primacy of the previous one, the whole seeming to disappear into oblivion.

Some Basics: Conventional Pitch Notation

YOU HAVE SEEN SEVERAL DIFFERENT REPRESENTATIONS FOR PITCH AND HOW THEY may be useful in various contexts. Now it is important to summarize the conventions for notating pitch used by musicians in reading, writing, and playing music.

Through the quirks of music history, just seven letters, A through G, are used to designate pitches. These seven letters are repeated through at least five *octaves*. Pitches that are an octave apart have the effect of "mutual duplication"—that is, they sound alike but at the same time different.* For instance, when men and women sing the same melody "in unison," the women are singing higher, the men are singing lower, but both groups are actually singing the same pitches one or more octaves apart.

Pitches that are related by an octave have the same name and are described as belonging to the same *pitch class.* Higher or lower pitches that belong to the same pitch class are described as being in a higher or lower *register.* A pitch that is one octave higher than another has twice as many vibrations per second; a pitch that is one octave lower than another has half as many vibrations per second.

In Impromptu, pitches that are members of the same pitch class but in different registers are notated by adding !'s either before or after the shared letter name. For example, a letter name by itself, G, is in the mid-

---

*J. A. Westrup, and F. L. Harrison, *The New College Encyclopedia of Music.* New York: W. W. Norton, 1960.

dle register, while !!G is two octaves below and !G is one octave below G; G! is an octave above G, and G!! is two octaves above G.

Same pitch class

There are several other more common conventions for notating the register of a pitch class. For instance, in one commonly used notation, the registers for the pitch class, G, are notated as follows:

Same pitch class

Pitch is most commonly shown by its position on the five-line *staff*. Each line and each space of the staff "holds" one note.*

notes in spaces   notes on lines

It is clear that there is not enough room on a single five-line staff to notate pitches in all registers. Moreover, each instrument and each singing voice has a specifically limited *range*—the highest and lowest pitches between which they can play or sing. To accommodate the range of particular instruments or voices, the pitches to which the lines and spaces refer can be adjusted to keep the players' notes mostly within a single staff. A *clef* symbol fixes the position of one absolute pitch on the staff, with all the others oriented in relation to it. There are three primary clefs used in CMN: the *G or treble clef,* the *F or bass clef,* and *the C clef.*

The treble clef is used to notate pitches for instruments or voices (often melody instruments) that generally play in the higher register (middle C and up), such as violin, oboe, or a soprano singing voice. The "swirl"

---

*While each note symbol refers to or "holds" two properties—a pitch and a duration—we focus only on pitch notation in this section.

of the treble clef fixes the position of the G above middle C on the second line:

Treble clef notation

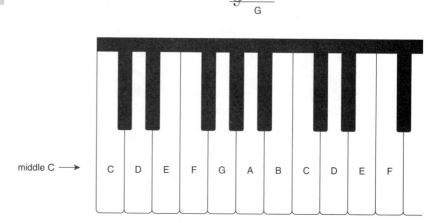

The *F or bass clef* is used to notate instruments or voices that are generally in a lower register (middle C and the octaves below) such as cello, bassoon, or a bass singing voice. The two dots of the bass clef fix the position of F below middle C on the fourth line.

Bass clef notation

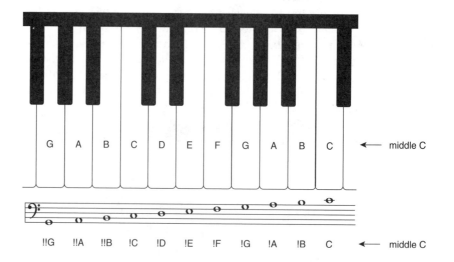

The C clef fixes the position of middle C. However, the C clef is moveable—that is, the position of middle C on the staff can vary depending on the range and register of the instruments or voices involved. The most commonly used C clefs are the *alto clef*, which fixes middle C on the third line, and the *tenor clef*, which fixes middle C on the fourth line. The alto clef is used most commonly in writing for the viola; the tenor clef is used most commonly in writing for the upper registers of the cello or bassoon.

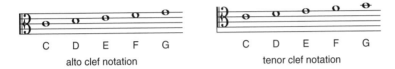

alto clef notation   tenor clef notation

Degrees of the Scale

Each degree of the scale has a conventional name:

Degree	Name
$\hat{1}$	*Tonic*
$\hat{2}$	*Supertonic* (above the tonic)
$\hat{3}$	*Mediant* (midway between tonic and dominant)
$\hat{4}$	*Subdominant* (the fifth under the tonic)
$\hat{5}$	*Dominant* (the fifth above the tonic)
$\hat{6}$	*Submediant* (midway between tonic and subdominant)
$\hat{7}$	*Leading tone* (leads toward the upper tonic)

Sharps and Flats

By adding *accidentals* [*sharps* (#) and *flats* (♭)] to the seven letters for pitches, all twelve pitches used in Western music notation can be named and can be positioned on a staff. Sharps raise a pitch by a half step; flats lower a pitch by a half step. Thus, A# is one half step higher than A, and A♭ is one half step lower than A. A natural sign (♮) cancels a previous flat or sharp. All 12 pitches played in order from low to high or high to low constitute a *chromatic scale*.

Chromatic scale: Treble
clef notation

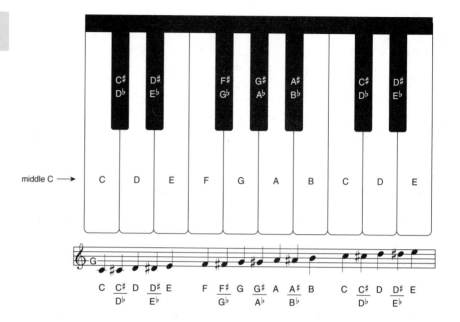

Chromatic scale: Bass
clef notation

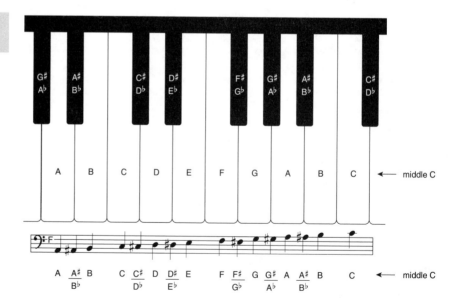

To notate pitches above or below the five-line staff, the staff is extended
by the addition of *ledger lines*. For example, in the bass clef, middle C is
written on the first ledger line above the staff, while in the treble clef,
middle C is written on the first ledger line below the staff.

Ledger lines

Enharmonic Equivalents

As discussed in Project 3.2 and shown in the preceding illustrations of the chromatic scale, a pitch that sounds the same when played on the piano can be notated in different ways, depending on its function within a key. For instance, A♭ is a half step lower than A, and G# is a half step higher than G, but both A♭ and G# are found in the same place on the keyboard. Pitches that sound the same but are notated differently are called *enharmonic equivalents*.

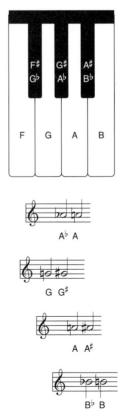

Enharmonic equivalents

Intervals

An *interval* is the distance between two pitches. Just as scale degrees are not actually numbers but rather names for the consecutive pitches in a major or minor scale, so intervals within a scale are conventionally named according to the number of scale degrees they span. For instance, the intervals between scale degrees $\hat{1}$ and $\hat{3}$ and between scale degrees $\hat{4}$ and $\hat{6}$ are *thirds*; the intervals between scale degrees $\hat{1}$ and $\hat{5}$ and between scale degrees $\hat{3}$ and $\hat{7}$ are *fifths*.

Notice that when you count the distance between pitches, you need to include the scale degrees on both sides of the interval—that is, from $\hat{3}$–$\hat{7}$ is a fifth, because counting from the lower to the higher you count up five pitches: $\hat{3}$-$\hat{4}$-$\hat{5}$-$\hat{6}$-$\hat{7}$. Intervals may be played simultaneously *(harmonic interval)* or one note after the other *(melodic interval)*:

Interval Types

There are four types or classes of intervals: *perfect, major/minor, diminished,* and *augmented*. The four types reflect the structure and function of pitch relations within scales and keys. Further, the types differentiate among the kinds of transformations that intervals can undergo.

Types of intervals

Perfect   Prime (the same note)
                   Fourth
                   Fifth
                   Octave

Major/minor	Second
	Third
	Sixth
	Seventh
Diminished	A perfect or minor interval lowered by a half step
Augmented	A major or perfect interval raised by a half step

The following illustration shows the kinds (names) of intervals formed by pitches ascending and descending from the tonic as found in all major scales. The C-major scale is used as an example.

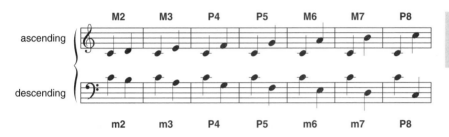

Intervals within the C-major scale starting on the tonic

Things to Notice

• Three types of intervals are included: major (M), minor (m), and perfect (P).

• All the intervals ascending (going up) from the tonic are either perfect or major.

• The distinction between perfect intervals on one hand and major or minor on the other aligns with the distinction between primary and secondary scale degrees.

> *Perfect intervals* (fourths, fifths, octaves) are found between the tonic and the other primary scale degrees: $\hat{1}$–$\hat{4}$, $\hat{1}$–$\hat{5}$, $\hat{1}$–$\hat{8}$.

> *Major intervals* (seconds, thirds, sixths, and sevenths) are found between the tonic and the secondary scale degrees: $\hat{1}$–$\hat{2}$, $\hat{1}$–$\hat{3}$, $\hat{1}$–$\hat{6}$, $\hat{1}$–$\hat{7}$.

• All intervals descending (going down) are either perfect or minor.

> Perfect intervals remain perfect—the tonic down to the primary scale degrees: $\hat{1}$–$\hat{5}$, $\hat{1}$–$\hat{4}$, $\hat{1}$–$\hat{1}$ (octave).

> *Major intervals* become minor—the tonic down to the secondary scale degrees: $\hat{1}$–$\hat{7}$, $\hat{1}$–$\hat{6}$, $\hat{1}$–$\hat{3}$, $\hat{1}$–$\hat{2}$.

Classification of Ascending Intervals within the Major Scale

Interval	Abbreviated	Composed of	Scale degrees
Minor second	m2	one half step	$\hat{3}$–$\hat{4}$; $\hat{7}$–$\hat{8}$
Major second	M2	two half steps	$\hat{1}$–$\hat{2}$; $\hat{2}$–$\hat{3}$; $\hat{4}$–$\hat{5}$; $\hat{5}$–$\hat{6}$; $\hat{6}$–$\hat{7}$
Minor third	m3	three half steps	$\hat{2}$–$\hat{4}$; $\hat{3}$–$\hat{5}$; $\hat{6}$–$\hat{8}$; $\hat{7}$–$\hat{2}$
Major third	M3	four half steps	$\hat{1}$–$\hat{3}$; $\hat{4}$–$\hat{6}$; $\hat{5}$–$\hat{7}$
Perfect fourth	P4	five half steps	$\hat{1}$–$\hat{4}$; $\hat{2}$–$\hat{5}$; $\hat{3}$–$\hat{6}$; $\hat{5}$–$\hat{8}$; $\hat{6}$–$\hat{2}$; $\hat{7}$–$\hat{3}$
Augmented fourth	A4	six half steps	$\hat{4}$–$\hat{7}$
Perfect fifth	P5	seven half steps	$\hat{1}$–$\hat{5}$; $\hat{2}$–$\hat{6}$; $\hat{3}$–$\hat{7}$; $\hat{4}$–$\hat{8}$; $\hat{5}$–$\hat{2}$; $\hat{6}$–$\hat{3}$
Diminished fifth	D5	six half steps	$\hat{7}$–$\hat{4}$
Minor sixth	m6	eight half steps	$\hat{3}$–$\hat{8}$ $\hat{6}$–$\hat{4}$; $\hat{7}$–$\hat{5}$
Major sixth	M6	nine half steps	$\hat{1}$–$\hat{6}$; $\hat{2}$–$\hat{7}$; $\hat{4}$–$\hat{2}$; $\hat{5}$–$\hat{3}$
Minor seventh	m7	ten half steps	$\hat{2}$–$\hat{8}$; $\hat{3}$–$\hat{2}$; $\hat{5}$–$\hat{4}$; $\hat{6}$–$\hat{5}$; $\hat{7}$–$\hat{6}$
Major seventh	M7	eleven half steps	$\hat{1}$–$\hat{7}$; $\hat{4}$–$\hat{3}$

Again there are several things to notice:

- *Seconds:* The minor seconds are, of course, the critical half steps between degrees $\hat{3}$–$\hat{4}$ and $\hat{7}$–$\hat{8}$ that define the major scale. All the other seconds are major.
- *Thirds:* The major thirds are those that begin on the primary scale degrees: $\hat{1}$, $\hat{4}$, and $\hat{5}$. The minor thirds are those that begin on the secondary degrees: $\hat{2}$, $\hat{3}$, $\hat{6}$, and $\hat{7}$.
- *Fourths and fifths:* All of the fourths and fifths are perfect except those that involve scale degrees $\hat{4}$ and $\hat{7}$. The interval between degrees $\hat{4}$ and $\hat{7}$ is a "large" fourth called an *augmented fourth.* An augmented fourth includes a half step more than a perfect fourth. The interval between $\hat{7}$ and $\hat{4}$ is a "small" fifth called a *diminished fifth.* A diminished fifth includes a half step less than a perfect fifth. These special intervals result from the half step between degrees $\hat{3}$–$\hat{4}$ and $\hat{7}$–$\hat{8}$ in the major scale. And, like the half steps, the augmented fourth and the diminished fifth are very important in defining tonal centers.

Inversions of Intervals

In general, to invert an interval you simply turn it upside down. However, there are two ways to do that and each involves pivoting around a fixed pitch.

Melodic Inversion
Examples of melodic inversion are shown in the following illustration. To make a melodic inversion, start on any pitch, go up along the scale a cer-

tain number of scale degrees, then turn from the initial pitch and go down along the scale the same number of scale degrees. For instance, with C as the starting pitch, go up from C to D (adjacent scale degrees) and then down from C to B (adjacent scale degrees). With this kind of inversion, the name of the interval will stay the same, but the type of interval will change—a M2 becomes a m2 (from C up to D, a M2, will become a m2 from C down to B). Once again, perfect intervals remain perfect.

Inverting intervals (melodic)

Rules of melodic inversion

- A major interval always becomes a minor interval; a minor interval always becomes a major interval; a perfect interval always remains a perfect interval.
- The name of the interval always stays the same:
  - The inversion of a M2 is a m2.
  - The inversion of a P5 is a P5 (except when the initial pitch is scale degree $\hat{4}$).
  - The inversion of a P4 is a P4 (except when the initial pitch is scale degree $\hat{7}$).
  - The inversion of a m6 is a M6.

Harmonic Inversion

To make a harmonic inversion, start on any pitch, let's say A, go up along the scale to a certain pitch above the initial pitch, let's say C; then, from the initial pitch, A, turn the other way (down) to find another pitch with the same name, C, an octave below. Thus, the inversion of the interval, A up to C, is the descending interval A down to C.

Inverting intervals (harmonic)

Rules of harmonic inversion

- A major interval always becomes a minor interval; a minor interval always becomes a major interval; a perfect interval always remains a perfect interval.

• The sum of an interval and its harmonic inversion always adds up to
  9. For instance:
    • The inversion of a m3 is a M6.
    • The inversion of a P4 is a P5.
    • The inversion of a M2 is a m7.
    • The inversion of a M6 is a m3.
    • The inversion of a m2 is a M7.

Composers sometimes invert a whole melody. To do so, each interval
through which the melody proceeds is replaced by its melodic inversion.
That is, each descending interval is replaced by an ascending interval of
the same size; each ascending interval is replaced by a descending interval of the same size. This can be easily seen in the following example from
Brahms' *German Requiem*: The original melody begins with a descending
minor third (A♭–F) followed by a descending major second (F–E♭). The inversion begins with an ascending major third (E♭–G), followed by an ascending minor second (G–A♭), and so on.

A melody and its inver-
sion

Brahms' German Requiem

original

inversion

Chromatic Notation

So far the discussion has been limited to notation of pitch and of intervals within major and minor scales. Scales (or better, pitch collections)
such as these that include just seven different pitches are called *diatonic*.
In turn, intervals that lie within these diatonic collections are called *diatonic intervals*.

The chromatic collection of pitches, as you know, includes all twelve
pitch classes. Pitch classes in the chromatic collection are numbered con-
secutively, with 0 always representing middle C. Thus, each chromatic

number represents a pitch that is related to those immediately adjacent to it by a chromatic interval of 1. Thus, chromatic numbers, unlike scale degree number-names, consistently measure the interval between any two pitches.

Chromatic and diatonic number notation

With this chromatic notation, the chromatic numbers that play the C-major scale are 0 2 4 5 7 9 11 12. This number sequence also represents a particular sequence of pitch intervals; this pattern of intervals always generates a major scale.

With chromatic notation, it is thus possible to label intervals in a more consistent fashion. Further, it is possible to use ordinary arithmetic to measure and describe intervals. For example, an interval of 3 is always three chromatic steps. Thus, the chromatic interval 0–3 is a minor third, and 2–5 and 3–6 are also minor thirds. In contrast, using the names of scale degrees, the diatonic interval $\hat{1}$–$\hat{3}$ is a major third, but $\hat{2}$–$\hat{4}$ is a minor third.

Impromptu provides chromatic notation in the Pitchset menu. To get a feel for the difference in these notations, open a familiar tuneblock and use the Pitchset menu to switch between Major and Chromatic.

Part 4

The paths of a structured physical space reflect the tonal paths of melodies that migrate among keys. (Image copyright © 1998 PhotoDisc, Inc.)

Making Music Out of Theory

Introduction: Paths and Landmarks

THROUGH THE EXPLORATIONS IN PROJECT 3.2, YOU MADE SOME ADVANCES TOWARD OUR CONtinuing effort to describe the logic that hides in even the simplest tunes and, implicitly, the logic hiding in the intuitions you use to make sense of them. By perturbing stability—juxtaposing, shifting, and sliding tonalities into one another—the norms of this stability became more palpable and their existence more convincing. The internal logic that you take for granted in your immediate apprehension of musical coherence is being exposed—put "out there"—to be interrogated and played with.

Working within the Practice Scales and Set Key environments, these processes have remained artificial and machine crafted. The projects in this chapter will involve working with real melodies that incorporate this process of playing with "normal stability" to create increased interest and complexity in more musical settings. These projects also give you an opportunity to circle back over the work you have done so far—the issues, puzzles, insights, and multiple views of organizing structures that you have encountered in previous projects.

First, working with tuneblocks again, you will build tunes as you did before but now using blocks that include shifting tonal centers. You will listen, in particular, for the critical links through which to join these migrating blocks together to become a coherent whole. Project 4.1 ends with an exploration in which you go back and listen again to the Bach Minuet (Listening Example 3.1), zooming in on and actively playing with the details.

Then, in Project 4.2, you will move down into the contents of blocks, using your heightened intuitions to create melodic coherence at the note level. Starting with pitches and durations that will initially sound quite incoherent, you will search for means through which to transform this chaos into coherence.

Finally, you will listen to examples of compositions that include and exploit, in extended and multidimensional ways, the networks that form the complex terrain we call tonality, as well as some that abandon the tonal terrain to map out other means of comprehensibility.

Project 4.1

Building Tunes That Migrate

THE TASK   Compose coherent tunes with blocks that migrate between keys.

There are three sets of blocks to work with:

- DUTCH
- BRITISH
- SALEM

You can choose to listen to a completed tune and reconstruct it using the given tuneblocks, or you can start with the tuneblocks and make your own tune. The practice sessions take you through each option.

Reconstructing Migrating Tunes: "Dutch"

INFO BOX
Starting Project 4.1
· In the Playrooms menu, select Tuneblocks
· In the Tunes Catalog, select DUTCH

Begin with the same steps for reconstructing tunes that you followed in Project 1.1. However, you now have an additional focus—changing key. You also have more tools with which to account for your hearings.

We will use "Dutch" as a practice example. Listen first to the whole tune (the DUTCH block) and be sure to keep track of your work in your log book. The questions and suggestions in the following lists bring together many of the issues that you have paid attention to throughout Parts 1–3.

- How are you segmenting the tune? Can you say what pitch and time relations are helping to generate the structural boundaries you hear?
- Are blocks repeated? If so, when are blocks repeated?
- Where/when does the tune move to a different key—that is, when do you hear a new pitch becoming the tonic?
- Make a preliminary sketch of the whole tune showing its hierarchical structure: motives, phrases, sections.

Next, listen to each of the blocks and consider the following:

- Do the given blocks segment the tune as you did in your sketch? If not, how do the blocks differ from yours?
- What is the contour of each block—going up; going down; going up and down? Make a sketch of the contour as you hear it.
- What is the possible function of each block—ending, beginning, middle? What features make it so?
- Consider blocks that you hear as having an ending function: Do your ending blocks center on different tonics? For instance, compare Blocks 1 and 5.

Next, listen to FP and then to SP.

- Is there a change of key in FP or in SP? Is there a change of key between FP and SP?
- Arrange the blocks so as to reconstruct FP and then SP.
- Pay attention to surprises that happen as you work.

When you have reconstructed the whole tune, look back at your structural sketch.

- Do you hear the structure differently now? If so, how and why?
- Compare your structural analysis with the structures of tunes in Project 1.1.
- What role does the change in key play in the larger structure of the tune?
- Are there repeated rhythmic motives (as in "America")?
- Are small, melodic motives repeated?

Pick out the tune on the keyboard using the blocks as units of work. The tune begins in the key of F.

- What key does it migrate to?

- What new pitch is introduced to make that migration work?
- Given the direction and the means of migration, how do they relate to the interleaved scales you worked with?
- Try composing your own tunes using the DUTCH blocks.

Before going on to the BRITISH and SALEM block sets, do the following explorations.

Key Change as Elaborating Structural Functions

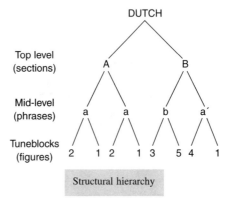

Structural hierarchy

"Dutch" is, of course, another embodiment of the familiar structural hierarchy shared by many of the tunes you reconstructed in Project 1.1. However, that structure is further elaborated in this tune. In partiular, contrast in the *B* section is enhanced by the move to a new key, and the return to *a'* is reinforced by a return to the original key. The specific direction of key changes—to the key of the dominant and back—is a further extension of the melodic moves between scale degrees $\hat{1}$-$\hat{5}$-$\hat{1}$ within a single key, as in "Star" or "Early." That is, the $\hat{1}$-$\hat{5}$-$\hat{1}$ melodic skeleton is extended and made more complex through its elaboration into a key area also related by a fifth. "Dutch," as played by Impromptu, begins in the key of F, staying there through the repeated *a* phrases, then moves to its dominant, the key of C, in the *b* phrase, and back again to F in *a'*.

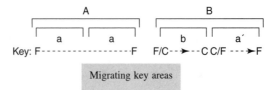

Migrating key areas

Our intuitive hearing of structural functions—tension and resolution—demonstrates the unambiguous tonal context of the A section. The first figure (Block 2) clearly needs resolution; the second figure (Block 1) just as clearly resolves to stability—the tonic. Moving in closer, we hear the first figure (Block 2) moving basically between scale degrees $\hat{1}$–$\hat{5}$, with the fifth degree extended and along with it the extension of instability. The second figure (Block 1) resolves this tension by moving stepwise, $\hat{4}$-$\hat{3}$-$\hat{2}$-$\hat{1}$, back to the tonic. (*Note:* Skeleton pitches are shown with larger dots.)

Phrase <u>a</u>:

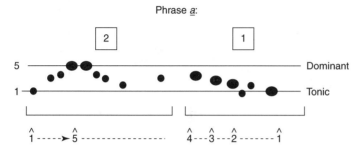

In the version of "Dutch" played by Impromptu, the moves from scale degrees $\hat{1}$–$\hat{5}$ are from F–C in in the first figure, followed by the stepwise progression back to the tonic, B♭-A-G-F, in the second figure:

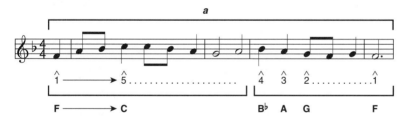

Going on to the *b* phrase, in the course of its two figures (Blocks 3 and 5), F as tonic is overthrown. By the time we arrive at the end of the *b* phrase, C, the relatively unstable fifth degree in F, has taken over to become the stable tonic.

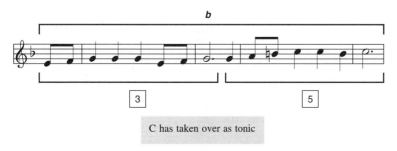

C has taken over as tonic

In fact, the means used to effect this transformation mimic your explorations with linked scales. Recall, specifically, the F scale linked with the C scale:

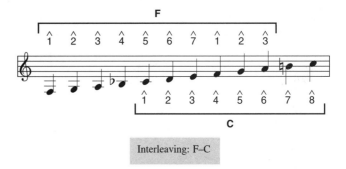

Interleaving: F–C

The top of the F scale (C-D-E-F) overlaps the bottom of the C scale. And continuing on up with the top of the C scale (G A B C), the one new note, B-natural, is enough to instantly establish C as the new tonic.

And that is exactly what happens in the *b* phrase of "Dutch." The *b* phrase begins with a figure (Block 3) that hovers around the existing tonic, F; starting with the seventh degree, the tonic, F, is surrounded—degrees $\hat{7}$-$\hat{1}$-$\hat{2}$, or E-F-G with the G repeated!

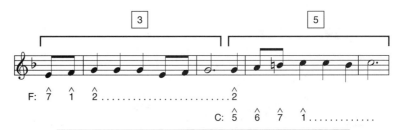

The *b* phrase: From the key of F to the key of C via linked scales

In the next figure (Block 5), that same pitch, G, which is scale degree $\hat{2}$ in F, and which was emphasized by repetition, transforms in retrospect to become $\hat{5}$ in C. Upon arriving at the C after hearing the pitches G-A-B-natural–C, the C has clearly become stable—the new tonic. Looking (or listening) back, the stepwise rising progression from G to C transforms the function of pitch G, and prepares us for the ascendancy of C to the tonic role. Theoretical structures come alive to be useful in melody making.

But scales and critical pitches are not enough to make either a convincing melody or even a convincing change of key. As illustration, try juxtaposing Blocks 1 and 5—the end of the *a* phrase joined with the end of the *b* phrase:

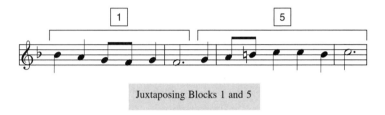

Juxtaposing Blocks 1 and 5

Does this make a convincing progression? Does the C at the end of Block 5 sound like a stable tonic? If not, why not? Why does the actual sequence of Blocks 2-1-3-5 make a more convincing progression? Think about pivot tones and the rate of change.

How about the return to the initial key, F? How is the transition effected? Do you find it convincing? Listen to the whole melody once more. Would you agree that the coherence of the tune rides on our ability to smoothly adjust to changing tonal contexts?

With these thoughts and questions in mind, go on to the next task—composing your own tunes with blocks that migrate.

Composing Migrating Tunes: "British" and "Salem"

To compose coherent tunes with these blocks, you will need to listen for blocks that share a common tonal center. This is sometimes difficult to do, because of our mental versatility in adapting to new tonal contexts—you are there even before you know that you have left here. Building tunes with these blocks will give you an opportunity to slow down this mercurial process—to hear tonal migration happening. Of course, it is sometimes more interesting to couple up blocks that belong to different keys—but you need to be able to hear the difference before you can take advantage of that possibility. This is a good example of developing your musical intuitions.

Begin with BRITISH. Listen, first, to the tuneblocks with colored icons; these are the blocks with which to compose. Black-and-white blocks are sample tunes that others have made; listen to them later. The following steps are intended to help you listen for and differentiate among blocks that declare a particular tonal center, blocks that are participants in one of these established key areas, and blocks that are "on the way" toward a new key area. Most important is the musical significance of these distinctions: Once you have differentiated among the blocks, how can you use these new possibilities to enhance the coherence and interest of your tunes? For instance, how can you use evolving tonal centers to create more lively structural functions such as arrivals and departures, contrast, ambiguity, and return? And how can these, in turn, help provide a bit more excitement in these rather minimal tune worlds?

Here are some suggestions for listening to the blocks:

- Listen for tuneblocks that sound as if they could be an ending, but with each ending in a different key—that is, each resolves to a different pitch.
- Pair an ending block with another block that is in the same key and helps to establish its tonal center.
- Use the Tuneblocks Scratchpad (in the Options menu) to make experiments with subtunes. For instance, drag sets of coupled blocks (those that belong to the same key) onto the Scratchpad. Experiment with joining coupled blocks together and joining sets of coupled blocks together in various ways.
- Do you prefer one key following the other in a particular way? What about Block 5? Where does it belong? Can you say why?
- What about proportions—that is, does your tune stay in one key too long? Is the key changing too rapidly or not rapidly enough? Repeating blocks will slow that process down.
- Use Block-It in the Scratchpad to build bigger blocks (subtunes) that you like. Drag bigger blocks into the PlayRoom to work at this more aggregated structural level.
- When you have a tune that makes sense, pick it out on the keyboard. Look at the contents of blocks if you like—that is, open them with the magnifying glass cursor.

The log of your experiments in composing your own tunes should include the following:

- Each of the arrangements of blocks that you tried.
- Your impressions of each of your tries—which you liked or didn't like and why.
- What keys are the blocks in? How do you know?

- What is the relationship between the keys?
- What means did you find to help make the tune migrate from one key to the other?
- How do these means relate to the interleaving scales you worked with before?
- An analysis of your final tune, including where the tune modulates and the role of the modulation within the structure.
- A comparison between these tunes and those you built in Projects 1.1 and 1.2.
- A comparison between your tune and the examples (black-and-white blocks) that others have composed.
- Which example do you like best? Why?
- Which one is most like yours?

Using the same kinds of procedures, go on now to compose one or more tunes using the SALEM set.

Playing with Bach's Minuet

EXPLORATIONS 2

After building your own tunes with tuneblocks that migrate between keys, you will hear and appreciate more how Bach migrates between keys in developing his Minuet. In these explorations you will move in on the details of Bach's Minuet. As you play with Bach's "tuneblocks" yourself, you will hear how he has played with them in composing this piece.

Before getting into the details, go back and listen again to the whole Minuet (Example 3.1). As you listen, follow along with the large structure shown here.

INFO BOX
Starting Explorations 2
· In the Playrooms menu, select 4-Voices
· In the Tunes Catalog, select BACHS

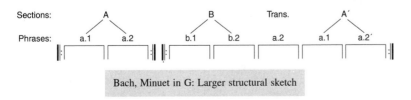

Bach, Minuet in G: Larger structural sketch

Then listen in more detail to just the A and B sections (Example 3.3), shown next.

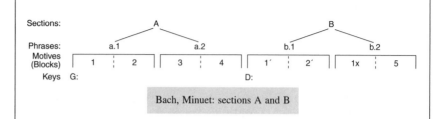

Bach, Minuet: sections A and B

With the BACHS screen in your workspace, notice that the blocks in the Tuneblocks area are labeled and grouped exactly as in the two preceding figures. Thus, the red blocks are the motives—those labeled 1, 2, 3, 4, 1', 2', 1x, 5, and 6. The purple blocks are the phrases—*a*.1, *a*.2, *b*.1, and *b*.2. The blue blocks are the sections—A, B, trans, A'. In addition, there are "bass blocks," each of which corresponds with and goes together with a melody block: Bs1, Bs2, and so on; Bsa1, Bsa2, and so on; and BsA, BsB, and so on.

Begin by listening to just the melody for section A (Block A) and section B (Block B). Drag Blocks A and B into Voice 1 of the Playroom and click Play.

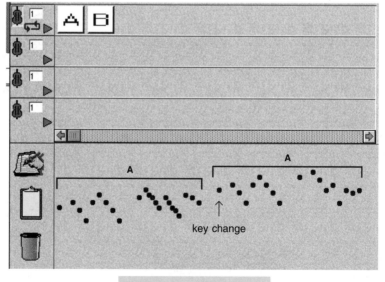

Bach, Minuet, Sections A and B

Can you hear that the tonic shifts at the beginning of section B? Listen several times. What is the effect? Do you lose your bearings? Probably not, but why not?

To play with this shift in key, you can move down in the structural ladder to the phrase level. Try juxtaposing the beginning phrase of section A (*a*.1) and the beginning phrase of section B (*b*.1). Turn off Voice 1. Drag the phrase blocks—*a*.1, which begins section A, and *b*.1, which begins section B—into Voice 2. Click Play.

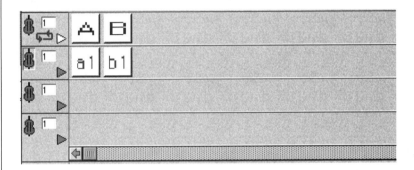

Now you will surely hear the abrupt shift. However, even though the shift is abrupt, it is not disorienting. This is mostly because the *b*.1 phrase is exactly the same as *a*.1, except now in the new key. You can see this clearly by comparing the two phrases in the graphics.

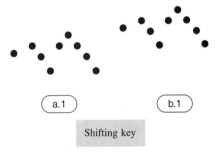

Shifting key

But there is another reason, too—namely, the relations between the two keys. Section A is in the key of G major and, as you might expect, section B shifts to the closely related key of the dominant, D major. While your experiments with changing the key of "America" in Project 3.2 were purely artificial, Bach has integrated just such moves into the structure of the Minuet to create contrast as well as coherence.

As you have already seen, the pitch contour graphics for Blocks *a*.1 and *b*.1 look the same, despite the difference in the actual pitches. Notice that in the staff notation in the next figure, there is a C# in phrase *b*.1—a foreign pitch in the key of G, but the critical seventh degree in D.

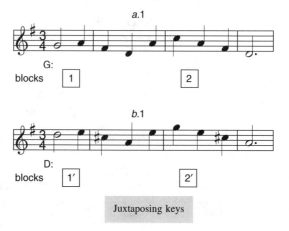

Juxtaposing keys

Notice, too, how pitches change function. For instance, in phrase *a*.1, the pitch D marks an unstable ending—it is scale degree $\hat{5}$ in the key of G. Phrase *b*.1 begins with the same pitch, D, only an octave higher. But by the time phrase *b*.1 is completed, D has become the stable tonic. However, you don't actually hear its stable arrival until the end of section B. Add Block *b*.2 to complete section B and to hear D functioning as the tonic.

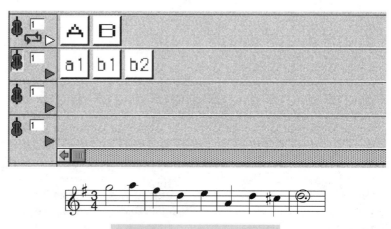

Phrase *b*.2: Arrival of D as the tonic

To put the phrases back into context, listen to sections A and B once more. Turn off Voice 2, turn on Voice 1, and click Play. To complete the whole context and to make the abrupt key shift even more striking, you can add Bach's bass line to the melody. (*Note:* Scroll the Blocks area to the right to see all the blocks.)

- Turn off Voice 2.
- Drag into Voice 3 the "bass blocks" BsA and BsB, which correspond with melody blocks A and B in Voice 1.
- Listen to sections A and B several times. Notice that when you start over (that is, go back to section A), you clearly hear the shift of key—this time from D major at the end of B to G major at the beginning of A.

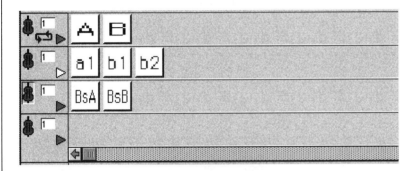

Bass blocks in Voice 3

- Indeed, you can turn Bach's Minuet into a simple A B A' piece. Simply add Block A' to Voice 1 and BsA' to Voice 3.

More Surprises

Another surprise comes from comparing Blocks 1 and 1x. Clear Voices, drag Blocks 1 and 1x into Voice 1, and listen.

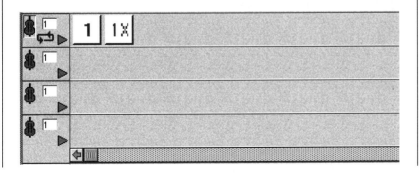

The melodies played by Blocks 1 and 1x turn out to be exactly the same pitches and durations, only this time the pitches are an octave apart. Why does this emerge only when the two blocks are lifted out of context and juxtaposed?

To answer that question, you need to put Blocks 1 and 1x back into context—that is, surrounded by the phrases of which they are a part.

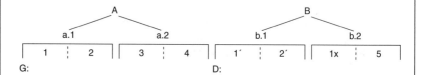

To do that:

- Clear Voices.
- Drag Block *a*.1 (Blocks 1–2), Block *b*.1 (Blocks 1′–2′), and Block *b*.2 (Blocks 1x–5) into the PlayRoom.
- Click Play.

Block 1 in the context of Block *a*.1 is in G major, but Block 1x (the same set of pitches and durations, only an octave higher), when embedded in Block *b*.2, is in D major! Indeed, with this arrangement you have three different versions of the opening motive: First, Block 1 in G major and in mid-range; second, Block 1′ shifted to D major; third, Block 1x exactly an octave higher than Block 1, but now sounding in D major. Listen to this example several times.

To make the context more complete and to make these transformations more convincing, drag the corresponding bass blocks into Voice 2: Bsa.1, Bsb.1, Bsb.2.

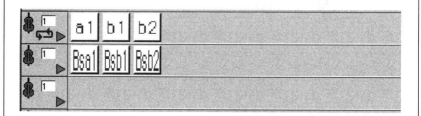

Re-embedded in the context of the bass line, the two blocks that are exactly an octave apart (Blocks 1 and 1x) sound unquestioningly different. This is a striking example of context influencing the meaning/function of the same pitches. Listen to this example several times.

You can make other interesting new pieces by playing with the punning possibilities of Bach's blocks. For instance, try the following experiments:

Blocks	*Structure*
1-2-3-6	Simple balanced phrases that stay in one key.
1-2-3-4; 1-2-3-6	Antecedent-consequent pair that stays in one key.
1-2; 1'-5	Antecedent-consequent with the consequent pair ending on the tonic but in the new key of the dominant (G → D).

For more convincing performances, add the bass blocks in Voice 2 that correspond with the each of the melody blocks.

Go back and listen once more to Bach's Minuet as he wrote it (Example 3.1). Did you notice that in the return, A', in the real Minuet, Blocks 1 and 2 are exactly the same as in the opening, but they are followed by a slightly transformed version of Block 3 (not included in the Impromptu version). This small change makes a smoother connection with the new Block 6. In turn, the new Block 6, substituting for the Block 4 that ended section A incompletely, functions to bring the Minuet to a close on the tonic, G.

For your log:

- Look back again at the questions you were asked when you first listened to the Minuet. What are your current impressions?
- How has your hearing of the Minuet changed?
- How have the explorations contributed to these changes?

Project 4.2

Grouping Boundaries

A RECURRING ISSUE THROUGHOUT THESE PROJECTS HAS BEEN, WHAT CREATES FIG-
ural groupings and their structural boundaries? We have returned often to
this issue because the musical means used to segment or "chunk" continuously unfolding streams of sound is a critical factor in generating the coherence we make (or seem to just find) in listening. Listening to the common music of our culture, we learn at an early age to recognize beginnings
and endings of motives and phrases, even though we are not able to say
what musical features (for example, pitch-time relations) contribute to the
groupings and boundaries that we are responding to. Conversely, when we
say of some piece that it "doesn't make sense" (for example, the music of
another culture), it is often because the features that are generating groupings and boundaries, those that are indigenous to that culture, are different
from those that we are used to and have come to take for granted. If we
cannot hear the goals of melodic motion—where to stop and start again—
we have the impression that this music just seems to "go on and on."

You may also have had this impression in listening to music of our own
culture that is composed in an unfamiliar style. Indeed, differences in style
can often be attributed to differences in the means that composers use to generate groupings and boundaries. For instance, as you have heard, some twentieth-century composers have developed means for generating groupings
and boundaries that do not include the network of pitch relations we have
called tonality. In learning to make sense of the music of another culture or
an unfamiliar style, the challenge is to find and hear the particular kinds of
features and relations indigenous to a particular style (or sometimes even to
a particular piece) that are meant to create boundaries, to define elements,
and also to generate stability and instability within a given universe.

Through the experiments in this project, your intuitions will again be both the source and the target of your work. And, in the course of the project, you will need to practice much of what you have learned in the previous projects and explorations to *make* new melodic coherence. For instance, in Part 2 you found that rhythm often plays a critical role in your intuitive boundary making—a longer duration tends to delimit a figure, group together preceding events, and separate them from what follows. And in Parts 3 and 4 you have heard that tonality plays a big role in generating structural boundaries—joining, separating, and confounding groupings through the construction and deconstruction of tonal centers. Indeed, it was proposed that in stretching the limits of coherence—getting lost—we can often grasp what it is we have been taking for granted, what it takes to know where we are. These experiments will be a good opportunity to test that conjecture.

In contrast to Project 4.1, where you were working at the block level, you will be working at the note level in Project 4.2. You will start by listening to a series of varied durations, all played on the same pitch. Your task will be to listen for figural groupings suggested by the durations and then to give pitches to the durations so as to bring out these groupings. The next task reverses the previous one: You will hear a series of varied pitches, all of the same duration. As in the first task, you will listen for possible figural groupings, and then make these potential groupings emerge by giving varied durations to the original pitches.

Turning back on your own intuitive decisions in each of these tasks, you will then try to account for the specific relations that generated the grouping boundaries you initially heard. Going on, you will also try to make explicit the pitch relations and the rhythmic means you found to project these groupings. Finally, by experimenting some more, you will try to make new and different grouping boundaries, thus creating a new coherence.

To work seriously on these projects, you will need to bring to them much of what you have learned so far—including a growing awareness of your own powerful intuitions, multiple representations for describing and for developing these intuitions, and the ability to experiment, reflect on, and inquire into the puzzles and surprises that emerge.

THE TASKS

1. Given only a set of varied durations, all played on the same pitch, listen for figural groupings. Then give varied pitches to the durations to bring out these groupings and to make a coherent melody.

2. Given only a set of varied pitches, all with the same duration, listen for figural groupings. Then give varied durations to the pitches to bring out these groupings and to make a coherent melody.

Figural Groupings: Varied Durations

<table>
<tr>
<td>

INFO BOX
Starting Project 4.2
· In the Playrooms
  menu, select
  Tuneblocks
· In the Tunes
  Catalog, select
  MAKETUNE.D

</td>
<td>

There are three sets of duration blocks to work with for the first Task. They are labeled DUR1, DUR2, and DUR3. The block labed DUR1.S is a sample solution for the DUR1 block. The blocks become more interesting and more complex as you go along. In working on both tasks listen to your intuitions in finding figural groupings; later, go back and try to account for your initial hearings. Remember to keep a running log of your work.

</td>
</tr>
</table>

Follow these steps for the first task:

1. Listen for possible groupings.
   a. Click DUR1 and just listen for possible figural groupings.
   b. Listen again, and this time clap back the rhythm.
2. Make a first accounting.
   a. Make a quick pencil sketch of the rhythm and the groupings you hear. For instance:

   b. Put DUR1 into the PlayRoom, and select Rhythm Bars in the Graphics menu. Compare your sketch with the graphics. What is the meter?
   c. Make a first guess at which features and relations within the durations of DUR1 seem to be generating the grouping boundaries you hear.
3. Design pitches to project your groupings.
   a. Use the magnifying glass cursor to open DUR1.

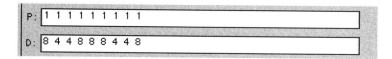

   Notice that all the pitches are the same ("1's" in the Pitch box). The durations (in the Durations box) are the givens.
   b. Using your initial hunch about grouping boundaries, experiment with possible pitches to project those groupings:

   • Delete the current pitches (1's in the Pitch box).

- Sing (improvise) a melody that projects the groupings you heard, using the given durations (or, as one student said, "So someone else will hear your groupings").
- Type in the pitches you improvised.
- The number of numbers you type will determine the number of pitch events you hear. For instance, if you type 1 2 3 4 and click Play It, you will hear just the first four durations (8 4 4 8) played with the pitches 1 2 3 4.

4. Create a new block and give it a name.

    a. With your new tune in the Edit window, choose a name for your tune and type it in the Name box—for example, "MY 1." Then click on Name → Icon. Your chosen name will appear on the block.

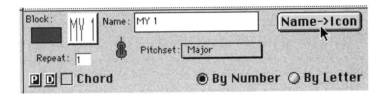

    b. Click New to create a new block and to return to the Tuneblocks screen.

    c. Your new block is now in the Tuneblocks area and can be played or dragged into the PlayRoom just like any other tuneblock.

5. Keep track in your log.

    a. Keep track of the pitches you try, your impressions of the results, what you changed, and why.

    b. When you have made a tune that works, write down the pitch numbers in your log book, and then translate the whole melody into staff notation.

    c. Listen especially to boundary conditions: how tonal functions (stablity-instability) intersect with rhythmic functions (accent/meter/short-long) to generate arrivals and departures of motion.

    d. Listen critically to the block DUR1.S, a melody made by a student using the durations of DUR1. Are the grouping boundaries the same as or different from yours? Which tune do you like better?

We will return to DUR1 and DUR1.S in Explorations 1. But in order not to get too analytical and self-conscious, go on now to work on the DUR2 and DUR3 blocks before doing Explorations 1. Be sure to name and save your melodies on your own floppy disk.

Interrogating Alternative Figural Groupings*

In accounting for the figural groupings you made and the means you used, it is important to remember that figural groupings are distinctly different from metric units. However, it is their interaction in boundary making that is of special interest. For instance, accent is an essential feature in both kinds of structures, but its function in each helps to differentiate between them. The position of the accent within figural groups can vary—going *to* an accent (end-accented figure) or taking off *from* an accent (beginning-accented figure) makes an important difference to the character of the figure. Indeed, as Arnold Schoenberg said, "The way the notes are joined is less important than where the center of gravity comes or the way the center of gravity shifts."† In contrast, by definition and function, metric accents always occur at the beginnings of metric units. And since metric accents occur at regular intervals, the number of beats in each unit (measure) is always the same. The interesting question is, how do figural groupings and metric units interact?

Even though the DUR1 rhythm seems trivial, two possible figural groupings emerge. Each grouping shapes different figures out of this single series of durations and in each, figural groups and metric units interact differently.

We can compare the possibility for alternative groupings to what are called *oronyms* in language: "strings of sound that can be carved into words in two different ways":

> The stuffy nose can lead to problems.
> The stuff he knows can lead to problems.
>
> The good can decay many ways
> The good candy came anyways.‡

Of course, when you read the written couplets, the differences in grouping and in meaning are perfectly clear. However, in talking and listening, that is not always the case. You can probably think of other examples where meanings were confused because the speaker was grouping sounds into words one way, while you were hearing the grouping another way. And the same is at least partially

---

*Explorations 1 and 2 in Part 4 are rather detailed, perhaps too much so for some students. However, the issues raised bring together, make use of, and also illustrate much that has gone before, so it is worthwhile to at least give them a try.
†A. Schoenberg, *Style and Idea,* ed. Leonard Stein. Berkeley: University of California Press, 1975, p. 348.
‡S. Pinker, *The Language Instinct.* New York: W. Morrow & Co., 1994, p. 160.

true in music. Given the totally uninflected "performance" by the computer synthesizer, listeners are apt to hear either one of two figural groupings for DUR1; each is equally possible. We can translate numeric rhythm notation into CRN with ♩ = 8, mark the unambiguous metric units with bar lines, and add grouping brackets. Once we have done so, the alternative figural groupings are quite clear, just as written language makes the spoken groupings clear.*

Grouping 1
weak beat ending

Grouping 2
upbeat ending

The differences have to do not only with the actual position of the grouping boundary, but also with the position of the accent within the figures. In Grouping 1, the first figure ends on a weak beat and the second figure begins on a metric accent. In Grouping 2, the second figure begins with an upbeat and goes to the metric accent. In Grouping 1, the beginning of the second figure coincides with a metric beginning. This means that the figures in Grouping 1 are contained within metric boundaries (the measure). In Grouping 2, the upbeat beginning of the second figure crosses over the metric boundary instead of being contained within it. Which grouping did you hear? Can you shift your focus from one grouping to the other? Which grouping do you prefer?

What about pitch relations? Listen to DUR1.S. Does the choice of pitches in DUR1.S make Grouping 1 or Grouping 2 clearly emerge? Or is the grouping still ambiguous even with these pitches?

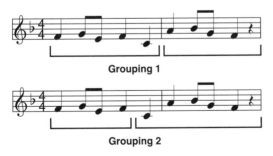

Grouping 1

Grouping 2

---

*Of course, *meaning* in spoken or written language has to do with the specific *referents* for words—*stuffy nose* refers to something quite specifically different from *stuff he knows*. Music differs from language in this important regard: There are no specific external referents such as *nose* or *knows* for notes or even figures. Like the generating of a tonal center, meaning in music is largely an internal affair.

If there is a difference in character between the two groupings, even though very small in this minimal melodic world, it results primarily from the greater contrast in Grouping 2. Grouping 1 makes for a more settled melody. The first figure ends incompletely on $\hat{5}$, the dominant, and on a weak beat. The second figure begins with an accent on $\hat{3}$, moves momentarily to $\hat{4}$, and moves solidly down to resolve on a relatively strong beat and on $\hat{1}$, the tonic.

Grouping 2 makes for a bit more lively melody. Both figures end on a relatively strong beat and on the tonic, suggesting a more stable, even stolid mood. However, the second figure in Grouping 2 begins with the more onward moving fifth degree as an upbeat, and continues on with a large upward leap over the bar line, going to the downbeat on a relatively unstable third degree. This tension is then quickly resolved as the melody briefly moves upward to $\hat{4}$ and downward to the tonic.

These may seem like very picky points, but it is exactly these kinds of differences in the hearing of groupings that strongly influence performers' decisions. For a pianist or violinist, each hearing would be played differently using instrumental means such as dynamic stress and/or slightly bending the beat, to project the intended hearing. Imagine yourself to be the performer. Play DUR1.S on the piano keyboard so that, unlike listening to the totally straight synthesizer, a listener could distinguish between each of the groupings.*

---

*For instance, to project Grouping 1, you can bring out the weak-beat ending of the first figure by playing it softer, and by making a slight pause at the bar line between the two figures. To project Grouping 2, you can settle a bit on the third beat (F), make a slight pause before beginning the second figure, and then rush a bit over the bar line toward the downbeat.

Go back now and reconsider the melodies you have made in the light of these explorations. Are your accountings still convincing? Do you notice aspects of your intuitive meaning-makers that you hadn't noticed before?

Figural Groupings: Varied Pitches

The second task for this project is in two parts—Task 2A and Task 2B. For both parts the task is basically the same. The blocks you will be given include a series of pitches all of the same duration. Listen for figural grouping boundaries, and then provide durations for the pitches so as to make a coherent melody. The difference between the two tasks is in the blocks themselves. The pitches included in the blocks for Task 2A are precomposed and clearly tonal. The pitches included in the blocks for Task 2B have been randomly selected by a computer from either a chromatic or major-scale collection of pitches.

> INFO BOX
> · In the Playrooms menu, select Tuneblocks
> · In the Tunes Catalog, select MAKETUNE.P

Task 2A: Figural Groupings: Precomposed Varied Pitches

There are three sets of pre-composed pitch blocks to work with for Task 2A, labeled PIT1, PIT2, and PIT3. PIT1 has 16 notes; PIT2 has 20; and PIT3 has 27. The block labeled PIT1.S is a sample solution for the PIT1 block.

The general procedure here is similar to the first task, with some notable exceptions.

1. Listen for figures:
   a. Click PIT1 and listen for possible figural groupings and boundaries. You may slow down or speed up the tempo and change instruments as you wish.
   b. On paper, draw lines that equal the number of pitch events in each block (for example, 16 in PIT1). Listen again (probably several times) and as you listen, mark off the groupings you hear.

$$\overline{|\;|}\;\overline{|\;|\;|\;|\;|\;|\;|\;|\;|\;|\;|\;|\;|\;|}\quad ?$$

Mark off possible groupings

2. Make a first accounting. Make a first guess at the features and relations within the pitches of PIT1 that seem to be generating the grouping boundaries you hear. Jot down your hunches in your log.

3. Design durations to project the groupings.

   a. Select the magnifying glass cursor and click PIT1 to open it.

   b. The numbers in the Pitch box are the given pitches. To experiment with durations for these pitches, first delete the 4's already in the Duration box.

   c. Experiment with possible durations by typing numbers in the Duration box. For instance, if you type 2 2 4 and click Play, you will hear the first three pitches played with the durations 2 2 4. The number of numbers you type will determine the number of pitch events you hear, up to the full 16.

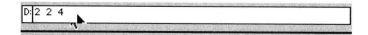

   d. Using your initial hunches about possible grouping boundaries, experiment with durations until you have a melody that projects the groupings you heard in step 1. Listen carefully to the results of your experiments; in the process of experimenting, you may find new groupings.

   e. Jot down in your log book the numbers of the durations you try, your impressions of the results, and if you change your hearings, how you would account for them.

   f. Create your own name for the new block you made, just as you did in the first task. Click New to make a new block. Save your new block on your own floppy disk.

4. Make a further accounting.

   a. Drag your new block into the PlayRoom and look carefully at the pitch contour graphics. Do you notice any new features that can help account for the grouping boundaries you heard?

   b. Open your new block again and look carefully at the given pitches while listening to your new block. You can choose to see pitches by number (scale degree) or by letter.

○ By Number ◉ By Letter

Looking at the pitches, what features and relations would you now say account for the groupings and boundaries you hear?

c. Transcribe the pitches and durations of your melody into standard notation and play it on the keyboard. (Your durations may sometimes be difficult to notate. We will return to that issue later; for now, don't worry about it.) Now that you see the pitches in standard notation and have played your melody on the keyboard, are new features liberated that suggest a different accounting for your hearing?

Look back at "Explorations 1: Interrogating Alternative Figural Groupings" for some aspects to pay attention to. For instance:

- Tonal center—its arrivals and departures
- Goals of motion at boundaries (for example, $\hat{1}$ and $\hat{5}$)
- Pitch contour (direction of motion, leaps or steps)
- Repeated notes, repeated figures, varied repetitions such as sequences

Before going on to Task2B, read and do the next exploration.

Normative Groupings

Listening for grouping boundaries in the preceding task, when only pitch is given, and trying to account for the boundaries you hear, turns out to bring forward many of the fundamental relations that have been the focus in previous projects. Thus, these explorations can serve as a forum to summarize what has gone before. We will explore PIT1 and the sample solution, PIT1.S, as embodiments of these fundamental relations. For example, the boundaries created by PIT1.S probably conform to your solution and to those made by others as well. This is because the pitches alone create boundaries that are intuitively shared. What are these normative figural groupings and what generates them?

The given pitches, all of the same duration, make two larger phrases. Within them, there are possibly two inner figures. Why?

Consider the following possibilities: The internal pitch relations clearly generate a tonic—a point of stable orientation—because:

- The pitches are all members of the same major scale collection (F major).
- The pitches progress through this collection in mostly stepwise motion, except for one significant leap.

- The range of the *skeleton pitches*, F–C, is marked by an interval of a fifth, which we hear as $\hat{1}$–$\hat{5}$.*
- The series begins and ends on what turns out to be the tonic.
- The opening figure "starts over again," creating a new beginning boundary:

tonic   dominant   start again   tonic

- Pitch direction is initially downward in the first phrase, arriving at the lowest pitch—the dominant—just before the opening figure starts again.
- The recurrence of the opening figure in the second phrase resolves this time to the tonic.
- The two phrases form the moves $\hat{1} \to \hat{5}$ and $\hat{1} \to \hat{1}$, respectively.

Thus the bare skeleton pitches embody the prototypical skeleton, $\hat{1}$-$\hat{5}$-$\hat{1}$, and also suggest an antecedent-consequent phrase relationship. To project these boundaries, and particularly the $\hat{1} \to \hat{5}$ and $\hat{1} \to \hat{1}$ coupled phrases, our intuitions are prone to do the following:

- Create a beat and meter—that is, an underlying pulse, proportional durations, and regularly recurring accents.
- Seek balance between phrases.
- Strengthen the feeling of arrival on the dominant by making it occur on an accented beat with a longer duration.
- Mark the second phrase, the figure that starts over, by beginning on a downbeat and ending on a strong beat as well.

Now listen again to PIT1 and to the solution, PIT1.S. Does PIT1.S work? Do the pitches seem to click into place? If so, do the characteristics just described make a convincing accounting for why? Check them out.

PIT 1.S

Skeleton pitches are the basic pitches upon which the melodic structure rests. They contrast with pitches that embellish or elaborate these basic pitches. In this example, for instance, G and A are embellishments of the skeleton pitch, F. See the analyses of "America" and "Star" in Project 3.1 for more.

Of course, it is just these normative simples that account for the tunes that we call "banal." To make melodies that are more interesting, even a little exciting, the norms need to be tampered with. For instance, you could build in some rhythmic conflict—syncopation, metric shift, and so on. Knowing what the norms are helps in learning how to bend them effectively.

All of the blocks for Task 2A have characteristics that lend themselves to such normative figural groupings. Listen again to your own tunes and look at your accountings. Did you make tunes that reinforce these intuitive norms, or did you make melodies that tamper with the norms in order to make more interesting melodies? If you did make "normative" tunes, try some other durations to liven them up.

Task 2B: Figural Groupings: Randomly Selected Pitches

Blocks RAND1, RAND2, and RAND3 include pitches that were randomly selected by a computer. Blocks RAND1 and RAND3 were selected from a chromatic collection of pitches; each has twelve pitches in all. RAND2 was randomly selected from a major scale collection; it has fifteen pitches in all. The blocks labeled R1.S, R1.1S, and R1.2S are sample solutions for RAND1. Blocks labeled R2.S and R2.1S are sample solutions for the RAND2 block, while the block labeled R3.S is a sample solution for RAND3.

While the procedure for Task2B is essentially the same as for Task 2A, you will confront some new issues, mostly because the pitches in these blocks may initially sound rather incoherent. That is, the relations among the pitches will not immediately suggest those normative figural boundaries that were quite apparent in the previous blocks. Yet, if you listen carefully, you will find that it is possible to hear figural groupings. You will not be able to depend on coherence-making features such as those generated by clear tonal functions, but this can liberate you to listen for other means of boundary making. And perhaps tonal functions will be lurking behind the apparent non-tonality, as well.

Notice that there is a new, final task within Task 2B. You are asked to design a second set of durations that will make the pitches in each of the RAND blocks regroup in new ways.

For Task 2B, follow the same steps as for Task 2A which are summarized here:

1. Listen for figures. Listen for possible figural groupings and boundaries. Draw lines that equal the number of pitch events (for example, twelve in RAND1), and mark off the groupings you hear.

> INFO BOX
> · In the Playrooms menu, select Tuneblocks
> · In the Tunes Catalog, select MAKETUNE.R

Mark off possible
groupings

| | | | | | | | | | | | | | | | | ?

2. Make a first guess at the features and relations that are generating grouping boundaries.

3. Design durations to project the groupings.

   a. Open RAND1, delete the 4's in the Duration box, and experiment with durations that project the groupings you heard in step 1.

   b. Account for changes you make.

   c. Name your new block and save it on your own floppy disk.

4. Make a further accounting.

   a. Drag your new block into the PlayRoom and look at the graphics to help account for your grouping boundaries.

   b. Open your new block. Looking at the pitches by letter will be more helpful. What features and relations account for the groupings and boundaries you hear?*

○ **By Number** ● **By Letter**

   c. Transcribe the pitches and durations of your melody into conventional notation and play it on the keyboard. Look for new features that might suggest a different accounting for your hearing.

5. Regroup.

   a. Design a new set of durations to make the pitches of each block group very differently.

   b. At this point you may change one or two pitches in the Pitch box if you want to. But if you do, you must say why you made these changes and comment on the effectiveness of the results.

   c. Remember, you can insert a rest in your tune. Type an "R" in the Pitch box and a duration number in the Duration box at the point you wish the rest to occur.

   d. Give your new melody a name similar to the name you chose for the first set of durations. Click New.

6. Follow the same procedures for RAND2 and RAND3. Remember, RAND2 has fifteen pitches.

---

*A pitch without an accidental (♭ or #) is assumed to be a natural.

Alternative Groupings, Once Again

This last task presented you with new challenges. Unlike the blocks for the previous task, most of the norms, the simples, that we depend on for coherence were missing or were at least hidden in the surface "randomness" of these randomly generated blocks. Consider RAND1, for example: There is no immediate sense of tonal center, which is not surprising considering that the pitches have been picked from the full chromatic collection. There is no obvious sense of regularly recurring accent, also not surprising since with no changes in duration, accent must be generated primarily by the functions of pitch. There are certainly no repeated figures. So what did you hear that could possibly generate figural groupings and their boundaries?

Given little else to go on, there is one aspect that seems to draw the listener in—the contrasts in register and the large leaps between these highs and lows. The sense of the pitches grouping into high and low configurations not only becomes apparent in listening, but is clearly visible in the pitch contour graphics. (The pitches look similar to the configurations formed by the proximities of stars—do you see the Big Dipper?)

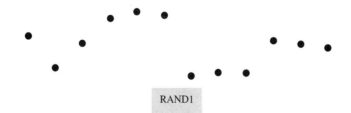

RAND1

The student who composed R1.S chose to use durations primarily to bring out the configurations delineated by the contrasts in register. Following the pitch contour graphics and listening to R1.S, he made longer durations to mark boundaries, thus separating the four configurations in both sound-space and screen-space.

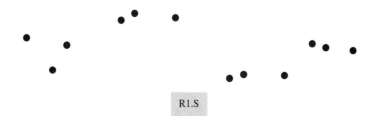

R1.S

Listening to R1.S again, notice that there is some ambiguity in the boundary between the third and fourth clusters. The relatively short duration of the last low note in the third cluster makes it belong to its close pitch neighbors in the third cluster, but also makes it join the higher pitches in the fourth cluster. This ambiguity is helped by repetition: The ambiguous event has the same pitch as the previous event. A repeated pitch often signals a new beginning.

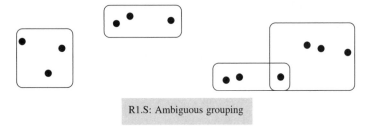

R1.S: Ambiguous grouping

While pitch contour graphics are useful for grasping the general figural grouping, we need a different kind of representation to account for the rhythmic details. Indeed, looking at the actual durations as represented in Impromptu numbers and in CRN holds some surprises:

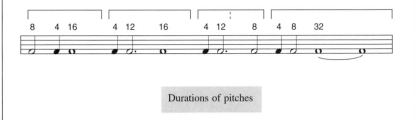

Durations of pitches

While the rhythm seems to be quite coherent as you listen, looking at the durations, it is difficult to say why. Each of the figures differs in total time, and while all of the durations are multiples of four and thus proportional to one another, it is difficult to find a meter—that is, to hear or clap a regularly recurring grouper beat. The student built his durations by ear and by experimenting. He made sure that figural boundaries were clearly marked, and he was attending particularly to the position of accents within figures as reinforcing important pitches. The result is a melodic rhythm that is coherent, rather improvisatory in feeling, but certainly not sounding "random." Indeed, if we were to take a regular beat as a norm, then the durations given to pitches in R1.S "bend the beat" much as a live performer does in projecting structural groupings.

This example seems particularly convincing evidence that we do, indeed, construct the coherence we think we just find, and what we construct is often different from what we see represented by the measured properties of time as shown in CRN or in Impromptu notation. It is enough, it seems, at least within some limits, to have clearly defined figural groups around which we can freely adjust our metric needs.

It is interesting to "clean up" the durations of R1.S to make them clearly metric. The block labeled Clean does just that. Play R1.S, then Clean, and listen for the difference.

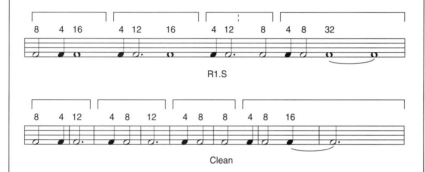

The two versions sound remarkably similar, despite the non-metric rhythm of R1.S. Since the figural grouping is clearly the same in both, the comparison is evidence once more for the importance we give to figural grouping in the structured hearings we spontaneously make. The difference between the two is more one of freedom versus constraints: Clean is constrained by its metric purity, while R1.S is freer in its projection of phrase motion. For a more musical example, go back and listen to Billie Holiday singing "Night and Day" (Example 2.3). Listen to how she bends the underlying beat to express the phrase motion. Imagine trying to capture Holiday's rhythm in CRN.

In contrast to the Clean block, in which the figural grouping remains the same as in R1.S, the durations in the R1.1S block result in a real figural regrouping. This alternative grouping disturbs the grouping in R1.S by causing the pitches to group across the registers and the leaps. You may at first have trouble shifting your focus to make sense of this alternative; listen to it closely. Notice that this student's durations encourage a hearing that make the three-note lower cluster go right on up into the higher cluster. In turn, the subsequent three-note lower cluster joins with the final higher one. The result is that we tend to hear just two big groups.

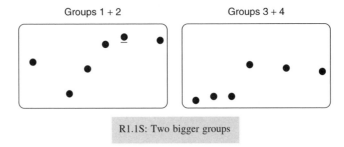

R1.1S: Two bigger groups

Notice also that the highest pitch (in the first bigger group) now gains a more noticeable accent. This is partly because of the clearly directed upward direction, of which this pitch is the apex, and also it has been given a longer duration to which the previous shorter durations cling. This accented high pitch falls off in what seems like a pseudo-resolution. But do you hear that this pitch also sounds somewhat like a stranger? Why? Or why not?

It was suggested earlier that stretching the limits of coherence—getting lost—can often help us grasp what it is we take for granted—what it means to know where we are. Perhaps in seeking to orient himself in a rather strange terrain, this student's durations propose a hearing in which each figural group suggests a tonal center, but the tonality could be migrating between groupings. Of course, this sense of key centers can only be a proposal, since certainly no tonic is unambiguously established. But the sense that the last note in the first large group sounds somewhat strange—like the kind of "cancellation" you heard in the linked-scales examples—would strengthen this proposal: In order for a pitch to sound out of place, there must be a location where it sounds "in place."

To pursue these possibilities, it is necessary to use a notation that shows the actual pitches. This will also help you make use of the ideas that emerged from your previous work in the Set Key and Practice Scales environments. Indeed, this is also a good example of the usefulness of moving among differing notations. Since each captures certain features that others ignore, each notation may lead to insights that are hidden by another. Make use of these notational comparisons as you try to account for your spontaneous hearings of figural groupings.

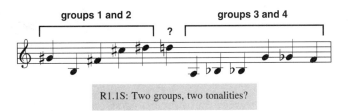

R1.1S: Two groups, two tonalities?

For instance, looking at the pitches within the two large groupings generated by R1.1S, you can see that the first group includes
only sharps, while the second includes only flats. But that is a notational reflection: a reflection that the "scribe" is hearing two different tonalities—the first tonality on the sharp side, the second
tonality on the flat side. On this hearing, the first group proposes
the key of B major. Why? All the pitches up to and including the
high point, D#, are members of the B-major pitch collection. Moreover, the leap up of a fifth from B to F# could suggest tonic to dominant. You can test this possibility intuitively by playing the first figure through the D# on the keyboard, and then playing a B. Does the
B sound like a resolution to a stable tonic?

A test for B major

If B does sound like the tonal center, the high D# is the third degree and the key is clearly B major. That could account for why the
D-natural sounds like a "cancellation": D# followed by D-natural
makes B major become b minor. D# is the third degree in the scale
of B major; lowering the third degree by a half step to D-natural
changes the mode from B major to b minor.

B major to b minor

Moving on to the second figure, the scribe's use of flats suggests
she is hearing a move to the flat side of the tonal scheme. The half
step from A to B$^\flat$ is critical; it suggests a move to the new key of B$^\flat$,
with the A → B$^\flat$ functioning as scale degree $\hat{7}$ going to $\hat{1}$. With that
proposal we hear the final F as unresolved, but still reaffirming B$^\flat$
as its tonic.

B-flat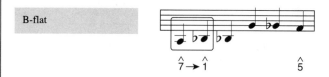

$\hat{7} \rightarrow \hat{1}$ $\hat{5}$

If this is a convincing hearing, the strangeness of D-natural becomes understandable—we are in the process of a tonal migration. The D-natural is a foreigner in the context of B major; it shares the tonal center of B major, but not the mode—that is, it suggests b minor. But B-natural is a pitch common both to b minor and to B♭ major, being the third degree in each. So B-natural serves as a transitional pitch, what is known as a pivot tone, carrying us from one mode (B major) to another mode (b minor) and thence to another key and mode (B♭ major). It is rather remarkable what can be heard in "randomness."

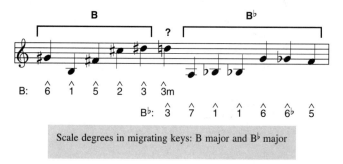

Scale degrees in migrating keys: B major and B♭ major

Finally, listen closely to R1.2S. This set of durations seems to make the sense of tonal centers and tonal migration even stronger. The durations of R1.2S create three figural groups. The first figure arrives quickly at the highest pitch, D#, and hovers there, creating a boundary.

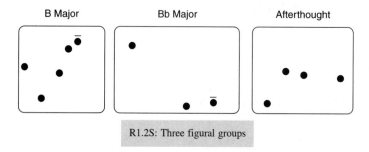

R1.2S: Three figural groups

The second figure lingers on the stranger, D-natural, giving the listener time to wonder, and then with a large leap makes the half-step move from the lower A to B♭, moving more convincingly to the B♭ as a boundary.

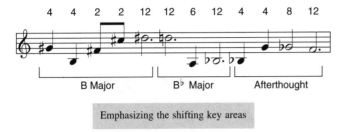

Emphasizing the shifting key areas

The third figure begins again with B♭, which now clearly has an upbeat feeling; moving through the next two events, hesitating on the "passing" G♭, the figure comes to rest on F, the dominant, and on what seems a weak beat. This last figure comes almost as an afterthought—a small coda.

Once again there is no clear meter, but the figural groupings and the accents within them are convincing. The bending of the beat to project structural functions is particularly evident in the second group where the migration occurs: The migrant D-natural is extended and suspended, moving quickly but hesitantly through the seventh degree, A, to the new tonic, B♭, which is also extended in time. In the last figure, the "passing" tone, G♭ (passing between the sixth and fifth scale degrees in F), is stressed, giving the dominant a sense of at least local resolution.

Most important in all of this is how each of these melodies creates such distinctly different feelings, despite all having the same pitches. Indeed, if you put them all in the Playroom, starting with RAND1, you have a kind of theme and variations. Close listening and reflecting on the differences you hear can reveal the inherent subtlety that composers depend on and expect of their listeners in appreciating the complexity of detail they have created.

The sample solutions for RAND2 raise some of the same issues as the samples for RAND1. However, there is a difference because RAND2 was randomly selected from a major scale collection, in contrast to the chromatic collection from which RAND1 was selected. But the pitches of RAND2 also seem to propose two different tonal centers. The sample solutions differ with respect to how each of these potential tonalities is emphasized. Listen to each of them carefully. Which do you find more convincing and why? Which grouping is more like yours?

Part 5

The varying textures seen in this old French tapestry help to define and shape its larger design. Similarly, the changing textures heard in a composition help define and shape its larger design. (Image: *Triumph of Eternity,* Loire Valley, 1500–1510. Cleveland Museum of Art, gift from various donors by exchange)

Harmony and Polyphony

Introduction

THROUGHOUT YOUR WORK ON PROJECT 4.2 YOU FOCUSED ON THE DETAILED LEVEL OF PITCHES and durations and how the relationships among them generate higher level structures such as grouping boundaries, structural functions, and the moves from one key to another. For the projects in Part 5 you will listen to and make larger structures generated by quite different kinds of entities and relations.

Project 5.1 is a brief introduction to harmony. Here, instead of working with single strands of pitches and durations to form motives and phrases, you will work with blocks of pitches played together—that is, chords. Listening to melodies, many of which you will recognize from Project 1.1, you will use these chords to harmonize the melodies as they go along—that is, in real time. Thus, you will be experimenting with a very different kind of accompaniment to tunes. The chords you work with will generate and elaborate structural functions with which you are already familiar and which are already implicit in the melodies: tonic, dominant, and subdominant functions.

For Project 5.2 your attention will turn to making music in which several melodies are playing, each "imitating" but moving independently of one another. Instead of a melody with a chordal and subsidiary accompaniment, each of the voices in these pieces is equally important, thus generating a very active texture. You will control each of the four voices as they cumulatively enter into the sound, continuously increasing the density and activity of the texture.

In working on the projects in Part 5, you will find that they both differ from all of the other projects in the following way: In all the other projects, you described what you wanted beforehand and then you waited to hear the results. In these projects you will be working more as a live performer—that is, actively listening and responding to the music as it is happening in real time.

Project 5.1

Harmonizing Tunes with Chord Blocks

THE TASKS

1. Harmonize the following melodies using the I, IV, and V chords:*

   "Lassie"

   "Austrian"

   "Bonnie"

   "Susanna"

   "Sweden"

2. For each melody, write down the chord progression following the given model.

Your materials for Project 5.1 are only three basic chord blocks called I, IV, and V: that is, tonic, subdominant, and dominant chord functions. These three chords are all you need to create chordal accompaniments for most common tunes. Putting it another way, most common tunes are, themselves, built on only these three chords. Indeed, if you are a guitar player, these are the three chords with which you are probably most familiar.†

---

*See Explorations 2 for discussion of files with an added H (e.g., LASSIE.H).
†See Some Basics at the end of Part 5 for a full discussion of the I, IV, and V chords.

Working in real time, you will listen to a tune and as it plays you "play" the appropriate chord blocks to accompany it. With a little practice, you will be able to hear the chord that fits with the melody quite intuitively even as it goes along.

Getting Started

Notice that in the Blocks area there are the usual tuneblocks for "Lassie," but also three chord blocks marked I, IV, and V, respectively.

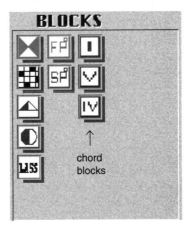

INFO BOX
Starting Project 5.1
· In the Playrooms menu, select Harmonize
· In the Tunes Catalog, select LASSIE

To play the chord blocks, you need to use the ear cursor. (You can use the ear cursor to play tuneblocks, as well.) Click the ear cursor to select it.

Using the ear cursor, click each of the chord blocks and listen for which one sounds most stable. Not surprisingly, it is the I chord, which is built on scale degree $\hat{1}$, the tonic. The chords you are working with are called *triads* because they are each made up of three pitches. The I chord is called the *tonic triad*. The chord built on scale degree $\hat{5}$, the V chord, is called the *dominant triad*. The triad built on the fourth degree, the IV chord, is called the *subdominant triad*. Try playing the chord sequence V–I. This chord sequence, or *chord progression,* is called a *full cadence* (or, more technically, a *perfect authentic cadence*). It creates a very solid, stable feeling—indeed, you will find that nearly all common tunes end with a V–I chord progression. Now reverse the order—try I–V. This progression of course sounds incomplete; it is called a *half cadence* (or, more technically, an *imperfect cadence.*)*

To get a feel for these three basic chords, experiment with them—play them in different orders, repeat them, and so on. For instance, try IV–I. This is called a *plagal cadence.* How would you compare this progression with the V–I cadence?

Harmonizing "Lassie"

Follow these steps, using the ear cursor:

1. Listen to the first part of "Lassie" by clicking the FP block using the ear cursor.
2. As you listen, try to hear where the harmony changes. Notice that "Lassie" begins with an upbeat.
3. Click FP again; this time, right on the first downbeat, click the I block.
4. When FP has finished playing, click FP again. This time go on to play the I block on every downbeat. As you do, pay attention to where and when the I chord sounds wrong—that is, where it doesn't seem to fit.
5. Click FP again; this time click the V chord where the I chord sounded wrong before. Try this several times.
6. Playing a chord on each downbeat (one chord for each measure), you should have found the following progression:

Notice that the harmonic progression (I–I–V–I) is repeated. Why does the repeated harmonic progression sound more final the second time? (*Hint:* Pay attention to the melody and the rhythm as well as the harmony.)

---

*For a full discussion of cadences, see Some Basics at the end of Part 5.

7. Now try harmonizing the second part (SP), following the same procedure.

8. Playing a chord on each downbeat, you should have found the following progression:

Notice that the harmonic progression follows the structure of the melody—*a a' b a'*.

a	a'	b	a'
Antecedent	Consequent	Contrast	Return

Harmonic structure follows melodic structure

Both the antecedent and consequent phrases (*a a'*) have the same harmonic progression; the contrasting section (*b*) has contrasting harmony, and the return to the consequent phrase (*a'*) returns to the initial harmonic progression.

Go on now to harmonize "Austrian," "Bonnie," "Susanna," and "Sweden." In your log:

• Keep track of the chord progressions that you make for each melody.
• Record progressions in diagrams like those shown for "Lassie."
• Keep a log of your progress—what chords you tried, where you had problems, and why.
• Pay attention to recurring patterns of chord progressions that you find.

Note: You will sometimes need to use more than one chord per measure. The rate at which chords change is called the *harmonic rhythm.* For instance, in "Austrian" you will find that the harmonic rhythm gets faster in the third measure, where you need two chords instead of the usual one chord per measure.

		IV V				

"Austrian" FP: Two chords per measure

Impromptu Triads

The following illustration shows the contents of the three primary triads, I, IV, and V, in the key of C Major. Keep in mind that the scale degrees, shown at the right of each chord, will be the same in every key, while the pitches will be specific to each key.

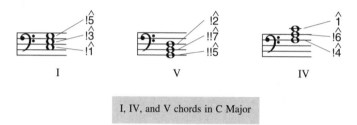

I, IV, and V chords in C Major

The next illustration shows the contents of the I, IV, and V chords in the key of c minor.*

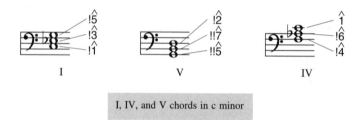

I, IV, and V chords in c minor

The pitch contents of Impromptu chord blocks are the same as in the triads shown here. However, the internal arrangement of pitches in the IV and V chords is somewhat different. As shown in the next illustration, the contents of the IV and V chords have been flipped over. The *root* of the IV chord (F in C major, shown in white) is in the middle of the triad, and the *fifth* of the triad (C) has been flipped over so that it is in the bass (lowest note).

When the fifth of a triad is in the bass, it is in *second inversion*. The root of the V chord (G in C major, shown in white) has been flipped over so that it is now on top and the third of the triad (B) is in the bass. When the third of a triad is in the bass, it is in *first inversion*.

---

*For more on triads, see Some Basics at the end of Part 5.

IV

Second Inversion

V

First Inversion

Impromptu's IV and V chords in C major

To see the actual pitches and the scale degrees for chords you have been working with, use the magnifying glass cursor to open the chord blocks. Start with chord block I. Notice the following:

- The Chord box is checked, which means that the pitches shown in the Pitch box (!1̂, !3̂, and !5̂ scale degrees) will be played together rather than one after the other.

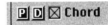

- Pitch set is set to Major.
- Click By Letter. In the Pitch box there are now three pitch letters—!C, !E, and !G.

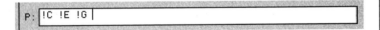

This means that the I chord block in the key of C major is playing pitches !C, !E, and !G. The ! in front of the pitches means that pitches are playing in the octave below middle C.

- Click By Number. The contents of the tonic triad in C major are pitches !C, !E, and !G, which are scale degrees !1̂, !3̂, and !5̂.

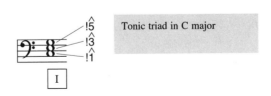

Tonic triad in C major

- Try playing this chord on the keyboard.

Next, use the magnifying glass cursor to open chord block V.

- The pitch contents of the V chord in C major are G, B, and D. But notice that in the Pitch box you see pitches !!B, !D, and !G, or scale degrees !!$\hat{7}$, !$\hat{2}$ and !$\hat{5}$—in that order from bottom to top. Thus, the V chord as played by Impromptu is in first inversion. That is, the root of the chord, scale degree $\hat{5}$ (G), has been flipped up to become the top of the chord, and the third of the chord (B) is now the bass. With the third of the chord in the bass, the V chord is in first inversion.

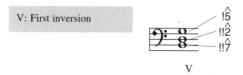

- Try playing this chord on the keyboard.

Finally, open chord block IV. Investigate its pitch contents and play it on the keyboard. The IV chord is in second inversion.

Looking Back

Several of the melodies that you harmonized for Project 5.1 are ones that you reconstructed in the very first project, Project 1.1. Looking back at these melodies from the view of their harmony will reveal interesting similarities and differences among them. Recall that the structures of "Austrian," "Lassie," and "Susanna" are very similar to one another.

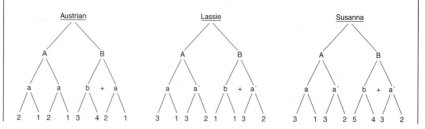

But looking now at the harmony of the three melodies, subtle differences emerge. These differences in harmony might also help account for differences in the characters of the melodies, as well.

To help you follow these explorations, the melodies have been harmonized for you.

Listen carefully to the A section (FP) of each tune, focusing particularly on the harmonic progressions. Start with "AUSTRIAN".H:

INFO BOX
Starting Explorations 2
· In the Playrooms
  menu, select
  Harmonize
· In the Tunes
  Catalog, select
  AUSTRIAN.H

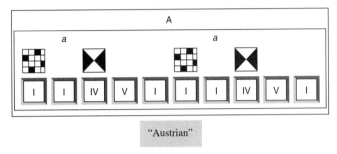

"Austrian"

In one sense, "Austrian" is the least varied of the three. Along with literal repetition of the melody in the A section (*a a*), the harmonic progression is also simply repeated. However, "Austrian" is the only one of the three melodies that includes the IV chord at the cadence— IV–V–I. The change from IV to V also occurs more rapidly—two different chords in the time of just one in the previous figure. This is described as an increase in the harmonic rhythm. You were probably quite aware of the more rapid change as you played the harmony since you, too, needed to move faster at the cadence of the *a* section.*

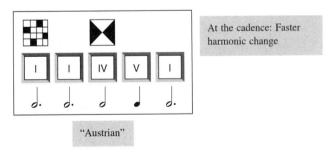

At the cadence: Faster
harmonic change

"Austrian"

Unlike "Austrian," both "Lassie" and "Susanna" include melodic contrast in their A sections—specifically, an antecedent-consequent pair (*a a'*).

---

*The change in harmonic rhythm is reflected in the varied durations of the **V** chords. You see a block, |**V.4**|, where the harmonic rhythm gets faster and the **V** chord gets a duration of only 4; and later a block, |**V.12**|, where the **V** chord gets a duration of 12.

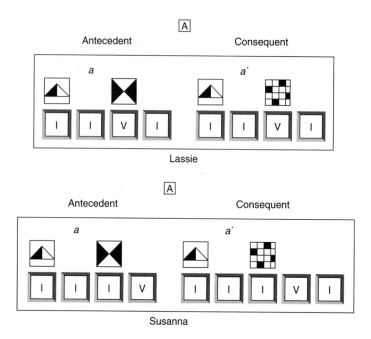

However, the cadential harmony of the two melodies differs. Listen to the harmonized A sections of "Lassie" and "Susanna" (LASSIE.H and SUSANNA.H), paying particular attention to the harmony at the cadences. Can you hear how they differ?

In "Lassie," just as in "Austrian," the harmonic progression is simply repeated—both phrases end with a full cadence, V–I. With "Susanna," there is a contrast between the two cadences. The antecedent phrase ends with a I–V progression, a half (or incomplete) cadence; the consequent phrase ends with a V–I progression—a full (or perfect) cadence. Thus, the cadential harmony of "Susanna" reinforces the antecedent-consequent relationship (unresolved to resolved phrases), while it does not in "Lassie." What, then, makes "Lassie"'s antecedent phrase sound unfinished, seeking resolution?

To answer this question we need to consider the confluence of musical dimensions that make up the perception of an event such as a cadence. Melody, harmony, and rhythm are always interacting to generate our intuitive perception of functional events. Indeed, it is only upon analysis—and if we ask the question, "I wonder why that happened?"—that we are able to extricate the dimensions from one another—and then, often only with the help of a symbolic representation. So consider the melody of "Lassie" as written in CMN along with the Impromptu chord blocks:

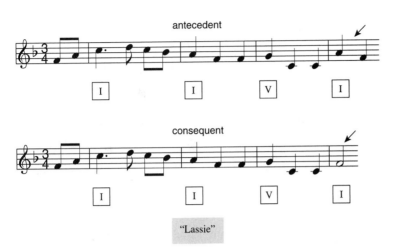

"Lassie"

What is the difference in the relations among dimensions between the cadences of the antecedent and consequent phrases? With respect to rhythm, the antecedent phrase sounds less final because it ends on a weak beat (the second beat of the measure), while the consequent phrase ends on the strong downbeat. With respect to harmony, the antecedent phrase ends with the tonic triad on the downbeat. However, it sounds less final because the third degree of the tonic triad (A), not the tonic (F), is in the melody on the downbeat. The consequent phrase sounds more final because here the root of the tonic triad (F) is in the bass and also in the melody.

"Lassie"

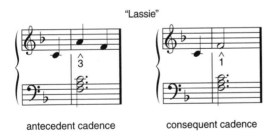

antecedent cadence   consequent cadence

The remarkable thing is that these very subtle, seemingly trivial differences are intuitively heard as making a significant difference in function. We hear a clear difference in the relations of stability/instability at the two cadences because we are selectively giving precedence to differences (in melody and rhythm) over the sameness of harmony.

How about the B sections of these three melodies? Since they all include a return to the material of the A section (*a* or *a'*), it is the contrasting B section that is of special interest. Listen to and compare the harmonized B sections of all three tunes. How do they differ and with what effect?

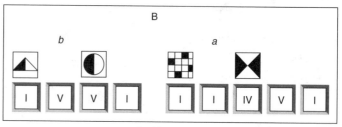

Austrian

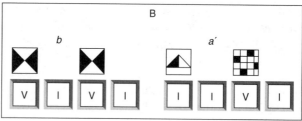

Lassie

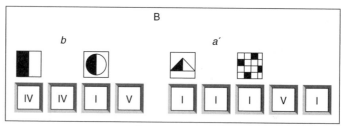

Susanna

Recall that the B section of "Austrian" was made up of a sequence. Notice that the sequence is harmonized symmetrically—I–V V–I. Thus, the two figures of the B section are, so to speak, reflective of one another in both melody and harmony. The melody in the B section of "Lassie," as you will remember, borrows from the previous A section—repetitions of the ending fig-

ure of *a*. The harmony simply follows suit with a repetition of
the harmony—V–I V–I. But, as you found in reconstructing the
melody of "Lassie," repetitions of the same figure in this new
context make the same figure, and now the harmony, seem different. In this context the same melody and harmony serve to
create an appropriately contrasting B section:

- The repetitions in B occur after the full cadence of A.

- The relatively unstable melodic and rhythmic ending of this figure, despite the V–I cadence, give a sense of moving onward.

- The moving onward movement leads into and is resolved by the return, A'.

The B section of "Susanna" presents the biggest contrast. While
the A section was harmonized with just I and V, the B section introduces the fresh sound of the IV chord. Indeed, listening to the
melody now, you may hear that the melody figure with which the
B section begins also moves into a whole different pitch area; the IV
harmony is simply reflecting and supporting that move. And unlike either of the other tunes, the *b* phrase ends on V (a half cadence),
making the return a more significant resolution than in the other
tunes. The greater contrast in melody and harmony in the B section
seems to reflect the change in mood expressed by the words of the
song at that moment.

A

a Oh I come from Alabama with my banjo on my knee

     I   I   I   V

a' And I'm goin' to Lou'siana my true love for to see.

        I   I   I   V   I

B

b Oh Susanna, oh don't you cry for me;

 IV   IV   I   V

a' For I come from Alabama with my banjo on my knee.

     I   I   IV V   I

Finally, "Bonnie" ("My bonnie lies over the ocean . . . ") is quite different from the other three tunes, both in melodic structure and in harmony.

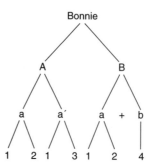

Here we have a single, large antecedent/consequent pair (A B), with three of the four phrases beginning with the same small figure (Block 1). As just touched on in "Susanna," the melody here more closely follows the lyrics. The repeated melodic figure (*a*) corresponds to the repetition of the same words, "My bonnie," at the beginning of each of the first three lines of the lyrics. The text for the last line finally breaks out of the repetition, and the melody does so as well:

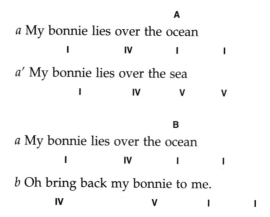

Now listen to the harmonized version of "Bonnie" (BONNIE.H). Notice that from the beginning there is much more emphasis on the subdominant, the IV chord. Befitting the lyrics, this progression has a more gentle, somewhat nostalgic quality as compared with the

I–V–I progressions that were more common in the other three tunes. The first three phrases begin with a move from I to IV. The first phrase (*a*), the beginning of the antecedent, immediately goes back to I, making a I–IV–I progression. The second part of the antecedent (*a'*) goes on from IV to V to make the unresolved (half) cadence that completes the antecedent.

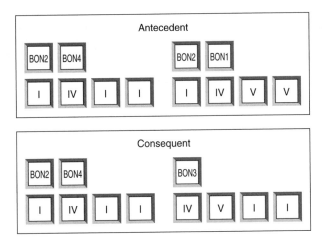

The consequent, of course, begins just as the antecedent did (*a*)—moving from I to IV to I. But new melodic and harmonic material is introduced at the end of the consequent (*b*), bringing the tune to a close with the most complete kind of cadence—IV moving to V and then to I. Once again, the change to new melodic and harmonic material in *b* expresses the change in the lyrics— from a description of a rather sad story in *a* and *a'* to the stronger expression of a wish in *b*: "Oh bring back my bonnie to me!" The stronger expression is reflected in the stronger IV–V–I cadence with which the song ends.

Indeed, the structure of the song is closely intertwined with the lyrics all the way through; the large melodic leap with which the melody begins and which is reiterated three times might suggest the distance that separates the narrator from his love. The tonic to subdominant harmony, as already mentioned, projects a softer feeling as compared with tonic to dominant. And finally, the IV–V–I cadence—a strong change of chord on each beat—reflects the narrator's plea for the return of his "bonnie."

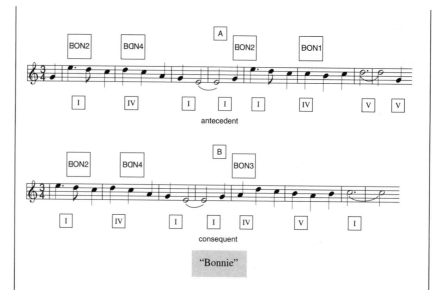

"Bonnie"

With all this in mind, now try to play the harmonic accompaniment for "Bonnie" on the keyboard. The I, IV, and V chords in C major as played by Impromptu are notated in the following illustration:

Practice using these chords to play various progressions—for example, I–IV; I–V; IV–V, IV–V–I, and so on. Then click the tuneblock BONNIE, and as you listen, accompany the song by playing the chords on the keyboard. Try to play the chords just by listening for the changes in the melody, just as you did with the chord blocks. If you have trouble, you can follow the chord changes as shown in the preceding illustration.

Finally, what about "Sweden"? "Sweden" is in the key of c minor. The I and IV chords in a minor key are minor, while the V chord is major. This means that the interval from the root to the third of the I and IV chords is a minor third rather than a major third.*

---

*For a more complete discussion of triads in minor mode, see Some Basics.

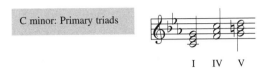

I IV V

As in the major mode, the V and IV Impromptu chord blocks are in first and second inversion, respectively.

I IV V

The structure of "Sweden" is probably simpler than any of the others: a single antecedent-consequent pair with lots of repetition both melodically and harmonically and thus very little contrast throughout.

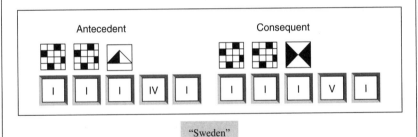

"Sweden"

The I–IV–I harmony of the antecedent phrase does create some contrast in relation to the I–V–I harmony of the consequent phrase. Indeed, this contrast also contributes to making the antecedent-consequent structural relationship. The tonic triad at the cadence of the antecedent phrase sounds incomplete, as in "Lassie." But here, it is the IV–I harmonic progression at the cadence as well as the fifth of the tonic triad in the melody (rather than the tonic) that creates this feeling of incompleteness. The V–I cadence of the consequent phrase, as well as the tonic in the melody, brings the little melody to a more solid close. Notice, too, that the harmonic rhythm becomes faster at the cadences—the changes from IV–I and from V–I occur quickly (on each beat), while there has been only the I chord and thus no change of harmony up till then. Interestingly, this faster harmonic rhythm occurs simultaneously with the faster triplet motion in the melody.

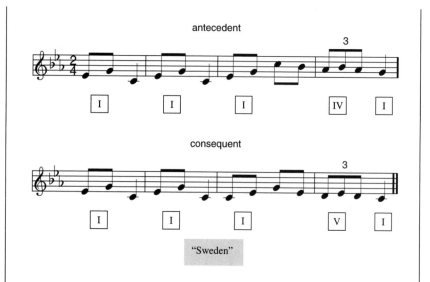

antecedent

| I | I | I | IV | I |

consequent

| I | I | I | V | I |

"Sweden"

You should find it relatively easy to accompany "Sweden" on the keyboard. Practice the I, IV, and V chord blocks in c minor, as shown in the preceding illustration labeled "C minor: Impromptu chord blocks." Then let the synthesizer play the tune for you while you accompany it on the keyboard.

LISTENING EXAMPLES: THE MANY VOICES OF I, IV, AND V

Listening carefully to these examples you will hear the familiar I, IV, and V chords embedded and put to use in very different contexts and with different effect.

Example 2.4: Lanner, "Styrian Dances" (1840)
Example 2.5: Sousa, "Stars and Stripes Forever" (1888)
Example 5.1: Wood, "Old Bedbug Blues" (Bessie Smith, vocal) (1927)
Example 5.2: Turner, "Fine and Mellow" (Billie Holiday, vocal) (1939)
Example 5.3: Rossini, *La Gazza Ladra*, Overture (1817)
Example 5.4: Rossini, *La Scala di Seta*, Overture (1812)

You are probably all too familiar with the Lanner and Sousa examples (Examples 2.4 and 2.5). But as you shift your listening attention now to their underlying harmonic structure, you may come to hear the same pieces in new ways.

> **Example 2.4: Lanner, "Styrian Dances" (1840)**
> **Example 2.5: Sousa, "Stars and Stripes Forever" (1888)**

Lanner's straightforward triple meter accompaniment includes only the basic I and V chords, as shown in the following illustration:

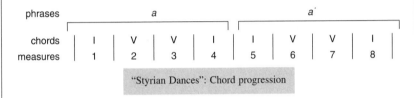

"Styrian Dances": Chord progression

As you focus your attention on the accompaniment, listen especially to the lowest pitches in the bass. These lowest pitches (the *oom* of the *oom-pah-pah*) mark the downbeats, and they also mark the changes between tonic and dominant chords. The tonic chord functions as our point of orientation—of departure and of return. The dominant defines the stability of the tonic by seeking resolution through its return.

Notice the symmetrical harmony (I–V–V–I) is identical in both phrases (*a* and *a'*). The symmetry creates an almost rocking feeling as the harmony moves from I to V and then back again from V to I. The use of only I and V chords, and the play between them, is similar to the harmony of "Lassie" and identical to the B section of "Austrian." And as in "Lassie," despite the return to I in both phrases, the second phrase sounds more final, more complete. Can you say why?

The excerpt from Sousa's march falls into two sections that form an antecedent-consequent pair. The harmonization of the antecedent involves primarily I and V chords, but the ending cadence on V is emphasized by quicker moves from I–IV–V. The consequent is a bit more complex: Beginning once again with I, the harmony wanders through more colorful secondary chords (II and VI) and then "clears up" to end with a strong V–I cadence. The following illustration shows the chords in each measure (except where the secondary chords are playing) along with the rhythm played by the low tuba.

Listening to the rhythm played by the tuba will also help you hear the chord changes.

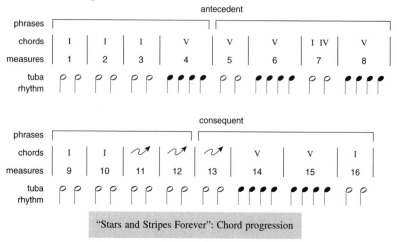

"Stars and Stripes Forever": Chord progression

Example 5.1: Wood, "Old Bedbug Blues" (Bessie Smith, vocal) (1927)
Example 5.2: Turner, "Fine and Mellow" (Billie Holiday, vocal) (1939)

Listening to Examples 5.1 and 5.2 takes you ahead into the twentieth century and into a whole different musical and social culture: from the string players of nineteenth-century coffeehouses in old Vienna and from U.S. marching bands to the early twentieth-century jazz combos in the clubs of New York; and to Bessie Smith and Billie Holiday, two of the great singers in the history of jazz.

> What I think about what makes the blues really good is when a fellow writes a blues and writes it with a feeling, with great harmony, and there are so many true words in the blues, of things that have happened to so many people, and that's why it makes the feelings in the blues.*

"Old Bedbug Blues" and "Fine and Mellow" are but two examples of many, many blues songs all of which are organized around a single underlying chord progression. The chord progression involves basically only the I, IV, and V chords. This collection of blues

---

*J. D. Short, as quoted in Samuel Charters, *The Poetry of the Blues.* New York: Avon, 1963, p. 17.

improvisations accounts for that large group of pieces called the *twelve-bar blues*. The underlying harmonic structure is internalized by jazz musicians as a kind of harmonic "felt path." Musicians from the early twentieth century up until the present have continued to play with it and on it.

While each improvisation, each song, differs in text, instrumentation, texture, rhythm, and type of melodic embellishment, the harmonic underpinning is essentially the same in all of them. Learning to hear this shared harmonic structure will help you hear and marvel at their extraordinary differences—the unique realization of the same basic chord progression, reinvented each time in a new way. Fortunately, many of these early jazz performances were recorded, since it was and is in the performance itself, not in any written form, that the music exists.

Listen to just the first stanza of "Old Bedbug Blues" following the text:*

a

Bedbugs as big as a jackass

Will bite you and stand and grin, [instrumental]

a'

Bedbugs as big as a jackass

Will bite you and stand and grin; [instrumental]

b

We'll trick all those bedbugs

'Fore them turn around and bite you again. [instrumental]

"Mean Old Bedbug Blues"

Focusing on the melody of the first stanza, you will hear that each phrase (*a*, *a'*, and *b*) is four measures long—that is, there are four downbeats in each phrase (downbeats are marked with an /). In turn, three phrases constitute a stanza or chorus. Thus, there are twelve measures or twelve bars in all—the twelve-bar blues. In "Mean Old Bedbug Blues" the singer, Bessie Smith, actually ends

---

*"Mean Old Bedbug Blues," lyrics and music by Jack Wood. © Copyright 1927 by Edwin H. Morris & Company. © Copyright renewed by Edwin H. Morris & Company, Inc. Used by permission.

each of her phrases at the beginning of the third measure, which leaves almost two full measures (end of the last phrase, beginning of the next) for the instrumentalists to fill in.

Listen once again just to the first stanza, and this time concentrate on the chord changes, which are shown under the text:

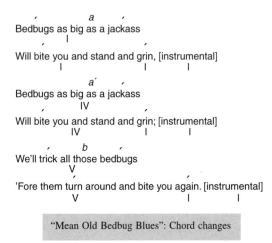

"Mean Old Bedbug Blues": Chord changes

This example represents the basic twelve-bar blues progression, shown in its essential form in the following illustration:

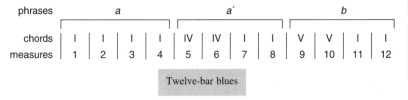

Twelve-bar blues

Characteristically, the text and melody are nearly the same in the first two phrases (*a* and *a'*), but there is an important change of harmony in the second phrase. As the second phrase begins, listen for the change from the I chord at the end of the *a* phrase, to the IV chord at the beginning of the *a'* phrase, and then back to I again. Can you hear that the move to IV gives the song a quite different feel at that moment? Recall the effect of the I–IV–I progression in the melodies you harmonized for Project 5.1—especially "Bonnie" and "Susanna."

Listen now for the differences between phrases *a'* and *b*. Notice particularly the more definitive V–I progression at the beginning of *b*. It is the V chord that gives this final phrase in each stanza its fresh quality—a freshness that coincides with the new words of the text.

Now listen to the whole song. There are three stanzas, each identical in harmony and melody except that the last is only eight bars long—possibly because of the time limitations of the old 78 rpm records. To hear the harmonic progressions clearly, concentrate on the instrumental accompaniment. Finally, listen to the piece once again and this time focus on what is most important—the singer herself.

Listening to Billie Holiday's "Fine and Mellow" (Example 5.2), you will hear that, as in her performance of "Night and Day," there is that wonderful flexibility of rhythm as she plays with, almost teases the underlying pulse. How would you compare Bessie Smith's feel for the beat with Billie Holiday's?

Recorded twelve years later than "Mean Old Bedbug Blues," "Fine and Mellow" is somewhat more elaborate in its harmony, but still the fundamental twelve-bar blues pattern is the same. We hear first a four-measure introduction on tonic harmony. The saxophones first repeat a short motive, then compress it, and then restore it to its original form. Focusing now on the harmony, listen as Billie Holiday comes in after the muted trumpet:*

```
                 a
My man don't love me,
     I

Treats me oh so mean [instrumental]
IV          I        I

                 a
My man he don't love me,
IV

Treats me awful mean [instrumental]
  IV        I       I

                 b
He's the lowest man
     II

That I've ever seen. [instrumental]
   V        I  IV  I
```

*Copyright Edward B. Marks Music Corporation. Used by permission.

Listen again closely to the harmony:

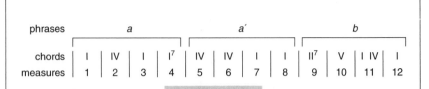

As in Bessie Smith's blues, notice that here the IV chord is introduced already in the first phrase. However, the way it is played, IV functions more as an elaboration or extension of the tonic harmony than as a new, fresh sound. For instance, compare the function of the IV chord in this first phrase with its function in the second phrase, *a'*, where it has a clear structural function of its own. In *b*, the V chord once again serves to move the harmony more decisively toward the return to the tonic. However, the expected V–I progression at the end of *b* in "Fine and Mellow" is somewhat softened by the quick interpolation of IV before the final I. The IV chord functions here more as a softly colored I than in a truly subdominant function.*

Even if you cannot hear each individual chord change in these examples, try to follow the fundamental progression in the twelve-bar structure: the move to IV at the beginning of the second phrase (*a'*), back to I at the end of the second phrase; the definitive move to V at the beginning of the last phrase (*b*), and once again back to I at the end.

It is interesting to compare the use of the I, IV, and V chords in the twelve-bar blues with the use of these same chords in the tunes that you harmonized earlier. Perhaps most important is the potentially different relationship between melody and harmony. Cer-

---

*For a more advanced analysis of the harmony, consider the following: In the progression I–IV, the I chord functions as the V or the dominant of the upcoming IV chord. For instance, as you found in working with scales, the tonic (I) in the key of C becomes the dominant (V) in the key of F. This dominant function is reinforced by adding the new pitch (B♭ in this case) to the C chord—thus, C E G B♭. Bottom to top, C–B♭, forms an interval of a seventh above the root of the chord, C, thus, I^7, as in the diagram above. The II chord plays the same role with regard to the V chord—that is, II (D in the key of C) becomes the dominant of V (G).

tainly the coherence we hear in both melody and harmony of the folk or folklike songs depends on the fifth relations that generate tonality—I–V; I–IV. However, the particular chord progressions in each of these songs follow more from the melodies and the harmony that these pitch relations implicitly generate. With the twelve-bar blues, it's the other way around—the melodies follow from the strongly felt and shared harmonic progression. Indeed, each melody can be heard as a unique elaboration of the same harmonic structure—the one that they all share.

Example 5.3: Rossini, *La Gazza Ladra*, Overture (1817)
Example 5.4: Rossini, *La Scala di Seta*, Overture (1812)

Rossini is known almost exclusively as an opera composer. These examples are excerpts from two opera overtures that he wrote relatively early in his career.* In these examples you will again hear the three fundamental chords, the harmonic simples of tonal music, used to create critical structural functions—stability and instability. At the same time, Rossini uses these harmonies to create the dramatic effects that we associate with opera—the feelings of tension and expectation, leading eventually to an anticipated arrival at resolution.

The excerpt from the overture to *La Gazza Ladra* ("The Thieving Magpie") exemplifies the use of a prolonged dominant harmony to create a feeling of expectation, of waiting. Over the reiterated dominant in the bass, Rossini increases the sense of suspense by writing fast, scalelike figures covering a large range, coupled with decorative embellishment by the high woodwinds.

All of this builds up to a unison passage in which the orchestra (predominantly woodwinds and brass) strongly marks both the dominant pitch and the beat. The unison passage is first played loudly (*fortissimo*) and then echoed softly (*pianissimo*). A slow dissipation of suspense follows, but with the dominant pitch still sustained in the bass.

The tension is finally resolved with the much-anticipated arrival on the tonic. The arrival is coupled with the entrance of a clear melody. The stability of the melody (played by the oboe) is created,

---

*The overture to an opera is a complete work meant to be played before the opera begins but it is often played by orchestras as a separate work.

in part, by its clear phrase structure, which stands out over the minimal accompaniment played by the plucked strings. The stability of the accompaniment, in turn, is generated by the familiar moves between tonic and dominant chords: the first phrase is harmonized by I, which moves to V just at the end, while the second phrase is harmonized by V, which moves back to I just at the end.

The next example, an excerpt from the very end of the overture to *La Scala di Seta* ("The Silken Ladder"), exemplifies just the opposite effect from the sense of expectation of the previous example; this is clearly an ending passage in contrast to the previous waiting passage. And, as one might expect, the ending function is created by emphasis on the tonic harmony in contrast to the waiting function generated by the dominant harmony.

Beginning with a brief melody harmonized by the I, IV, and V chords, the rest of the excerpt involves almost entirely dominant going to tonic harmony. Once again Rossini writes quickly moving figures played by the woodwinds, under which we hear the alternations between dominant and tonic getting faster and faster. The increased rate of detailed change, in the midst of dominant-tonic stasis, culminates in a cadential passage where the typical progression IV–V–I is repeated in a rousing climax, bringing us unquestionably to the end of the overture.

Project 5.2

Rounds

THE TASKS

1. Experiment with playing familiar rounds in four voices. For each tune, find the moments when each voice should come in and successfully perform the round in real time.

2. Experiment with unfamiliar and more challenging rounds using the already-set-up solution to help.

Project 5.2 is a performance activity played in real time, as you did in the Harmonize Playroom in Project 5.1. However, instead of using chords to accompany melodies, you will be working with a melody played "against itself." You are probably familiar with rounds such as "Frère Jacques" and "Row, Row, Row Your Boat." And if you have participated in singing rounds (or *canons,* as they are sometimes called), you will recall that everybody sings exactly the same melody. Of course, if everyone came in at the same time, they would be singing in unison. Instead, each singer or group of singers comes in one after the other. Thus, both entrances and exits are staggered—the first group in is also the first group out, and the last group in is the last group out. The result, as mentioned earlier, is a performance in which the texture becomes cumulatively more dense and more active as each singer joins in "imitating" those who came before. A picture of these staggered entrances and exits would look something like this:

Staggered entrances and exits

| Voice 1: TUNE |
| Voice 2: TUNE |
| Voice 3: TUNE |
| Voice 4: TUNE |

Since each singer "imitates" the previous singer, the whole canon is described as singing in *exact imitation*. Of course, not any tune will work as a round; the tune must be specially composed so that it will sound well when sung against itself. Moreover, each person needs to know exactly when to come in—when to start singing. For example, in "Row, Row, Row Your Boat," each person must come in just after the previous person has sung the words "Row, row, row your boat." That is, each new person starts singing the beginning of the tune when the previous person is right at the beginning of the next line—on the word "Gently." Thus, as each person enters, the texture becomes thicker and more active, and as each person finishes, the texture becomes symmetrically thinner and less active.

Row row row your boat, Gently down the stream...

　　　　　Row row row your boat, Gently down the stream...

　　　　　　　　　Row row row your boat, Gently down the stream...

In the eighteenth century, a favorite pastime was playing a game called "riddle canon." Mozart, for instance, would write a letter to a friend, and at the end add a canon tune that he composed—probably right on the spot. When Mozart's friend received the letter, he had to listen to the tune and try to figure out when each voice should come in to make the canon work. That is, he had to find the exact place of entry so that all four voices, when singing together, would sound right.

Mozart, being a trickster, tried to compose tunes that would make it as difficult as possible for his friends to solve the riddle in their heads. Impromptu makes things easier because you can experiment with entrances of each voice in real time. Listening to the performance by the synthesizer, you will be able to hear right away if your "performance" of the round works well. Just as in experimenting with arrangements of tuneblocks or with rhythm accompaniments, your musical intuitions will tell you if your experiments are successful.

Later on you will have an opportunity to solve some of Mozart's riddle canons, as well as others that you will find in the Tunes Catalog. But first try playing riddle canon with tunes that are familiar. Impromptu includes the following rounds that you may know already:

• "Row, Row, Row Your Boat" (Row Your Boat)
• "Frère Jacques"

- "Three Blind Mice"
- "Sumer Is Icumin In"

Playing Riddle Canon

Riddle canon is played in the Blocks area itself, not in the Playroom. Looking at the Rounds screen, you see four blocks in the Blocks area all marked TUNE.

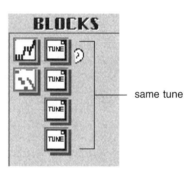

same tune

INFO BOX
Playing Riddle Canon
· In the Playrooms
  menu, select Rounds
· In the Tunes
  Catalog, select
  ROW YOUR BOAT

As you might expect, each of these blocks plays the same tune—in this example, the tune is "Row, Row, Row Your Boat." Notice that the ear cursor is selected. As in the Harmonize Playroom, you use the ear cursor to play riddle canon in real time.

When playing rounds, it is as if you were actually all four singers making a performance in real time. Click the first block labeled TUNE to start the first singer. As you listen, get ready to come in just as if you were the second singer. But instead of singing, click the second TUNE block exactly when the second singer should enter. Continue this process for the third and fourth singers clicking each block at the right moment until all four singers are in. Just as in singing a round with live singers, to successfully play rounds with Impromptu, you must be both a careful listener and an accurate performer.

To play riddle canon

1. Select a tune in the Tunes Catalog (FRERE JACQUES, THREE BLIND MICE, and so on)
2. Select the ear cursor.
3. In the Blocks area, click the top TUNE block and listen.

4. Listen again to the same block; this time, try to guess where the second voice should come in.

5. Click the first TUNE block once more; this time, listening carefully, try to click the second TUNE block at the exact right moment.

6. Follow the same procedure for the third and fourth voices.

When you have successfully "performed" "Row Your Boat," go on to "Frère Jacques" and "Three Blind Mice."

You have to be really on your toes to get each "singer" to come in at the right moment. If the second voice doesn't fit on your first try, click Stop and try again before going on to the third and fourth voices. If you hear that the second voice doesn't sound well, there are two kinds of possibilities to listen for:

• You may simply have selected the wrong moment to start the second voice.
• You may have chosen the right moment but been a bit inaccurate in your performance—clicked a little too soon or a little too late.

  You need to listen closely because it's not always easy to tell which of these possibilities is creating the problem. Once you succeed with the second voice, you can get into a kind of rhythm, since each voice enters in the same place with respect to the voice just before it.

Before going on to the Mozart canons, practice with the familiar tunes until you get pretty good at it.

EXPLORATIONS 1

Singing and Playing Along

It is interesting and fun to practice singing along with the synthesized voices. To do so, start up the first TUNE block, and then instead of clicking the second block, sing the tune, coming in at just the right moment. Or you can bring in all four voices and add your own as a fifth. Using the keyboard (or any other instrument you are familiar with), you can also play along with the synthesized voices in the same way.

Experimenting with Instrumentation

Experimenting with the instrumentation of a round can be revealing. The Instrument menus next to each voice in the Playroom correspond to the ordering of TUNE blocks in the Blocks area. Thus, if you select Recorder in the Instrument menu for Voice 1, the first

TUNE block in the Blocks area will be played by the synthesizer's recorder; if you choose Horn in the Instrument menu for Voice 2, the second TUNE block will be played by the synthesizer's horn; and so forth. As you experiment with instruments, notice how your choice can dramatically influence the effectiveness of the round.

Graphics

What does a round look like in a pitch contour graphics representation? Since the graphics window shows only what is in the Playroom, to find out you need to use the hand cursor to drag each of the TUNE blocks into one of the Voices in the Playroom. Use "Row Your Boat" again as an example.

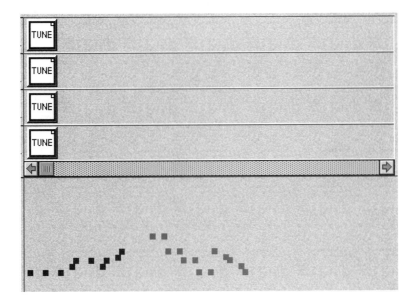

You may at first be surprised at the graphics you see—only one voice rather than four seems to be represented. And if you click Play, you will hear four voices and four instruments, but they are all playing together in unison. Why? What do you need to do to see and hear all four voices individually? Answers will once again reveal the power of your musical intuitions, and also important differences between what you know how to do and what the computer "knows" how to do.

The Playroom is set up so that the computer expects to start all four voices at the same time. And since all four voices of a round are playing the same tune, you naturally hear four instruments playing that same tune in unison. In turn, since the graphics just trace the action of each voice, you see one voice on top of the other. So the question is, how can you stagger the entrances of the voices so each enters one after the other at just the right moment?

When you were playing rounds "in action"—listening to a tune and experimenting with entrances—you developed an intuitive feel for how long to wait before each voice should come in. And with a little practice, you could just do it. But the computer doesn't come equipped with musical intuitions; you need to tell it exactly how long to wait before beginning to play each voice. And that means you will need to measure the wait time in some kind of specific units that the computer can "understand" with the help of Impromptu.

Measuring, counting, and units were probably not things you needed to think about at all when playing in real time. But if you were to count and measure, what are the time units you could use? Recall that the functional way of measuring musical time is in relation to the underlying beat or tactus. So, to measure the wait time, you need to count beats—specifically, the number of beats that each voice must wait before it comes in. That means that you must listen to the first TUNE block, and while listening count the number of beats Voice 1 plays before Voice 2 comes in. Try it with "Row Your Boat."

Of course, the number of beats you count will depend on the beat level you choose as the tactus. However, it is most likely (and we will assume for this example) that in listening to the first TUNE block, you counted four beats, and then Voice 2 comes in. And since each voice waits the same number of beats with respect to the previous voice, you only have to figure out the wait time for the second voice and then add. So we have a picture like this:

"Row, Row, Row Your Boat": Wait times

In the Rounds Playroom, Impromptu is programmed so that you can indicate in terms of beats how long you would like each voice to wait before coming in. In the Options menu, select Wait Times. Then indicate for each voice how many beats it should wait before coming in.* Notice that the value of the beat (Rounds Wait Unit) is also shown.

Standard Settings

Select Wait Times for each Voice:

Voice 1: `0`

Voice 2: `4`

Voice 3: `8`

Voice 4: `12`

Rounds Wait Unit: `4`

[OK]   [Cancel]

Options menu: Wait time

Insert the wait times as shown in the illustration and click OK. Now click Play and listen while following the graphics.

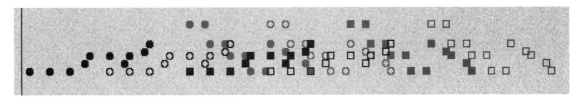

Notice that, as each voice enters, you can clearly see the texture becoming thicker, more dense. And after the middle when all four voices are in, the texture becomes symmetrically thinner as each voice finishes and drops out, until only one voice is left.

Try counting the wait times for other rounds that you have already played with. As you do, notice that the limitations of the computer are

---

*Notice that wait time is different here than in the other Playrooms—the Drummer Playroom, for instance. In the other Playrooms, wait time refers simply to durations, not to beats. Thus, in the Drummer Playroom, a wait time of 4 tells Impromptu to make a rest of duration 4. In the Rounds Playroom, a wait time of 4 tells Impromptu to wait 4 *beats*. Notice that the assumed value of the beat is also indicated in the Wait Times window as Rounds Wait Unit.

serving a useful purpose. As you need to count and measure in order to "talk" to the computer, the computer helps you appreciate and also make explicit what you were able to do in action through your own intuitive know-how. At the same time, the computer's "know-how," together with Impromptu's graphics capabilities, makes visible what was invisible as you worked in real time—the shape of a round. The graphics hold still in space what disappears as it happens in time; you can see what you hear.

Go on now to play riddle canon with some of the other familiar tunes. When you are ready for a challenge, try one of Mozart's riddle canons. There are three canons by Mozart: MOZART1, MOZART2, and BO-NANOX. These canons are already set up in the Playroom. Listen to the completed canon, watch the graphics, and then, by ear, try to play it in action. Or, alternatively, look at the wait times in the Options menu and then, as you listen, count the number of beats shown there. Go through the Tunes Catalog and try the canon by Lawes as well.

LISTENING EXAMPLES: CANONS AND FUGUES

Example 5.5: Mozart, *Bona nox, bist a rechta ox* (1788)
Example 5.6: Haydn, Sonata in E-flat, Tempo di Minuetto (1773)
Example 5.7: Handel, Concerto Grosso, Op. 6, #2, Fourth Movement (opening) (1739)
Example 5.8: Handel, Concerto Grosso, Op. 6, #2, Fourth Movement (1739)
Example 5.9: Beethoven, String Quartet, Op. 59, #3, Fourth Movement (1806)
Example 5.10: Bartók, Sonata for Two Pianos and Percussion, First Movement (1938)

Of the compositions you have listened to so far, most shared a relatively inactive texture—a single melody with clearly subsidiary accompaniment. For instance, the songs of the twelve-bar blues; the solo melody of the Mozart Concerto for Piano, and the dances such as *"Bulerias,"* Lanner's "Styrian Dance," and the Haydn Minuet. By contrast, all of the examples for Project 5.2 share a relatively active texture—several melodies with each playing an equally important role.

This difference in texture creates another kind of contrast, as well: The songs and dances are also clearly *sectional.* That is, boundaries of motives, phrases, and sections are clearly marked; they are nested into hierarchical structures; and the sections often cumulate to form an A B A' shape. In contrast, the examples included here are more *continuous*: their imitative and active texture, with voices overlapping one another, results in the blurring of boundaries, leaving only rare moments when there is a full stop-and-start-again feeling.

You already encountered this distinction between sectional and continuous pieces in the listening examples for Part 1. For instance, sectional pieces such as Beethoven's "Ode to Joy" were contrasted with more continuous pieces such as Vivaldi's "Winter." Go back and listen to some of the pieces that are more continuous in their unfolding: Vivaldi's "Winter" (Example 1.5), the Gigue from Bach's Partita #2 (Example 1.6), and the excerpt from Liszt's Faust Symphony (Example 1.7). Recall that the focus in each of these excerpts was on the composer's use of sequential passages, the spinning out of a brief motive, as a primary mode of development.

Terms such as *sectional* and *continuous* are useful for differentiating among contrasting ways of organizing pitch and time. However, extended, complex compositions are rarely just sectional or just continuous. Sectional and continuous structures are better described as the extremes of a continuum. As Arnold Schoenberg said, "Theory must be stricter than reality. It is forced to generalize, and that means reduction on the one hand, exaggeration on the other."[*]

Indeed, creating contrast between sectional and continuous passages is a powerful resource for composers in their development of large, complex works. For example, the theme of Beethoven's "Ode" is clearly sectional, and the larger structure of the variations on "Ode" is also obviously sectional (each variation clearly bounded and separated from the next). However, moving from one variation to the next, Beethoven also moves between relatively active and inactive textures. For instance, moving from the theme to Variation 1, the texture becomes more active: the bassoon plays a countermelody, competing for attention as it weaves in and around the melody of the theme, played by the violas and cellos. Go back and listen to the excerpts from Beethoven's Symphony #9 in the light of these comments (Example 1.2). And in this proposed continuum extending between active and inactive textures at the extremes, think about where you would place the Bach Minuet in contrast to the March (Examples 3.1 and 3.2).

---

[*]A. Schoenberg, *Fundamentals of Musical Composition,* London: Faber & Faber, 1967, p. 103.

Examples 5.5 through 5.10 are clearly at the active end of this continuum. However, they differ from the examples of more active texture in Part 1 in that they all include imitation. Mozart's *Bona nox*, which you may recognize from the Impromptu version, and the Minuet from Haydn's piano sonata are both *canons*. The Handel and Beethoven examples are both *fugues*. Fugues include imitation but, as you will hear, not in the same fashion as a canon.

Canons

> **Example 5.5: Mozart, *Bona nox, bist a rechta ox* (1788)**
> **Example 5.6: Haydn, Sonata in E-flat, Tempo di Minuetto (1773)**

Bona nox is one of many canons for which Mozart wrote comic and rather bawdy verses. For instance, the opening line is sung to the words *"Bona nox, bist a rechta ox,"* which translated into English says, "Good night, you're a real ox." As you already know, all the voices participating in a canon sing or play exactly the same melody throughout. Beginning with just one voice alone, as each subsequent voice enters, the cumulating "points of imitation" create a texture that grows continuously thicker and more animated from within. When *Bona nox* is performed by live singers as Mozart intended, the canon gains decidedly in vigor and also in humor, compared with Impromptu's relatively dull synthesized version. And notice that unlike Impromptu, the singers in the recorded performance "round off" the canon by stopping all together.

Haydn's Minuetto is the third movement of one of his many piano sonatas, but surprisingly it is also a canon. Haydn gives this canon, the minuet movement in a piano sonata, a distinctly different function from the canons Mozart wrote as comic riddles to be sung. Listening to the Haydn Minuetto, you may find it difficult at first to hear that it is, in fact, an almost exact canon in two "voices"—that is, between the pianist's right and left hands. Indeed, despite the exact imitation, Haydn's canon sounds more sectional than continuous. Haydn creates an interesting mix of styles and types—relatively distinct phrases and sections, combined with the exact imitation of a canon. How has Haydn created this mix?

The movement begins, as all canons do, with one voice alone. Here, it is the upper voice played by the pianist's right hand. The upper voice is quickly followed by the entrance of the lower voice in imitation, played by the left hand. But this initial feeling of continuousness is interrupted by a phrase boundary: Haydn has composed the canon melody so that the first voice has time to pause briefly while the second voice finishes the imitation alone. This marks a phrase boundary. The second phrase, again begun by the upper voice, introduces a new rhythm, and again the upper voice (right hand) pauses to articulate a phrase boundary while the left hand finishes the imitation alone.

Haydn marks the end of the first part of the canon by breaking the exact imitation; there is a rapid, ascending, scalelike figure that is played in rhythmic unison. This is followed by a typical cadential figure outlining V/I harmony. And, as in the Bach and Haydn minuets that you heard earlier, the piece migrates to the key of the dominant during this third phrase. The first section is repeated, which also contributes to the sectional feeling of the piece.

There follows a contrasting middle section, again in exact imitation. Beginning now with the left hand alone in the lower voice, the piece becomes more continuous, there are fewer pauses rhythmically, and the tonality is continuously shifting as well. This more continuous passage is followed by a big pause in anticipation of the return. But as the return begins, Haydn, with his endless ingenuity, reverses the imitative entries—beginning this time with the lower voice, which the upper voice now imitates. The return restates the whole first part in this upside-down way, but this time staying in the same key throughout. This second part is also repeated. And when he is finished, Haydn has made an A B + A' minuet while at the same time composing a canon in almost entirely strict imitation.

Fugues

> **Example 5.7: Handel, Concerto Grosso, Op. 6, #2, Fourth Movement, opening (1739)**
> **Example 5.8: Handel, Concerto Grosso, Op. 6, #2, Fourth Movement, complete (1739)**

Before reading further, listen to Example 5.7, the beginning of the final movement of a concerto grosso by Bach's contemporary, George Frideric Handel.* Example 5.7 is the opening of a fugue.

---

*A *concerto grosso* is a work in several movements that exploits the contrast between a small group of solo instruments (called the *concertino* section) and the full orchestra (called the *tutti* section).

Think about how this opening differs from the canons you have been working with and listening to.

This opening portion of a fugue is called the *exposition*. All the participants are introduced here, each having a go at a complete statement of the same melody. This opening melody, played by each of the participants, is called the *subject* of the fugue. As its name suggests, the whole fugue is concerned with it in one way or another.

The exposition of this fugue includes five statements of the subject: the violins playing in a middle register state the subject first, then the violas and cellos play it in a lower register, then there is a statement in the lowest register by cellos and basses. Then, as if starting once more, Handel gives the subject to the violins again, now in the highest register (an octave higher than the first time), and finally the violins play the subject once more in a middle register.

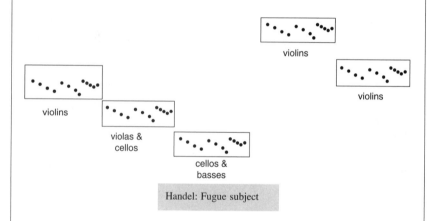

Handel: Fugue subject

Listen to the exposition of the fugue once more. Notice that, while there are similarities between a canon and a fugal exposition, there is an important difference: In a canon, instruments or voices sing or play exactly the same melody—thus, they "imitate" one another exactly throughout. In a fugal exposition, voices or instruments (as in this fugue) enter one after the other in imitation, but unlike the imitation in a canon, in a fugue *the imitation is not exact*.

The subject as first stated by the violins is clearly recognizable in each of its statements because of its "pitch shape." Like the silhouette of a carved sculpture, the "jagged" beginning—disjunct, with each note marking the beat—is set off against the second part (faster, with the primarily conjunct motion profiled by a leap and contrary motion).

disjunct   conjunct

Handel: Fugal exposition

The second statement of the subject, played by the violas and cellos, is almost exactly the same in its interval relations and thus in its pitch shape. However, the actual pitches are entirely different.

So what we have, of course, is a tune that *migrates*. Not surprisingly, these two opening statements of the subject are in keys related by a fifth: the first statement in the key of F, the second statement in its dominant, C. As the exposition unfolds, the entrances of the subject continue to alternate between these two keys: the third statement is in F, and, beginning again, the fourth is also in F, with the last in C. The exposition ends with a sequential passage based on a melodic fragment from the "tail" of the subject, resolving into a clear cadence in the key of the dominant, C.

```
tail                           sequence
```

Listen now to Example 5.8, the entire fourth movement of the Concerto Grosso. Pay attention especially to the stark contrasts in texture as the movement continues. With the cadence at the end of the fugal exposition, Handel introduces a new, slower, more lyrical melody together with a "pulsing" chordal accompaniment played by the lower strings in rhythmic unison. As the movement continues, this new melody with its relatively inactive texture occurs in abrupt alternation with the imitative texture of the exposition and its clearly marked fugal subject. Indeed, the movement is a brilliant example of how contrast between active and inactive texture, rather than exclusive use of one or the other, can serve as a powerful resource in the development of a large and complex work such as this.

Listening more closely, you will hear that, as the piece evolves, the two "characters" in this drama come closer and closer together. Contrasts between the fugal subject and the slowly moving lyrical melody occur more rapidly, and soon you hear the two melodies superimposed on one another. Using his virtuoso ability to compose melodies that can combine and interact in multiple ways, Handel plays off the lyrical melody against the more stark and vigorous fugal subject—sometimes placing the slower melody below and sometimes above the fugal subject.

In this way, Handel creates rich varieties of sound and texture, but also new embeddings for the two recurring and contrasting melodic ideas. Near the end of the movement, the fugal subject is played in closer and closer imitation; instruments enter virtually tumbling over one another, as if they can't wait for each other to finish. This is a culmination of the movement's growing intensity—the ever-increasing rate of contrast between the two melodies and textures, melodies superimposed upon one another. It is as if the music were speeding up, yet the tempo remains the same throughout.

It is interesting to compare this sense of structurally growing faster with other means that composers have used to create a similar effect. For example, go back and listen to the Minuet from the Haydn Quartet (Example 2.10), where the meter shifts from triple to duple, and the Beethoven variations on "Ode to Joy" (Example 1.1), where the texture becomes more active from one variation to the next.

Comparing Fugal Expositions

Example 5.9: Beethoven, String Quartet, Op. 59, #3, Fourth Movement (1806)
Example 5.10: Bartók, Sonata for Two Pianos and Percussion, First Movement (1938)

Throughout the listening examples, a point has been made of juxtaposing pieces that come from differing periods and/or from differing cultures. At the same time, juxtaposed examples, despite their differences, always share some underlying principle—for instance, sequence, rhythmic conflict/complexity, tonic-dominant harmony, or imitation and active texture. The last two examples are no exception; they come from quite different moments in time and place—eighteenth-century Vienna and twentieth-century Hungary—and yet each is a fugal exposition. And just as the other examples, through their juxtaposition, brought out similarities as a result of their differences, so the structure of the fugal exposition is revealed through quite different musical contexts of each example.

Along with the Handel movement, both the Beethoven and Bartók excerpts include the critical statement of the subject by each of the participants in turn—a fugal exposition. But the expositions are obviously quite different in nearly every other respect. Perhaps the most striking difference is in the unique character of the fugal subjects themselves. Each subject, in turn, carries critical implications for the shape of the unfolding exposition.

These two examples also illustrate in a dramatic fashion that the shaping of a composition, be it sectional or continuous, a dance, a fugue, or variations on a theme, depends on the confluence of particular situational factors. Starting from the most general and moving toward the unique, some of these factors are the following:

- The general characteristics common to music at the time and the place in which the piece was written—the *style* of the period
- The *form* the composer may adopt as an organizing frame—minuet, sonata, rondo, fugue, and so on
- The unique *voice* of this composer—his or her personal style
- The germinal motives composed for this piece and from which this particular composition uniquely evolves

These differences are immediately evident in listening to Examples 5.9 and 5.10. Example 5.9 is the opening of the last movement of a Beethoven string quartet written in the early nineteenth century. Example 5.10 is an excerpt from near the end of the first movement of a piece by Béla Bartók written 132 years later in the mid–twentieth century. The instrumentation of the two works could not be more different. The Beethoven quartet is composed for two violins, viola, and cello; the Bartók sonata is composed for two pianos and percussion, including timpani, xylophone, snare drums, cymbal, bass drum, triangle, and tam-tam.

Despite their dramatic differences (in harmonic relations, rhythmic structure, melodic contours, and instrumentation), the two excerpts share even more than the fugal exposition procedure; one feels in both pieces a sense of energy, of driving momentum. What is it in each piece that generates this excitement?

Unfortunately, the limits of the CD's time/space do not permit this momentum to continue on to the completion of the movements. Perhaps that can become a reason to move out and beyond the boundaries of this book and its recorded examples—to listen to the entire movements of which these short excerpts are only brief moments, and even to the whole pieces of which these movements are but a small part.

Some Basics

THE BUILDING BLOCKS OF TONAL HARMONY ARE *TRIADS*. TRIADS, IN THE SPECIFIC meaning used here, are the three-tone chords that are built upon and that elaborate each degree of a major or minor scale. The lowest tone of the triad is called the *root*. (Perhaps the name stems from an analogy with a plant, the root of a triad being likened to the tone from which the triad "grows.")

Each triad is labeled according to the scale degree that is its root. Roman numerals are used to label triads. This is in contrast to the Arabic numerals used to indicate the scale degree of a single pitch. For instance, the triad built on the first degree of the scale is called the I chord; the triad built on the fourth degree of the scale is called the IV chord. Triads and their functions within a key are also referred to by the following names:

Scale Degree	Name
I	Tonic triad
II	Supertonic triad
III	Mediant triad
IV	Subdominant triad
V	Dominant triad

VI   Submediant triad
VII   Leading Tone triad

Types of Triads

A triad is built up by adding to its root pitches that lie a third and a fifth above it in the scale. Thus, the middle tone of the triad is called the *third*, the top tone is called the *fifth*. These labels reflect the intervallic relationship of the upper two tones to the root.

The three primary triads, those which define a tonality, are the I chord, or *tonic* triad, made up of scale degrees 1, 3, and 5; the V chord, or *dominant* triad, made up of scale degrees 5, 7, and 2; and the IV chord, or *subdominant* triad, made up of scale degrees 4, 6, and 8.

I, V, and IV chords in C major

Notice that the tonic triad in a given key (here, C major) is surrounded by the V chord a fifth above it, and the IV chord a fifth below it. These chords, related once again by fifths, form the pillars of a tonality.

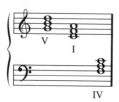

There are four basic types of triads and they have the same names as the four types of intervals:

• Major (M)
• Minor (m)
• Diminished (D)
• Augmented (A)

The types of triads and their names reflect their intervallic relations: the interval from the root to the middle pitch (third), and from the root to the top pitch (fifth). The four types of triads and their intervallic relations are shown in the following figure. The information is summarized in Table 5.1.

Four types of triads

Table 5.1   Intervallic Relations Within Types of Triads

	Root → Third	Root → Fifth
Major triad	M3	P5
Minor triad	m3	P5
Diminished triad	m3	D5
Augmented triad	M3	A5

The figure below shows the triads built on each of the scale degrees in the keys of C major and G major, along with their types. Table 5.2 summarizes this information.

Triads in the keys of C major (left) and G major (right)

Table 5.2   Types of Triads in the Major Scale

Scale Degree	Type
I	Major
II	Minor
III	Minor
IV	Major
V	Major
VI	Minor
VII	Diminished

The following figure shows the triads built on each of the scale degrees in the minor mode along with their types—here, in the keys of c minor and g minor.*

---

*Notice that the triad types result from building triads up on the scale degrees of the *harmonic minor scale.*

Triads in the keys of c
minor (left) and g minor
(right)

I	II	III	IV	V	VI	VII		I	II	III	IV	V	VI	VII
m	D	Aug	m	M	M	D		m	D	Aug	m	M	M	D

Things to Notice

- Within a major key, the primary triads (I IV and V) are all major; the secondary triads (II III, VI) are minor, and VII, alone, is diminished.

- Within a minor key, using the harmonic minor scale, the primary triads, I and IV are minor but V is major; of the secondary triads, II and VII are diminished, VI is major, and III is augmented.

- Just as the same pitch may change its function when embedded in a new context or key, so a triad may change its function. For example, two major keys related by the critical interval of a fifth have two of their functional chords in common, but these chords have different functions in each context. The same triad that functions as the tonic triad (I) in G major (G-B-D) functions as the dominant triad (V) when embedded in the key of C major. Similarly, the same chord that functions as the IV (subdominant) chord in G major (C-E-G) functions as the I chord when embedded in C major.

G major

       I   IV

C major

       V   I

- Composers use triads shared by more than one key as "pivot chords" to make easy moves from one key to the other. Closely related keys (e.g., adjacent around the circle of fifths) always share two of their primary chords.

Inversions

Triads can be inverted just as intervals can. A triad can assume three different positions:

1. Root position: The root is in the bass
2. First inversion: The third is in the bass
3. Second inversion: The fifth is in the bass

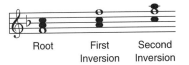

Tonic triad in F major: root, first inversion, and second inversion

Thus, inversions of triads, like inversions of intervals, are made by simply flipping the currently lowest pitch, the bass note, to its upper octave. Notice the distinction between the *root* of the triad (shown in white) and the *bass* of the triad: The root is also the bass only when the triad is in root position; the *bass* of the triad (the lowest note) varies in pitch with each inversion: the bass is the third of the chord when in first inversion, or the fifth of the chord in second inversion.

Each position of a triad has a characteristic quality, including its degree of relative stability, but all positions of a triad include the same pitch classes and all have the same *harmonic function within a given key.* For instance, the D major triad in all of its inversions will always function as the tonic triad in D major. However, in the key of B major, the same triad in all its inversions will function as the dominant, and in the key of A major, it will function as the subdominant triad.*

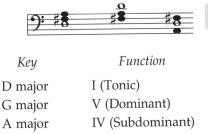

D major triad

Key	Function
D major	I (Tonic)
G major	V (Dominant)
A major	IV (Subdominant)

---

*There is an exception to this general statement: The second inversion tonic triad often takes on a dominant function (with the fifth degree in the bass) when followed by the dominant triad and then the tonic in root position.

Voicing

All the examples of triads so far have been in "closed position." That is, pitches of the triad were placed above one another as close together as possible. Thus, the maximum interval from bass to top was a sixth (in first and second inversions). Triads can also be written in "open position" where the root, third, or fifth is positioned in different octaves and in different combinations. For example, the pitches of a triad may be spread out so that the span from bass to top is several octaves. Further, since there are only three tones to work with, if four voices are used (e.g., soprano, alto, tenor, bass), one of the tones must be repeated or "doubled." The following figure shows the G major triad in closed position and in open position with the root doubled.

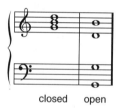

closed   open

Cadences

Cadence is the term used to describe the end of a phrase or section. The term may be used in relation to the phrase-endings of a melody and/or to refer to the harmonic progression that supports these phase-endings. Speaking now of these harmonic progressions, there are three basic types of cadences:

Cadence Type	Chord Progression
Perfect	V I; or IV V I (sounds final)
Imperfect	I V (sounds incomplete)
Plagel	IV I (sounds softly final)

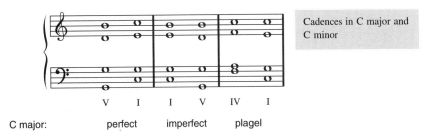

Cadences in C major and C minor

	V	I	I	V	IV	I
C major:		perfect		imperfect		plagel

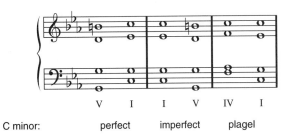

	V	I	I	V	IV	I
C minor:		perfect		imperfect		plagel

Notice that in these examples of cadences, triads are written in four voices, in open position, and with the root of the triad doubled.

List of Listening Examples and CD Track Numbers

Listening Example Number	CD Track Number	Composer, Title, and Artists
1.1	1	Beethoven, *Symphony No. 9*, fourth movement, *Ode to Joy* New York Philharmonic; Leonard Bernstein, conductor
1.2	2	Beethoven, *Symphony No. 9*, fourth movement, Variations New York Philharmonic; Leonard Bernstein, conductor
1.3	3	Haydn, *Symphony No. 99, Minuet*, A section New York Philharmonic; Leonard Bernstein, conductor
1.4	4	Haydn, *Symphony No. 99, Minuet* New York Philharmonic; Leonard Bernstein, conductor
1.5	5	Vivaldi, *The Seasons*, "Winter" Tafelmusik; Jeanne Lamon, violin and conductor © 1992 Sony Classical GmbH
1.6	6	Bach, *Partita No. 2 for Solo Violin*, "Gigue" Hilary Hahn, violin © 1997 Sony Music Entertainment Inc.
1.7	7	Liszt, *Faust Symphony*, opening New York Philharmonic; Leonard Bernstein, conductor
2.1	8	"Bhimpalasi" Ravi Shankar
2.2	9	Hindemith, *Kleine Kammermusik*, fourth movement Ensemble Wien © 1996 Sony Classical GmbH
2.3	10	Porter, "Night and Day" Billie Holiday
2.4	11	Lanner, "Styrian Dances" Wiener Biedermeier Solisten © 1991 Camerata. Courtesy of Camerata
2.5	12	Sousa, "Stars and Stripes Forever" Columbia All-Star Band; Gunther Schuller, conductor © 1975 Sony Music Entertainment Inc.

Listening Example Number	CD Track Number	Composer, Title, and Artists
2.6	13	Stravinsky, *Petrouchka* (excerpt) New York Philharmonic; Pierre Boulez, conductor
2.7	14	Mozart, *Concerto for Piano*, K. 467 English Chamber Orchestra; Murray Perahia, piano and conductor © 1978 Sony Music Entertainment Inc.
2.8	15	*Mi Capona* (Bulerias) Tomas Pavon with Melchor de Marchena, guitar © Arhoolie Productions Inc. El Cerrito, CA 94530. From Arhoolie Records CD-326 "Early Cante Flamenco"
2.9	16	Ziporyn, "What She Saw There" Evan Ziporyn, bass clarinet; Danny Tunick, William Winant, marimbas © 1993 Composers Recordings, Inc. Courtesy of Composers Recordings, Inc.
2.10	17	Haydn, *String Quartet*, Op. 76 No. 5 Tokyo String Quartet © 1981 Sony Music Entertainment Inc.
2.11	18	*Balai Pusing*
2.12	19	Stravinsky, *The Rite of Spring*, "Dance of the Adolescents" (excerpt) Cleveland Orchestra; Pierre Boulez, conductor
3.1	20	Bach, *Minuet in G*, Notebook for Anna Magdalena Bach No. 11 Jeanne Bamberger, piano
3.2	21	Bach, *March in D*, Notebook for Anna Magdalena, Bach No. 16 Jeanne Bamberger, piano
3.3	22	Bach, *Minuet in G* (excerpt) Jeanne Bamberger, piano
3.4	23	Chopin, *Mazurka*, Op. 67 No. 2 Alexander Brailowsky, piano © 1984 Sony Music Entertainment Inc.
3.5	24	Helps, *Gossamer Noons*, No. 2 American Composers Orchestra; Bethany Beardslee, soprano; Gunther Schuller, conductor © 1978 Composers Recordings, Inc.
5.1	25	"Mean Old Bedbug Blues" Bessie Smith
5.2	26	"Fine and Mellow" Billie "Holiday

Listening Example Number	*CD Track Number*	*Composer, Title, and Artists*
5.3	27	Rossini, *La Gazza Ladra,* Overture RAI Symphony Orchestra of Turin; Gianluigi Gelmetti, conductor
5.4	28	Rossini, *La Scala di Seta,* Overture New York Philharmonic; Leonard Bernstein, conductor
5.5	29	Mozart, *Bona nox, bist a rechta ox* Tölz Boys Choir © 1993 Koch International L.P. Courtesy of Koch International L.P.
5.6	30	Haydn, *Sonata in E-flat,* Hob. XVI 25, Tempo di Minuetto Lola Odiaga, piano Courtesy of Albany Records
5.7	31	Handel, *Concerto Grosso,* Op. 6. No. 2, fourth movement, opening La Grande Ecurie et la Chambre du Roy; Jean-Claude Malgoire, conductor © 1975 Sony Music Entertainment Inc.
5.8	32	Handel, *Concerto Grosso,* Op. 6. No. 2, fourth movement, complete La Grande Ecurie et la Chambre du Roy; Jean-Claude Malgoire, conductor © 1975 Sony Music Entertainment Inc.
5.9	33	Beethoven, *String Quartet,* Op. 59 No. 3, fourth movement The Juilliard String Quartet © 1983 Sony Music Entertainment Inc.
5.10	34	Bartók, *Sonata for Two Pianos and Percussion,* first movement Murray Perahia, Georg Solti, piano; David Corkhill, Evelyn Glennie, percussion © 1988 Sony Music Entertainment Inc.

Index

Only the elements of the *Impromptu* computer program that are mentioned in this book are indexed here. The * is used here as a wildcard character in *Impromptu* filenames. A complete index and map of *Impromptu's* functions, folders, tunes, and environments appears on the first page of its Help function.

Composers' names and titles of works are given here in Library of Congress form (AACR2), under which they will be found in most libraries' catalogs. This form of the title is a logical but sometimes artificial form (called the "uniform title"), which causes all versions of a work to be filed together in the catalog. Where these forms differ significantly from commoner spellings and translations and transliterations, cross-references are usually given in a library's catalog; but the user should also check under common variant spellings (for instance, "Schönberg" and "Schoenberg" should both be checked). In this index, *see* references that lead from more familiar forms and translations to the standard forms are included as needed for clarity and convenience.